Honore De Balzac His Life And Writings

by

Mary F. Sandars

Honore De Balzac
His Life And Writings
by Mary F. Sandars

ISBN: 978-93-61152-57-3

Published by

DOUBLE 9 BOOKS

2/13-B, Ansari Road
Daryaganj, New Delhi – 110002
info@double9books.com
www.double9books.com
Tel. 011-40042856

ABOUT THE AUTHOR

Mary Frances Sandars was an outstanding English writer and biographer, best known for her literary works from the late nineteenth and early twentieth century. Sandars took a particular intellectual approach to her writing, devoting herself to in-depth research and thorough analysis of the topics she chose to investigate. Her important work 'Honore de Balzac, His Life and Writings' (1904) exemplifies her influence, as it delves into the life of one of the finest authors and playwrights of the French realist style. Sandars not only presented a fascinating biography of Balzac, but also insights into his complicated personality and the social background of his time. Her narrative deftly weaves through Balzac's vast literary output, drawing crucial links between his personal experiences and the great psychological depth seen in his characters and stories. Sandars' biographical approach is distinguished by her clear, precise wording and ability to humanize historical individuals while maintaining the intellectual rigor of her work. While Sandars has less biographical material than her subjects, her contribution to English literary research, particularly in making French literary giants available to an English-speaking public, is an important aspect of her legacy.

CONTENTS

PREFACE

Books about Balzac would fill a fair-sized library. Criticisms on his novels abound, and his contemporaries have provided us with several amusing volumes dealing in a humorous spirit with his eccentricities, and conveying the impression that the author of "La Cousine Bette" and "Le Pere Goriot" was nothing more than an amiable buffoon.

Nevertheless, by some strange anomaly, there exists no Life of him derived from original sources, incorporating the information available since the appearance of the volume called "Lettres a l'Etrangere." This book, which is the source of much of our present knowledge of Balzac, is a collection of letters written by him from 1833 to 1844 to Madame Hanska, the Polish lady who afterwards became his wife. The letters are exact copies of the originals, having been made by the Vicomte de Spoelberch de Lovenjoul, to whom the autographs belong.

It seems curious that no one should yet have made use of this mine of biographical detail. In English we have a Memoir by Miss Wormeley, written at a time when little as known about the great novelist, and a Life by Mr. Frederick Wedmore in the "Great Writers" Series; but this, like Miss Wormeley's Memoir, appeared before the "Lettres a l'Etrangere" were published. Moreover, it is a very small book, and the space in it devoted to Balzac as a man is further curtailed by several chapters devoted to criticism of his work. The introduction to the excellent translation of Balzac's novels undertaken by Mr. Saintsbury, contains a short account of his life, but this only fills a few pages and does not enter into much detail. Besides these, an admirable essay on Balzac has appeared in "Main Currents of Nineteenth-century Literature," by Mr. George Brandes; the scope of this, however, is mainly criticism of his merits as a writer, not description of his personality and doings.

Even in the French language, there is no trustworthy or satisfactory Life of Balzac—a fact on which numerous critical writers make many comments, though they apparently hesitate to throw themselves into the breach and to undertake one. Madame Surville's charming Memoir only professes to treat of Balzac's early life, and even within these limits she intentionally conceals as much as she reveals. M. Edmond Bire, in his interesting book, presents

Balzac in different aspects, as Royalist, playwriter, admirer of Napoleon, and so on; but M. Bire gives no connected account of his life, while MM. Hanotaux and Vicaire deal solely with Balzac's two years as printer and publisher. The Vicomte de Spoelberch de Lovenjoul is the one man who could give a detailed and minutely correct Life of Balzac, as he has proved by the stores of biographical knowledge contained in his works the "Roman d'Amour," "Autour de Honore de Balzac," "La Genese d'un Roman de Balzac, 'Les Paysans,'" and above all, "L'Histoire des Oeuvres de Balzac," which has become a classic. The English or American reader would hardly be able to appreciate these fascinating books, however, unless he were first equipped with the knowledge of Balzac which would be provided by a concise Life.

In these circumstances, helped and encouraged by Dr. Emil Reich, whose extremely interesting lectures I had attended with much enjoyment, and who very kindly gave me lists of books, and assisted me with advice, I engaged in the task of writing this book. It is not intended to add to the mass of criticism of Balzac's novels, being merely an attempt to portray the man as he was, and to sketch correctly a career which has been said to be more thrilling than a large proportion of novels.

I must apologise for occasional blank spaces, for when Balzac is with Madame Hanska, and his letters to her cease, as a general rule all our information ceases also; and the intending biographer can only glean from scanty allusions in the letters written afterwards, what happened at Rome, Naples, Dresden, or any of the other towns, to which Balzac travelled in hot haste to meet his divinity.

The book has been compiled as far as possible from original sources; as the Vicomte de Spoelberch de Lovenjoul—whose collection of documents relating to Balzac, Gautier, and George Sand is unique, while his comprehensive knowledge of Balzac is the result of many years of study—has most kindly allowed me to avail myself of his library at Brussels. There, arranged methodically, according to some wonderful system which enables the Vicomte to find at once any document his visitor may ask for, are hundreds of Balzac's autograph writings, many of them unpublished and of great interest. There, too, are portraits and busts of the celebrated novelist, letters from his numerous admirers, and the proofs of nearly all his novels—those sheets covered with a network of writing, which were the despair of the printers. The collection is most remarkable, even when we remember the large sums of money, and the patience and ability, which have for many years been focussed on its formation. It will one day be deposited in the museum at Chantilly, near Paris, where it will be at the disposal of those who wish to study its contents.

The Vicomte has kindly devoted much time to answering my questions, and has shown me documents and autograph letters, the exact words of which have been the subject of discussion and dispute, so that I have been able myself to verify the fact that the copies made by M. de Spoelberch de Lovenjoul are taken exactly from the originals. He has warned me to be particularly careful about my authorities, as many of Balzac's letters — printed as though copied from autographs — are incorrectly dated, and have been much altered.

He has further added to his kindness by giving me several illustrations, and by having this book translated to him, in order to correct it carefully by the information to which he alone has access. I gladly take this opportunity of acknowledging how deeply I am indebted to him.

I cannot consider these words of introduction complete without again expressing my sense of what I owe to Dr. Reich, to whom the initial idea of this book is due, and without whose energetic impetus it would never have been written. He has found time, in the midst of a very busy life, to read through, and to make many valuable suggestions, and I am most grateful for all he has done to help me.

I must finish by thanking Mr. Curtis Brown most heartily for the trouble he has taken on my behalf, for the useful hints he has given me, and for the patience with which he has elucidated the difficulties of an inexperienced writer.

MARY F. SANDARS.

CHAPTER I

At a time when the so-called Realistic School is in the ascendant among novelists, it seems strange that little authentic information should have been published in the English language about the great French writer, Honore de Balzac. Almost alone among his contemporaries, he dared to claim the interest of the world for ordinary men and women solely on the ground of a common humanity. Thus he was the first to embody in literature the principle of Burns that "a man's a man for a' that"; and though this fact has now become a truism, it was a discovery, and an important discovery, when Balzac wrote. He showed that, because we are ourselves ordinary men and women, it is really human interest, and not sensational circumstance which appeals to us, and that material for enthralling drama can be found in the life of the most commonplace person—of a middle-aged shopkeeper threatened with bankruptcy, or of an elderly musician with a weakness for good dinners. At one blow he destroyed the unreal ideal of the Romantic School, who degraded man by setting up in his place a fantastic and impossible hero as the only theme worthy of their pen; and thus he laid the foundation of the modern novel.

His own life is full of interest. He was not a recluse or a bookworm; his work was to study men, and he lived among men, he fought strenuously, he enjoyed lustily, he suffered keenly, and he died prematurely, worn out by the force of his own emotions, and by the prodigies of labour to which he was impelled by the restless promptings of his active brain, and by his ever-pressing need for money. Some of his letters to Madame Hanska have been published during the last few years; and where can we read a more pathetic love story than the record of his seventeen years' waiting for her, and of the tragic ending to his long-deferred happiness? Or where in modern times can more exciting and often comical tales of adventure be found than the accounts of his wild and always unsuccessful attempts to become a millionaire? His friends comprised most of the celebrated French writers of the day; and though not a lover of society, he was acquainted with many varieties of people, while his own personality was powerful, vivid, and eccentric.

Thus he appears at first sight to be a fascinating subject for biography; but if we examine a little more closely, we shall realise the web of difficulties in which the writer of a complete and exhaustive Life of Balzac would involve himself, and shall understand why the task has never been attempted. The great author's money affairs alone are so complicated that it is doubtful whether he ever mastered them himself, and it is certainly impossible for any one else to understand them; while he managed to shroud his private life, especially his relations to women, in almost complete mystery. For some years after his death the monkish habit in which he attired himself was considered symbolic of his mental attitude; and even now, though the veil is partially lifted, and we realise the great part women played in his life, there remain many points which are not yet cleared up.

Consequently any one who attempts even in the most unambitious way to give a complete account of the great writer's life, is confronted with many blank spaces. It is true that the absolutely mysterious disappearances of which his contemporaries speak curiously are now partially accounted for, as we know that they were usually connected with Madame Hanska, and that Balzac's sense of honour would not allow him to breathe her name, except to his most intimate friends, and under the pledge of the strictest secrecy. His letters to her have allowed a flood of light to pour upon his hitherto veiled personality; but they are almost our only reliable source of information. Therefore, when they cease, because Balzac is with his ladylove, and we are suddenly excluded from his confidence, we can only guess what is happening.

In this way, we possess but the scantiest information about the journeys which occupied a great part of his time during the last few years of his life. We know that he travelled, regardless of expense and exhaustion, as quickly as possible, and by the very shortest route, to meet Madame Hanska; but this once accomplished, we can gather little more, and we long for a diary or a confidential correspondent. In the first rapture of his meeting at Neufchatel, he did indeed open his heart to his sister, Madame Surville; but his habitual discretion, and his care for the reputation of the woman he loved, soon imposed silence upon him, and he ceased to comment on the great drama of his life.

The great versatility of his mind, and the power he possessed of throwing himself with the utmost keenness into many absolutely dissimilar and incongruous enterprises at the same time, add further to the difficulty of understanding him. An extraordinary number of subjects had their place in his capacious brain, and the ease with which he dismissed one and took up another with equal zest the moment after, causes his doings to seem unnatural to us of ordinary mind. Leon Gozlan gives a curious instance of this on the occasion of the first reading of the "Ressources de Quinola."

Balzac had recited his play in the green-room of the Odeon to the assembled actors and actresses, and before a most critical audience had gone through the terrible strain of trying to improvise the fifth act, which was not yet written. He and Gozlan went straight from the hot atmosphere of the theatre to refresh themselves in the cool air of the Luxembourg Gardens. Here we should expect one of two things to happen. Either Balzac would be depressed with the ill-success of his fifth act, at which, according to Gozlan, he had acquitted himself so badly that Madame Dorval, the principal actress, refused to take a role in the play; or, on the other hand, his sanguine temperament would cause him to overlook the drawbacks, and to think only of the enthusiasm with which the first four acts had been received. Neither of these two things took place. Balzac "n'y pensait deja plus." He talked with the greatest eagerness of the embellishments he had proposed to M. Decazes for his palace, and especially of a grand spiral staircase, which was to lead from the centre of the Luxembourg Gardens to the Catacombs, so that these might be shown to visitors, and become a source of profit to Paris. But of his play he said nothing.

The reader of "Lettres a l'Etrangere," which are written to the woman with whom Balzac was passionately in love, and whom he afterwards married, may, perhaps, at first sight congratulate himself on at last understanding in some degree the great author's character and mode of life. If he dives beneath the surface, however, he will find that these beautiful and touching letters give but an incomplete picture; and that, while writing them, Balzac was throwing much energy into schemes, which he either does not mention to his correspondent, or touches on in the most cursory fashion. Therefore the perspective of his life is difficult to arrange, and ordinary rules for gauging character are at fault. We find it impossible to follow the principle, that because Balzac possessed one characteristic, he could not also show a diametrically opposite quality—that, for instance, because tenderness, delicacy of feeling, and a high sense of reverence and of honour were undoubtedly integral parts of his personality, the stories told by his contemporaries of his occasional coarseness must necessarily be false.

His own words, written to the Duchesse d'Abrantes in 1828, have no doubt a great element of truth in them: "I have the most singular character I know. I study myself as I might study another person, and I possess, shut up in my five foot eight inches, all the incoherences, all the contrasts possible; and those who think me vain, extravagant, obstinate, high-minded, without connection in my ideas,—a fop, negligent, idle, without application, without reflection, without any constancy; a chatterbox, without tact, badly brought up, impolite, whimsical, unequal in temper, — are quite as right as those who perhaps say that I am economical, modest, courageous, stingy, energetic, a worker, constant, silent, full of delicacy, polite, always gay. Those who consider that I am a coward will not be more wrong than those who say that I am extremely brave; in short, learned or ignorant, full of talent or absurd, nothing astonishes me more than myself. I end by believing that I am only an instrument played on by circumstances. Does this kaleidoscope exist, because, in the soul of those who claim to paint all the affections of the human heart, chance throws all these affections themselves, so that they may be able, by the force of their imagination, to feel what they paint? And is observation a sort of memory suited to aid this lively imagination? I begin to think so."[*]

[*] "Correspondance," vol. i. p. 77.

Certainly Balzac's character proves to the hilt the truth of the rule that, with few exceptions in the world's history, the higher the development, the more complex the organisation and the more violent the clashing of the divers elements of the man's nature; so that his soul resembles a field of battle, and he wears out quickly. Nevertheless, because everything in Balzac seems contradictory, when he is likened by one of his friends to the sea, which is one and indivisible, we perceive that the comparison is not inapt. Round the edge are the ever-restless waves; on the surface the foam blown by fitful gusts of wind, the translucent play of sunbeams, and the clamour of storms lashing up the billows; but down in the sombre depths broods the resistless, immovable force which tinges with its reflection the dancing and play above, and is the genius and fascination, the mystery and tragedy of the sea.

Below the merriment and herculean jollity, so little represented in his books, there was deep, gloomy force in the soul of the man who, gifted with an almost unparalleled imagination, would yet grip the realities of the pathetic and terrible situations he evolved with brutal strength and insistence. The mind of the writer of "Le Pere Goriot," "La Cousine Bette," and "Le Cousin Pons," those terrible tragedies where the Greek god Fate marches on his victims relentlessly, and there is no staying of the hand for pity, could not have been merely a wide, sunny expanse with no dark places. Nevertheless, we are again puzzled, when we attempt to realise the personality of a man whose imagination could soar to the mystical and philosophical conception of "Seraphita," which is full of religious poetry, and who yet had the power in "Cesar Birotteau" to invest prosaic and even sordid details with absolute verisimilitude, or in the "Contes Drolatiques" would write, in Old French, stories of Rabelaisian breadth and humour. The only solution of these contradictions is that, partly perhaps by reason of great physical strength, certainly because of an abnormally powerful brain and imagination, Balzac's thoughts, feelings, and passions were unusually strong, and were endowed with peculiar impetus and independence of each other; and from this resulted a versatility which caused most unexpected developments, and which fills us of smaller mould with astonishment.

Nevertheless, steadfastness was decidedly the groundwork of the character of the man who was not dismayed by the colossal task of the Comedie Humaine; but pursued his work through discouragement, ill health, and anxieties. Except near the end of his life, when, owing to the unreasonable strain to which it had been subjected, his powerful organism had begun to fail, Balzac refused to neglect his vocation even for his love affairs—a self-control which must have been a severe test to one of his temperament.

This absorption in his work cannot have been very flattering to the ladies he admired; and one plausible explanation of Madame de Castries' coldness to his suit is that she did not believe in the devotion of a lover who, while paying her the most assiduous court at Aix, would yet write from five in the morning till half-past five in the evening, and only bestow his company on her from six till an early bedtime. Even the adored Madame Hanska had to take second place where work was concerned. When they were both at Vienna in 1835, he writes with some irritation, apparently in answer to a remonstrance on her part, that he cannot work when he knows he has to go out; and that, owing to the time he spent the evening before in her society, he must now shut himself up for fourteen hours and toil at "Le Lys dans la Vallee." He adds, with his customary force of language, that if he does not finish the book at Vienna, he will throw himself into the Danube!

The great psychologist knew his own character well when, in another letter to Madame Hanska, who has complained of his frivolity, he cries, indignantly: "Frivolity of character! Why, you speak as a good *bourgeois* would have done, who, seeing Napoleon turn to the right, to the left, and on all sides to examine his field of battle, would have said, 'This man cannot remain in one place; he has no fixed idea!'"[*]

[*] "Lettres a l'Etrangere."

This change of posture, though consonant, as Balzac says, with real stability, is a source of bewilderment to the reader of his sayings and doings, till it dawns upon him that, through pride, policy, and the usual shrinking of the sensitive from casting their pearls before swine, Balzac was a confirmed *poseur*, so that what he tells us is often more misleading than his silence. Leon Gozlan's books are a striking instance of the fact that, with all Balzac's jollity, his camaraderie, and his flow of words, he did not readily reveal himself, except to those whom he could thoroughly trust to understand him. Gozlan went about with Balzac very often, and was specially chosen by him time after time as a companion; but he really knew very little of the great man. If we compare his account of Balzac's feeling or want of feeling at a certain crisis, and then read what is written on the same subject to Madame Hanska, Balzac's enormous power of reserve, and his habit of deliberately misleading those who were not admitted to his confidence, may be gauged.

George Sand tells us an anecdote which shows how easily, from his anxiety not to wear his heart upon his sleeve, Balzac might be misunderstood. He dined with her on January 29th, 1844, after a visit to Russia, and related at table, with peals of laughter and apparently enormous satisfaction, an instance which had come under his notice of the ferocious exercise of absolute power. Any stranger listening, would have thought him utterly heartless and brutal, but George Sand knew better. She whispered to him: "That makes you inclined to cry, doesn't it?"[*] He answered nothing; left off laughing, as if a spring in him had broken; was very serious for the rest of the evening, and did not say a word more about Russia.

[*] "Autour de la Table," by George Sand.

Balzac looked on the world as an arena; and as the occasion and the audience arose, he suited himself with the utmost aplomb to the part he intended to play, so that under the costume and the paint the real Balzac is often difficult to discover. Sometimes he would pretend to be rich and prosperous, when he thought an editor would thereby be induced to offer him good terms; and sometimes, when it suited his purpose, he would make the most of his poverty and of his pecuniary embarrassments. Madame Hanska, from whom he required sympathy, heard much of his desperate situation after the failure of Werdet, whom he likens to the vulture that tormented Prometheus; but as it would not answer for Emile de Girardin, the editor of *La Presse*, to know much about Balzac's pecuniary difficulties, Madame de Girardin is assured that the report of Werdet's supposed disaster is false, and Balzac virtuously remarks that in the present century honesty is never believed in.[*] Sometimes his want of candour appears to have its origin in his hatred to allow that he is beaten, and there is something childlike and naive in his vanity. We are amused when he informs Madame Hanska that he is giving up the *Chronique de Paris* —which, after a brilliant flourish of trumpets at the start, was a complete failure—because the speeches in the Chambre des Deputes are so silly that he abandons the idea of taking up politics, as he had intended to do by means of journalism. In a later letter, however, he is obliged to own that, though the *Chronique* has been, of course, a brilliant success, money is lacking, owing to the wickedness of several abandoned characters, and that therefore he has been forced to bring the publication to an end.

[*] "La Genese d'un Roman de Balzac," p. 152, by Le Vicomte de Spoelberch de Lovenjoul.

Of one vanity he was completely free. He did not pose to posterity. Of his books he thought much—each one was a masterpiece, more glorious than the last; but he never imagined that people would be in the least interested in his doings, and he did not care about their opinion of him. Nevertheless there was occasionally a gleam of joy, when some one unexpectedly showed a spontaneous admiration for his work. For instance, in a Viennese concert-room, where the whole audience had risen to do honour to the great author, a young man seized his hand and put it to his lips, saying, "I kiss the hand that wrote 'Seraphita,'" and Balzac said afterwards to his sister, "They may deny my talent, if they choose, but the memory of that student will always comfort me."

His genius would, he hoped, be acknowledged one day by all the world; but there was a singular and lovable absence of self-consciousness in his character, and a peculiar humility and childlikeness under his braggadocio and apparent arrogance. Perhaps this was the source of the power of fascination he undoubtedly exercised over his contemporaries. Nothing is more noticeable to any one reading about Balzac than the difference between the tone of amused indulgence with which those who knew him personally, speak of his peculiarities, and the contemptuous or horrified comments of people who only heard from others of his extraordinary doings.

He had bitter enemies as well as devoted friends; and his fighting proclivities, his objection to allow that he is ever in the wrong, and his habit of blaming others for his misfortunes, have had a great effect in obscuring our knowledge of Balzac's life, as the people he abused were naturally exasperated, and took up their pens, not to give a fair account of what really happened, but to justify themselves against Balzac's aspersions. Werdet's book is an instance of this. Beneath the extravagant admiration he expresses for the "great writer," with his "heart of gold," a glint can be seen from time to time of the animus which inspired him when he wrote, and we feel that his statements must be received with caution, and do not add much to our real knowledge of Balzac.

Nevertheless, though there are still blank spaces to be filled, as well as difficulties to overcome and puzzles to unravel, much fresh information has lately been discovered about the great writer, notably the "Lettres a l'Etrangere," published in 1899, a collection of some of the letters written by Balzac, from 1833 to 1848, to Madame Hanska, the Polish lady who afterwards became his wife. These letters, which are the property of the Vicomte de Spoelberch de Lovenjoul, give many interesting details, and alter the earlier view of several points in Balzac's career and character; but the volume is large, and takes some time to read. It is therefore thought, that as those who would seem competent, by their knowledge and skill, to overcome the difficulties of writing a complete and exhaustive life are silent, a short sketch, which can claim nothing more than correctness of detail, may not be unwelcome. It contains no attempt to give what could only be a very inadequate criticism of the books of the great novelist; for that, the reader must be referred to the many works by learned Frenchmen who have made a lifelong study of the subject. It is written, however, in the hope that the admirers of "Eugenie Grandet" and "Le Pere Goriot" may like to read something of the author of these masterpieces, and that even those who only know the great French novelist by reputation may be interested to hear a little about the restless life of a man who was a slave to his genius— was driven by its insistent voice to engage in work which was enormously difficult to him, to lead an abnormal and unhealthy life, and to wear out his exuberant physical strength prematurely. He died with his powers at their highest and his great task unfinished; and a sense of thankfulness for his own mediocrity fills the reader, when he reaches the end of the life of Balzac.

CHAPTER II

According to Theophile Gautier, herculean jollity was the most striking characteristic of the great writer, whose genius excels in sombre and often sordid tragedy. George Sand, too, speaks of Balzac's "serene soul with a smile in it"; and this was the more remarkable, because he lived at a time when discontent and despair were considered the sign-manual of talent.

Physically Balzac was far from satisfying a romantic ideal of fragile and enervated genius. Short and stout, square of shoulder, with an abundant mane of thick black hair—a sign of bodily vigour—his whole person breathed intense vitality. Deep red lips, thick, but finely curved, and always ready to laugh, attested, like the ruddiness in his full cheeks, to the purity and richness of his blood. His forehead, high, broad, and unwrinkled, save for a line between the eyes, and his neck, thick, round, and columnar, contrasted in their whiteness with the colour in the rest of the face. His hands were large and dimpled —"beautiful hands," his sister calls them. He was proud of them, and had a slight prejudice against any one with ugly extremities. His nose, about which he gave special directions to David when his bust was taken, was well cut, rather long, and square at the end, with the lobes of the open nostrils standing out prominently. As to his eyes, according to Gautier, there were none like them.[*] They had inconceivable life, light, and magnetism. They were eyes to make an eagle lower his lids, to read through walls and hearts, to terrify a wild beast—eyes of a sovereign, a seer, a conqueror. Lamartine likens them to "darts dipped in kindliness." Balzac's sister speaks of them as brown; but, according to other contemporaries, they were like brilliant black diamonds, with rich reflections of gold, the white of the eyeballs being tinged with blue. They seemed to be lit with the fire of the genius within, to read souls, to answer questions before they were asked, and at the same time to pour out warm rays of kindliness from a joyous heart.

[*] "Portraits Contemporains—Honore de Balzac," by Theophile Gautier.

At all points Balzac's personality differed from that of his contemporaries of the Romantic School—those transcendental geniuses of despairing temper, who were utterly hopeless about the prosaic world in which, by some strange mistake, they found themselves; and from which they felt that no possible inspiration for their art could be drawn. So little attuned were these unfortunates to their commonplace surroundings that, after picturing in their writings either fiendish horrors, or a beautiful, impossible atmosphere, peopled by beings out of whom all likeness to humanity had been eliminated, they not infrequently lost their mental balance altogether, or hurried by their own act out of a dull world which could never satisfy their lively imaginations. Balzac, on the other hand, loved the world. How, with the acute powers of observation, and the intuition, amounting almost to second sight, with which he was gifted, could he help doing so? The man who could at will quit his own personality, and invest himself with that of another; who would follow a workman and his wife on their way home at night from a music-hall, and listen to their discussions on domestic matters till he imbibed their life, felt their ragged clothing on his back, and their desires and wants in his soul,—how could he find life dull, or the most commonplace individual uninteresting?

In dress Balzac was habitually careless. He would rush to the printer's office, after twelve hours of hard work, with his hat drawn over his eyes, his hands thrust into shabby gloves, and his feet in shoes with high sides, worn over loose trousers, which were pleated at the waist and held down with straps. Even in society he took no trouble about his appearance, and Lamartine describes him as looking, in the salon of Madame de Girardin, like a schoolboy who has outgrown his clothes. Only for a short time, which he describes with glee in his letters to Madame Hanska, did he pose as a man of fashion. Then he wore a magnificent white waistcoat, and a blue coat with gold buttons; carried the famous cane, with a knob studded with turquoises, celebrated in Madame de Girardin's story, "La Canne de Monsieur de Balzac"; and drove in a tilbury, behind a high-stepping horse, with a tiny tiger, whom he christened Anchise, perched on the back seat. This phase was quickly over, the horses were sold, and Balzac appeared no more in the box reserved for dandies at the Opera. Of the fashionable outfit, the only property left was the microscopic groom—an orphan, of whom Balzac took the greatest care, and whom he visited daily during the boy's last illness, a year or two after. Thenceforward he reverted to his usual indifference about appearances, his only vanity being the spotless cleanliness of his working costume—a loose dressing-gown of white flannel or cashmere, made like the habit of a Benedictine monk, which was kept in round the waist by a silk girdle, and was always scrupulously guarded from ink-stains.

Naive as a child, anxious for sympathy, frankly delighted with his own masterpieces, yet modest in a fashion peculiar to himself, Balzac gave a dominant impression of kindliness and bonhomie, which overshadowed even the idea of intellect. To his friends he is not in the first place the author of the "Comedie Humaine," designed, as George Sand rather grandiloquently puts it, to be "an almost universal examination of the ideas, sentiments, customs, habits, legislation, arts, trades, costumes, localities—in short, of all that constitutes the lives of his contemporaries"[*]—that claim to notice recedes into the background, and what is seen clearly is the *bon camarade*, with his great hearty laugh, his jollity, his flow of language, and his jokes, often Rabelaisian in flavour. Of course there was another side to the picture, and there were times in his hardset and harassing life when even *his* vivacity failed him. These moods were, however, never apparent in society; and even to his intimate men friends, such as Theophile Gautier and Leon Gozlan, Balzac was always the delightful, whimsical companion, to be thought of and written of afterwards with an amused, though affectionate smile. Only to women, his principal confidantes, who played as important a part in his life as they do in his books, did he occasionally show the discouragement to which the artistic nature is prone. Sometimes the state of the weather, which always had a great effect on him, the difficulty of his work, the fatigue of sitting up all night, and his monetary embarrassments, brought him to an extreme state of depression, both physical and mental. He would arrive at the house of Madame Surville, his sister, who tells the story, hardly able to drag himself along, in a gloomy, dejected state, with his skin sallow and jaundiced.

[*] "Autour de la Table," by George Sand.

"Don't console me," he would say in a faint voice, dropping into a chair; "it is useless—I am a dead man."

The dead man would then begin, in a doleful voice, to tell of his new troubles; but he soon revived, and the words came forth in the most ringing tones of his voice. Then, opening his proofs, he would drop back into his dismal accents and say, by way of conclusion:

"Yes, I am a wrecked man, sister!"

"Nonsense! No man is wrecked with such proofs as those to correct."

Then he would raise his head, his face would unpucker little by little, the sallow tones of his skin would disappear.

"My God, you are right!" he would say. "Those books will make me live. Besides, blind Fortune is here, isn't she? Why shouldn't she protect a Balzac as well as a ninny? And there are always ways of wooing her. Suppose one of my millionaire friends (and I have some), or a banker, not knowing what to do with his money, should come to me and say, 'I know your immense talents, and your anxieties: you want such-and-such a sum to free yourself; accept it fearlessly: you will pay me; your pen is worth millions!' That is *all I want,* my dear."[*]

[*] "Balzac, sa Vie et ses Oeuvres, d'apres la Correspondance," by Mme. L. Surville (nee de Balzac).

Then the "child-man," as his sister calls him, would imagine himself a member of the Institute; then in the Chamber of Peers, pointing out and reforming abuses, and governing a highly prosperous country. Finally, he would end the interview with, "Adieu! I am going home to see if my banker is waiting for me"; and would depart, quite consoled, with his usual hearty laugh.

He lived, his sister tells us, to a great extent in a world of his own, peopled by the imaginary characters in his books, and he would gravely discuss its news, as others do that of the real world. Sometimes he was delighted at the grand match he had planned for his hero; but often affairs did not go so well, and perhaps it would give him much anxious thought to marry his heroine suitably, as it was necessary to find her a husband in her own set, and this might be difficult to arrange. When asked about the past of one of his creations, he replied gravely that he "had not been acquainted with Monsieur de Jordy before he came to Nemours," but added that, if his questioner were anxious to know, he would try to find out. He had many fancies about names, declaring that those which are invented do not give life to imaginary beings, whereas those really borne by some one endow them with vitality. Leon Gozlan says that he was dragged by Balzac half over Paris in search of a suitable name for the hero of a story to be published in the *Revue Parisienne.* After they had trudged through scores of streets in vain, Balzac, to his intense joy, discovered "Marcas" over a small tailor's shop, to which he added, as "a flame, a plume, a star," the initial Z. Z. Marcas conveyed to him the idea of a great, though unknown, philosopher, poet, or silversmith, like Benvenuto Cellini; he went no farther, he was satisfied—he had found "*the* name of names."[*]

[*] "Balzac en Pantoufles," by Leon Gozlan.

Many are the amusing anecdotes told of Balzac's schemes for becoming rich. Money he struggled for unceasingly, not from sordid motives, but because it was necessary to his conception of a happy life. Without its help he could never be freed from his burden of debt, and united to the *grande dame* of his fancy, who must of necessity be posed in elegant toilette, on a suitable background of costly brocades and objects of art. Nevertheless, in spite of all his efforts, and of a capacity and passion for work which seemed almost superhuman, he never obtained freedom from monetary anxiety. Viewed in this light, there is pathos in his many impossible plans for making his fortune, and freeing himself from the strain which was slowly killing him.

Some of his projected enterprises were wildly fantastic, and prove that the great author was, like many a genius, a child at heart; and that, in his eyes, the world was not the prosaic place it is to most men and women, but an enchanted globe, like the world of "Treasure Island," teeming with the possibility of strange adventure. At one time he hoped to gain a substantial income by growing pineapples in the little garden at Les Jardies, and later on he thought money might be made by transporting oaks from Poland to France. For some months he believed that, by means of magnetism exercised on somnambulists, he had discovered the exact spot at Pointe a Pitre where Toussaint-Louverture hid his treasure, and afterwards shot the negroes he had employed to bury it, lest they should betray its hiding-place. Jules Sandeau and Theophile Gautier were chosen to assist in the enterprise of carrying off the hidden gold, and were each to receive a quarter of the treasure, Balzac, as leader of the venture, taking the other half. The three friends were to start secretly and separately with spades and shovels, and, their work accomplished, were to put the treasure on a brig which was to be in waiting, and were to return as millionaires to France. This brilliant plan failed, because none of the three adventurers had at the moment money to pay his passage out; and no doubt, by the time that the necessary funds were forthcoming, Balzac's fertile brain was engaged on other enterprises.[*]

[*] "Portraits Contemporains—Honore de Balzac," by Theophile Gautier.

The foundation of his pecuniary misfortunes was laid before his birth, when his father, forty-five years old and unmarried, sank the bulk of his fortune in life annuities, so that his son was in the unfortunate position of starting life in very comfortable circumstances, and of finding himself in want of money just when he most needed it.

Balzac's father was born in Languedoc in 1746, and we are told by his son that he had been Secretary, and by Madame Surville, advocate, of the Council under Louis XVI. Both these statements however appear to be incorrect, and may be considered to have been harmless fictions on the part of the old gentleman, as no record of his name can be found in the Royal Calendar, which was very carefully kept. Almanacs are awkward things, and his name *is* mentioned in the National Calendar of 1793 as a "lawyer" and "member of the general council for the section of the rights of man in the Commune." But he evidently preferred to draw a veil over his revolutionary experiences, and it seems rather hard that, because he happened to possess a celebrated son, his little secrets should be exposed to the light of day.

Later on he became an ardent Royalist, and in 1814 he joined with Bertrand de Molleville to draw up a memoir against the Charter, which Balzac says was dictated to him, then a boy of fifteen; and he also mentions that he remembers hearing M. de Molleville cry out, "The Constitution ruined Louis XVI., and the Charter will kill the Bourbons!" "No compromise" formed an essential part of the creed of the Royalists at the Restoration.

When M. de Balzac[*] married, in 1797, he was in charge of the Commissariat of the Twenty-second Military Division; and in 1798 he came to live in Tours, where he had bought a house and some land near the town, and where he remained for nineteen years. Here, on May 16, 1799, St. Honore's day, his son, the celebrated novelist, was born, and was christened Honore after the saint.

[*] The Balzac family will be accorded the "de" in this account of them.

Old M. de Balzac was in his own way literary, and had written two or three pamphlets, one on his favourite subject—that of health. He seems to have been a man of much originality, many peculiarities, and much kindness of heart. He was evidently impulsive, like his celebrated son, and he certainly made a culpable mistake, and a cruel one for his family, when he rashly concluded that he would always remain a bachelor, and arranged that his income should die with him. He afterwards hoped to repair the wrong he had thus done to his children, by outliving the other shareholders and obtaining a part of the immense capital of the Tontine. Fortunately for himself he possessed extraordinary optimism, and power of excluding from his mind the possibility of all unpleasant contingencies—qualities which he handed on in full measure to Honore. He therefore kept himself happy in the monetary disappointments of his later life, by thinking and talking of the millions his children would inherit from their centenarian father. For their sakes it was necessary that he should take care of his health, and he considered that, by maintaining the "equilibrium of the vital forces," there was absolutely no doubt that he would live for a hundred years or more. Therefore he followed a strict regimen, and gave himself an infinite amount of trouble, as well as amusement, by his minute arrangements.

Unfortunately, however, the truth of his theories could never be tested, as he died in 1829, at the age of eighty-three, from the effects of an operation; and Madame de Balzac and her family were left to face the stern facts of life, denuded of the rose-coloured haze in which they had been clothed by the kindly old enthusiast. Balzac's mother certainly had a hard life, and from what we hear of her nervous, excitable nature—inherited apparently from her mother, Madame Sallambier—we can hardly be astonished when Balzac writes to Madame Hanska, in 1835, that if her misfortunes do not kill her, it is feared they will destroy her reason. Nevertheless, she outlived her celebrated son, and is mentioned by Victor Hugo, when he visited Balzac's deathbed, as the only person in the room, except a nurse and a servant.[*]

[*] "Choses Vues," by Victor Hugo.

She was many years younger than her husband—a beauty and an heiress; and she evidently had her own way with the easy-going old M. de Balzac, and was the moving spirit in the household: so that the ease and absence of friction in her early life must have made her subsequent troubles and humiliations especially galling. Besides Honore, she had three children: Laure, afterwards Madame Surville; Laurence, who died young; and Henry, the black sheep of the family, who returned from the colonies, after having made an unsatisfactory marriage, and who, during the last years of Honore de Balzac's life, required constant monetary help from his relations.

Her two young children were Madame de Balzac's favourites, and they and their affairs gave her constant trouble. In 1822 Laurence married a M. Saint-Pierre de Montzaigle, apparently a good deal older than herself; and Honore gives a very *couleur de rose* account of his future brother-in-law's family, in a letter written at the time of the engagement to Laure, who was already married. He does not seem so charmed with the bridegroom, *il troubadouro*, as with his surroundings, and remarks that he has lost his top teeth, and is very conceited, but will do well enough—as a husband. Every one is delighted at the marriage; but Laure can imagine *maman's* state of nervous excitement from her recollection of the last few days before her own wedding, and can fancy that he and Laurence are not enjoying themselves. "Nature surrounds roses with thorns, and pleasures with a crowd of troubles. Mamma follows the example of nature."[*]

[*] "H. de Balzac—Correspondence," vol. i. p. 41.

Laurence's death, in 1826, must have been a terrible grief to the poor mother; but she may have realised later on that her daughter had escaped much trouble, as in 1836 the Balzac family threatened M. de Montzaigle with a lawsuit on the subject of his son, who was left to wander about Paris without food, shoes, or clothes. We cannot suppose that any one with such sketchy views of the duties of a father could have been a particularly satisfactory husband; but perhaps Laurence died before she had time to discover M. de Montzaigle's deficiencies.

Henry, the younger son, appears to have been brought up on a different method from that pursued with Honore, as we hear in 1821 that Madame de Balzac considered that the boy was unhappy and bored with school, that he was with canting people who punished him for nothing, and must be taken away. Evidently the younger son was the mother's darling; but her mode of bringing him up was not happy in its effects, as he seems to have given continual anxiety and trouble. He came back from the colonies with his wife; and by threatening to blow out his brains, he worked on his mother's feelings, and induced her to help him with money, and nearly to ruin herself. In consequence she was obliged for a time to take up her abode with Honore, an arrangement which did not work well. Even when Henry was at last shipped off to the Indies, he continued to agitate his family by sending them pathetic accounts of his distress and necessities, and these letters from her much-loved son must have been peculiarly painful to Madame de Balzac.

Honore and his mother seem never to have understood each other very well; and she was stern with him and Laure in their youth, while she lavished caresses on her younger children. Likeness to a father is not always a passport to a mother's favour, and Madame de Balzac does not appear to have realised her son's genius, and evidently feared that, without due repression in youth, the paternal type of imaginative optimist would be repeated.

She was not a tender mother in childhood, when indeed she saw little of Honore, as she left him out at nurse till he was four years old, and sent him to school when he was eight; but later on in all practical matters she did her best for him, lending him money when he was in difficulties, and looking after his business affairs when he was away from Paris. She was evidently easily offended, and rather absurdly tenacious of her maternal dignity; so that sometimes the deference and submission of the great writer are surprising and rather touching. On the other hand it must be remembered that Honore made great demands on his friends, that they were expected to accord continual sympathy and admiration, to be perfectly tactful in their criticisms, and were only very occasionally allowed to give advice. Therefore his opinion of his mother's coldness may have sprung from her failure to answer to the requirements of his peculiar code of affection, and not from any real want of love on her part.

Certainly her severity in his youth had the effect of concentrating the whole devotion of Honore's childish heart on Laure, the *cara sorella* of his later years. She was a writer, the author of "Le Compagnon du Foyer." To her we owe a charming sketch of her celebrated brother, and she was the confidante of his hopes, ambitions, and troubles, of his sentimental friendships, and of the faults and embarrassments which he confided to no one else. Expressions of affection for her occur constantly in his letters, and in 1837 he writes to Madame Hanska that Laure is ill, and therefore the whole universe seems out of gear, and that he passes whole nights in despair because she is everything to him. The friendship between the brother and sister was deep, devoted, and faithful, as Balzac's friendships generally were—he did not care, as he said in one of his letters, for *amities d'epiderme*—and the restriction put on his intercourse with his sister by the jealousy of M. Surville was one of the many troubles which darkened his later years.

Occasionally, indeed, there were disagreements between the brother and sister, when Honore did not approve of Laure's aspirations for authorship. The only subject which really caused coldness on both sides, however—and this was temporary—was Laure's want of sympathy for Balzac's attachment to Madame Hanska; because she, like many of his friends, felt doubtful whether his passionate love was returned in anything like equal measure. Perhaps, too, there may have lurked in the sister's mind a slight jealousy of this alien *grande dame*, who had stolen away her brother's heart from France, who moved in a sphere quite unlike that of the Balzac family, and whose existence prevented several advantageous and sensible marriages which she could have arranged for Honore. Balzac, it must be allowed, was not always tactful in his descriptions of the perfections of the Hanska family, who were, of course, in his eyes, surrounded with aureoles borrowed from the light of his "polar star." It must have been distinctly annoying, when the virtues, talents, and charms of the young Countess Anna were held up as an object lesson for Madame Surville's two daughters, who were no doubt, from their mother's point of view, quite as admirable as Madame Hanska's ewe lamb. Nevertheless, there was never any real separation between the brother and sister; and it is to Laure that—certain of her participation in his joy—poor Balzac penned his delighted letter the day after his wedding, signed "Thy brother Honore, at the summit of happiness."

Laure's own career was chequered. In 1820 she married an engineer, M. Midy de la Greneraye Surville, and from the first the marriage was not very happy, as Honore writes, a month after it took place, to blame Laure for her melancholy at the separation from her family, and to counsel philosophy and piano practice. Possibly Balzac's habits of ascendency over those he loved, and his wonderful gift of fascination —a gift which often provides its possessor with bitter enemies among those outside its influence— made matters difficult for his brother-in-law, and did not tend to promote harmony between Laure and her husband. M. Surville probably became exasperated by useless attempts to vie in his wife's eyes with her much-beloved brother—at any rate, in later years he was tyrannical in preventing their intercourse, and we hear of the unfortunate Laure coming in secret to see Balzac, on her birthday in 1836, and holding a watch in her hand, because she did not dare to stay away longer than twenty minutes. There were other worries for Laure and her husband, for, like the rest of the Balzac family, they were in continual difficulty about money matters. M. Surville seems to have been a man of enterprise, and to have had many schemes on hand—such as making a lateral canal on the Loire from Nantes to Orleans, building a bridge in Paris, or constructing a little railway. Speaking of the canal, Balzac cheerfully and airily remarked in 1836 that only a capital of twenty-six millions of francs required collecting, and then the Survilles would be on the high road to prosperity. This trifling matter was not after all arranged, if we may judge from the fact that in 1849 the Survilles moved to a cheap lodging, and were advised by Balzac, in a letter from Russia, to follow his habit of former days, and to cook only twice a week. In fact, they were evidently passing through one of those monetary crises to which we become used when reading the annals of the Balzacs, and which irresistibly remind the reader of similar affairs in the Micawber family.

In spite of the friction on the subject of Madame Surville, there was never any actual breach between Honore and his brother-in-law; indeed, he speaks several times of working amicably with M. Surville, in the vain attempt to put in order the hopelessly involved web of family affairs. He evidently had great faith in his brother-in-law's plans for making his fortune, and took the keenest interest in them, even offering to go over to London, to sell an invention for effecting economy in the construction of inclined planes on railways. But M. Surville changed his mind at the last, and Balzac never went to England after all.

Honore and Laure were together during the time of their earliest childhood, as they were left at the cottage of the same foster-mother, and did not come home till Honore was four years old. His sister says, "My recollections of his tenderness date far back. I have not forgotten the headlong rapidity with which he ran to save me from tumbling down the three high steps without a railing, which led from our nurse's room to the garden. His loving protection continued after we returned to our father's house, where, more than once, he allowed himself to be punished for my faults, without betraying me. Once, when I came upon the scene in time to accuse myself of the wrong, he said, 'Don't acknowledge next time—I like to be punished for you.'"[*]

[*] "Balzac, sa vie et ses oeuvres, d'apres sa correspondance," by Madame L. Surville (nee de Balzac).

Both children were in great awe of their parents, and Honore's fear of his mother was extreme. Years after, he told a friend that he was never able to hear her voice without a trembling which deprived him of his faculties. Their father treated them with uniform kindness, but Honore's heart was filled with love for his kind grandparents, to whom he paid a visit in Paris in

1804. He came back to Tours with wonderful stories of the beauties of their house, their garden, and their big dog Mouche, with whom he had made great friends. The news of his grandfather's death a few months later was a great grief to him, and made a deep impression on his childish mind. His sister tells us that long afterwards, when the two were receiving a reprimand from their mother, and he saw Laure unable to control a wild burst of laughter, which he knew would lead to serious consequences, he tried to stop her by whispering in tragic tones, "Think about your grandfather's death!"

He was a child of very deep affections and warmth of heart, but he did not show any special intelligence. He was lively, merry, and extremely talkative, but sometimes a silent mood would fall on him, and perhaps, as his sister says, his imagination was then carrying him to distant worlds, though the family only thought the chatterbox was tired. In all ways, however, he was in these days a very ordinary child, devoted to fairy stories, fond of the popular nursery amusement of making up plays, and charmed with the excruciating noise he brought out of a little red violin. This he would sometimes play on for hours, till even the faithful Laure would remonstrate, and he would be astonished that she did not realise the beauty of his music.

This happy childish life, chastened only by the tremors which both children felt when taken by their governess in the morning and at bedtime into the stern presence of their mother, did not last very long for Honore. When he was eight years old (his sister says seven, but this seems to be a mistake), there was a change in his life, as the home authorities decided that it was time his education should begin in good earnest. He was therefore taken from the day school at Tours, and sent to the semi-military college founded by the Oratorians in the sleepy little town of Vendome. On page 7 of the school record there is the following notice: "No. 460. Honore Balzac, age de huit ans un mois. A eu la petite verole, sans infirmites. Caractere sanguin, s'echauffant facilement, et sujet a quelques fievres de chaleur. Entre au pensionnat le 22 juin, 1807. Sorti, le 22 aout, 1813. S'adresser a M. Balzac, son pere, a Tours."[*] Thus is summed up the character of the future writer of the "Comedie Humaine," and there was apparently nothing remarkable or precocious about the boy, as his quick temper is his most salient point in the eyes of his masters. It will be noticed, too, that the "de," about which Balzac was very particular, and which was the occasion of many scoffing remarks on the part of his enemies, does not appear on this register.

[*] "Balzac au College," by Champfleury.

Honore was a small boy to have been completely separated from home, and the whole scheme of education as devised by the Oratorian fathers appears to have been a strange one. One of the rules forbade outside holidays, and Honore never left the college once during the six years he was at school; so that there was no supervision from his parents, and no chance of complaint if he were unhappy or ill treated. His family came to see him at Easter and also at the prize-givings; but on these occasions, to which he looked forward, his sister tells us, with eager delight, reproaches were generally his portion, on account of his want of success in school work. In "Louis Lambert" he gives an interesting account of the college, which was in the middle of the town on the little river Loir, and contained a chapel, theatre, infirmary, bakery, and gardens. There were two or three hundred pupils, divided according to their ages or attainments into four classes—*les grands, les moyens*, les petits_, and *les minimes* —and each class had its own class-room and courtyard. Balzac was considered the idlest and most pathetic boy in his division, and was continually punished. Reproaches, the ferule, the dark cell, were his portion, and with his quick and delicate senses he suffered intensely from the want of air in the class-rooms. There, according to the graphic picture in "Louis Lambert," everything was dirty, and eighty boys inhabited a hall, in the centre of which were two buckets full of water, where all washed their faces and hands every morning, the water being only renewed once in the day. To add to the odours, the air was vitiated by the smell of pigeons killed for fete days, and of dishes stolen from the refectory, and kept by the pupils in their lockers. The boy who, in the future, was to awaken actual physical disgust in his readers by his description of the stuffy and dingy boarding-house dining-room in "Le Pere Goriot," was crushed and stupefied by his surroundings, and would sit for hours with his head on his hand, not attempting to learn, but gazing dreamily at the clouds, or at the foliage of the trees in the court below. No wonder that he was the despair of his masters, and that his famous "Traite de la volonte," which he composed instead of preparing the ordinary school work, was summarily confiscated and destroyed. So many were the punishment lines given him to write, that his holidays were almost entirely taken up, and he had not six days of liberty the whole time that he was at college.

In addition to the troubles incident to Honore's peculiar temperament and genius, he had in the winter, like the other pupils, to submit to actual physical suffering. The price of education included also that of clothing, the parents who sent their children to the Vendome College paying a yearly sum, and therewith comfortably absolving themselves from all trouble and responsibility. But the results were not happy for the boys, who dragged themselves painfully along the icy roads in miserable remnants of boots, their feet half dead, and swollen with sores and chilblains. Out of sixty children, not ten walked without torture, and many of them would cry with rage as they limped along, each step being a painful effort; but with the invincible physical pluck and moral cowardice of childhood, would hide their tears, for fear of ridicule from their companions.

Nevertheless, even to Balzac, who was peculiarly unfitted for it, life at the college had its pleasures. The food appears to have been good, and the discipline at meals not very severe, as a regular system of exchange of helpings to suit the particular tastes of each boy went on all through dinner, and caused endless amusement. Some one who had received peas as his portion would prefer dessert, and the proposition "Un dessert pour des pois" would pass from mouth to mouth till the bargain had been made. Other pleasures were the pet pigeons, the gardens, the sweets bought secretly during the walks, the permission to play cards and to have theatrical performances during the holidays, the military music, the games, and the slides made in winter. Best of all, however, was the shop which opened in the class-room every Sunday during playtime for the sale of boxes, tools, pigeons of all sorts, mass-books (for these there was not much demand), knives, balls, pencils—everything a boy could wish for. The proud possessor of six francs—meant to last for the term—felt that the contents of the whole shop were at his disposal. Saturday night was passed in anxious yet rapturous calculations, and the responses at Mass during that happy Sunday morning mingled themselves with thoughts of the glorious time coming in the afternoon. Next Sunday was not quite so delightful, as probably there were only a few sous left, and possibly some of the purchases were broken, or had not turned out quite satisfactorily. Then, too, there was a long vista of Sundays in the future, without any possibility of shopping; but after all a certain amount of compounding is always necessary in life, and an intense short joy is worth a grey time before and after.

When Balzac was fourteen years old, his life at the college came suddenly to an end, as, to the alarm of his masters, he was attacked by coma with feverish symptoms, and they begged his parents to take him home at once. It is curious to notice that the Fathers make no reference to this failure in their educational system in the school record, where there is no reason given for Honore's departure from school. Certainly his life at Vendome was not very healthy, as sometimes for idleness, inattention, or impertinence he was for months shut up every day in a niche six feet square, with a wooden door pierced by holes to let in air. When Champfleury visited the college years afterwards, the only person who remembered Balzac was the old Father who had charge of these cells, and he spoke of the boy's "great black eyes." Confinement in these *culottes de bois*, as they were called, was much dreaded by the boys, and the punishment seems barbarous and senseless, except from the point of view of getting rid of troublesome pupils. Balzac, however, welcomed the relief from ordinary school life, and indeed manoeuvred to be shut up. In the cells he had leisure to dream as he pleased, he was free from the drudgery of learning his lessons, and he managed to secrete books in his cage, and thus to absorb the contents of most of the volumes in the fine library collected by the learned Oratorian founders of the college. The ideas in many of the learned tomes were far beyond his age, but he understood them, remembered them afterwards, and could recall in later years not only the thought in each book, but also the disposition of his mind when he read them. Naturally this precocity of intellect caused brain fatigue, though this would never have been suspected by the Fathers of their idlest pupil.

Honore, his sister tells us, came home thin and puny, like a somnambulist sleeping with open eyes, and his grandmother groaned over the strain of modern education. At first he heard hardly any of the questions that were put to him, and his mother was obliged to disturb him in reveries, and to insist on his taking part in games with the rest of the family; but with the fresh air and the home life he soon recovered his health and spirits, and became again a lively, merry boy. He attended lectures at a college near, and had tutors at home; but great efforts were necessary in order to get into his head the requisite amount of Greek and Latin. Nevertheless, at times, he was astonishing, or might have been to any one with powers of observation. On these occasions he made such extraordinary and sagacious remarks that Madame de Balzac, in her character of represser, felt obliged to remark sharply, "You cannot possibly understand what you are saying, Honore!" When Honore, who dared not argue, looked at her with a smile, she would, with the ease of absolute authority, escape from the awkwardness of the situation by remarking that he was impertinent. He was already ambitious, and would tell his sisters and brother about his future fame, and accept with a laugh the teasing he received in consequence.

It must have been during this time that he grew to love with an enduring love the scenery of his native province of Touraine, with its undulating stretches of emerald green, through which the Loire or the Indre wound like a long ribbon of water, while lines of poplars decked the banks with moving lace. It was a smiling country, dotted with vineyards and oak woods, while here and there an old gnarled walnut tree stood in rugged independence. The susceptible boy, lately escaped from the abominations of the stuffy school-house, drank in with rapture the warm scented air, and often describes in his novels the landscape of the province where he was born, which he loves, in his own words, "as an artist loves art." Another lasting memory[*] was that of the poetry and splendour of the Cathedral of Saint-Gatien in Tours, where he was taken every feast-day. There he watched with delight the beautiful effects of light and shade, the play of colour produced by the rays of sunlight shining through the old stained glass, and the strange, fascinating effect of the clouds of incense, which enveloped the officiating priests, and from which he possibly derived the idea of the mists which he often introduces into his descriptions.

[*] See "Balzac, sa Vie et ses Oeuvres, d'apres sa Correspondance" par Madame L. Surville (nee de Balzac).

CHAPTER III

1814 - 1820

At the end of 1814 the Balzac family moved to Paris, as M. de Balzac was put in charge of the Commissariat of the First Division of the Army. Here they took a house in the Rue de Roi-Dore, in the Marais, and Honore continued his studies with M. Lepitre, Rue Saint-Louis, and MM. Sganzer and Benzelin, Rue de Thorigny, in the Marais. To the influence of M. Lepitre, a man who, unlike old M. de Balzac and many other worthy people, was an ardent Legitimist *before* as well as *after* 1815, we may in part trace the strength of Balzac's Royalist principles. On the 13th Vendemiaire, M. Lepitre had presided over one of the sections of Paris which rose against the Convention; and though on one occasion he failed in nerve, his services during the Revolution had been most conspicuous. On his reception at the Tuileries by the Duchesse d'Angouleme, she used these words, never to be forgotten by him to whom they were addressed: "I have not forgotten, and I shall never forget, the services you have rendered to my family."[*]

[*] "Biographie Universelle," by De Michaud.

We can imagine the enthusiasm and delight with which the man who, whatever might be his shortcomings in courage, had always remained firm to his Royalist principles, and who had been a witness of the terrible anguish of the prisoners in the Temple, would hear these words from the lips of the lady who stood to him as Queen—the Antigone of France—the heroine whose sufferings had made the heart of every loyal Frenchman bleed, the brave woman who, according to Napoleon, was the one man of her family. Lepitre's visit to the Tuileries took place on May 9th, 1814, the year that Balzac began to take those lessons in rhetoric which first opened his eyes to the beauty of the French language. During Lepitre's tuition he composed a speech supposed to be addressed by the wife of Brutus to her husband, after the condemnation of her sons, in which, Laure tells us, the anguish of the mother is depicted with great power, and Balzac shows his wonderful faculty for entering into the souls of his personages. Lepitre had evidently a powerful influence over his pupil, and as a master of rhetoric he would naturally be eloquent and have command of language, and in consequence would be most probably of fiery and enthusiastic temperament. We can imagine the fervour with which the impressionable boy drank in stories of the sufferings of the royal family during their imprisonment in the Temple, and strove not to miss a syllable of his master's magnificent exordiums, which glowed with the light and heat of impassioned loyalty.

No doubt Balzac's "Une Vie de Femme," a touching account of the life of the Duchesse d'Angouleme, which appeared in the *Reformateur* in 1832, was partly compiled from the reminiscences of his old master; and when we hear of his ardent defence of the Duchesse de Berry, or that he treasured a tea-service which was not of any intrinsic value, because it had belonged to the Duc d'Angouleme, we see traces of his intense love and admiration for the Bourbon family.

Nevertheless, in that big, well-balanced brain there was room for many emotions, and for a wide range of sympathies. The many-sidedness which is a necessary characteristic of every great psychologist, was a remarkable quality in Balzac. He may have been present at Napoleon's last review on the Carrousel—at any rate he tells in "La Femme de Trente Ans" how the man "thus surrounded with so much love, enthusiasm, devotion, prayer— for whom the sun had driven every cloud from the sky—sat motionless on his horse, three feet in advance of the dazzling escort that followed him," and that an old grenadier said, "My God, yes, it was always so; under fire at Wagram, among the dead in the Moskowa, he was quiet as a lamb—yes, that's he!" Balzac's admiration for Napoleon was intense, as he shows in many of his writings, and his proudest boast is to be found in the words, said to have been inscribed on a statuette of Napoleon in his room in the Rue Cassini, "What he has begun with the sword, I shall finish with the pen."

None of Balzac's masters thought much of his talents, or perceived anything remarkable about him. He returned home in 1816, full of health and vigour, the personification of happiness; and his conscientious mother immediately set to work to repair the deficiencies of his former education, and sent him to lectures at the Sorbonne, where he heard extempore speeches from such men as Villemain, Guizot, and Cousin. Apparently this teaching opened a new world to him, and he learned for the first time that education can be more than a dull routine of dry facts, and felt the joy of contact with eloquence and learning. Possibly he realised, as he had not realised before—Tours being, as he says, a most unliterary town—that there were people in the world who looked on things as he did, and who would understand, and not laugh at him or snub him. He always returned from these lectures, his sister says, glowing with interest, and would try as far as he could to repeat them to his family. Then he would rush out to study in the public libraries, so that he might be able to profit by the teaching of his illustrious professors, or would wander about the Latin Quarter, to hunt for rare and precious books. He used his opportunities in other ways. An old lady living in the house with the Balzacs had been an intimate friend of the great Beaumarchais. Honore loved to talk to her, and would ask her questions, and listen with the greatest interest to her replies, till he could have written a Life of the celebrated man himself. His powers of acute observation, interest, and sympathy—in short, his intense faculty for human fellowship, as well as his capacity for assimilating information from books—were already at work; and the future novelist was consciously or unconsciously collecting material in all directions.

In 1816 it was considered necessary that he should be started with regular work, and he was established for eighteen months with a lawyer, M. de Guillonnet-Merville, who was, like M. Lepitre, a friend of the Balzac family, and an ardent Royalist. Eugene Scribe—another amateur lawyer—as M. de Guillonnet-Merville indulgently remarked, had just left the office, and Honore was established at the desk and table vacated by him. He became very fond of his chief, whom he has immortalised as Derville in "Une Tenebreuse Affaire," "Le Pere Goriot," and other novels; and he dedicated to this old friend "Un Episode sous la Terreur," which was published in 1846, and is a powerful and touching story of the remorse felt by the executioner of Louis XVI. After eighteen months in this office, he passed the same time in that of M. Passez, a notary, who lived in the same house with the Balzacs, and was another of their intimates.

Balzac does not appear to have made any objection to these arrangements, though his legal studies cannot have been congenial to him; but they were only spoken of at this time as a finish to his education—old M. de Balzac, *homme de loi* himself, remarking that no man's education can be complete without a knowledge of ancient and modern legislation, and an acquaintance with the statutes of his own country. Perhaps Honore, wiser now than in his school-days, had learnt that all knowledge is equipment for a literary life. He certainly made good use of his time, and the results can be seen in many of his works, notably in the "Tenebreuse Affaire," which contains in the account of the famous trial a masterly exposition of the legislature of the First Empire, or in "Cesar Birotteau," which shows such thorough knowledge of the laws of bankruptcy of the time that its complicated plot cannot be thoroughly understood by any one unversed in legal matters.

Honore was very well occupied at this time, and his mother must have felt for once thoroughly satisfied with him. In addition to his study of law, he had to follow the course of lectures at the Sorbonne and at the College of France; and these studies were a delightful excuse for a very fitful occupation of his seat in the lawyer's office. Besides his multifarious occupations, he managed in the evening to find time to play cards with his grandmother, who lived with her daughter and son-in-law. The gentle old lady spoilt Honore, his mother considered, and would allow him to win money from her, which he joyfully expended on books. His sister, who tells us this, says, "He always loved those game in memory of her; and the recollection of her sayings and of her gestures used to come to him like a happiness which, as he said, he wrested from a tomb."

Other recollections of this time were not so pleasant. Honore wished to shine in society. No doubt the two "immense and sole desires—to be famous and to be loved"—which haunted him continually, till he at last obtained them at the cost of his life, were already at work within him, and he longed for the tender glances of some charming *demoiselle*. At any rate he took dancing-lessons, and prepared himself to enter with grace into ladies' society. Here, however, a terrible humiliation awaited him. After all his care and pains, he slipped and fell in the ball-room, and his mortification at the smiles of the women round was so great that he never danced again, but looked on henceforward with cynicism which he expresses in the "Peau de Chagrin." That wonderful book, side by side with its philosophical teaching, gives a graphic picture of one side of Balzac's restless, feverish youth, as "Louis Lambert" does of his repressed childhood. Neither Louis Lambert nor the morbid and selfish Raphael give, however, the slightest indication of Balzac's most salient characteristic both as boy and youth—the healthy *joie de vivre*, the gaiety and exuberant merriment, of which his contemporaries speak constantly, and which shone out undimmed even by the wretched health and terrible worries of the last few years of his life. In his books, the bitter and melancholy side of things reigns almost exclusively, and Balzac, using Raphael as his mouthpiece, says: "Women one and all have condemned me. With tears and mortification I bowed before the decision of the world; but my distress was not barren. I determined to revenge myself on society; I would dominate the feminine intellect, and so have the feminine soul at my mercy; all eyes should be fixed upon me, when the servant at the door announced my name. I had determined from my childhood that I would be a great man. I said with Andre Chenier, as I struck my forehead, 'There is something underneath that!' I felt, I believed the thought within me that I must express, the system I must establish, the knowledge I must interpret." In another place in the same book the bitterness of his social failure again peeps out: "The incomprehensible bent of women's minds appears to lead them to see nothing but the weak points in a clever man and the strong points of a fool."

Reading these words, we can imagine poor Honore, a proud, supersensitive boy, leaning against the wall in the ball-room, and watching enviously while agreeable nonentities basked in the smiles he yearned for. It was a hard lot to feel within him the intuitive knowledge of his genius; to hear the insistent voice of his vocation calling him not to be as ordinary men, but to give his message to the world; and yet to have the miserable consciousness that no one believed in his talents, and that there was a huge discrepancy between his ambition and his actual attainments.

In 1820 Honore attained his majority and finished his legal studies. Unfortunately the pecuniary misfortunes which were to haunt all this generation of the Balzac family were beginning—as old M. de Balzac had lost money in two speculations, and now at the age of seventy-four was put on the retired list, a change which meant a considerable diminution of income. He therefore explained to his son—Madame Surville tells us—that M. Passez, to whom he had formerly been of service, had in gratitude offered to take Honore into his office, and at the end of a few years would leave him his business, when, with the additional arrangement of a rich marriage, a prosperous future would be assured to him. Old M. de Balzac did not specify the nature of the service which was to meet with so rich a reward; and as he was a gentleman with a distinct liking for talking of his own doings, we may amuse ourselves by supposing that it had to do with those Red Republican days which he was not fond of recalling.

Great was Honore's consternation at this news. In the first place, owing to M. de Balzac's constant vapourings about the enormous wealth he would leave to his children, it is doubtful whether Honore, who was probably not admitted to his parents' confidence, had realised up to this time that he would have to earn his own living. Then, if it *were* necessary for him to work for his bread, he now knew enough of the routine of a lawyer's office to look with horror on the prospect of drawing up wills, deeds of sale, and marriage settlements for the rest of his life. He never forgave the legal profession the shock and the terror he experienced at this time, and his portraits of lawyers, with some notable exceptions, are marked by decided animus. For instance, in "Les Francais peints par eux-memes," edited by Cunmer, the notary, as described by Balzac, has a flat, expressionless face and wears a mask of bland silliness; and in "Pamela Giraud" one of the characters remarks, "A lawyer who talks to himself—that reminds me of a pastrycook who eats his own cakes." It was rather unfair to decry all lawyers, because of the deadly fear he felt at the prospect of being forced into their ranks, as there is little doubt that he would have shrunk with like abhorrence from any business proposed to him. His childish longing for fame had developed and taken shape, and for him, if he lacked genius, there was no alternative but the dragging out of a worthless and wearying existence. Conscious of his powers, it was a time of struggle, of passionate endeavour, possibly of bewilderment; with the one great determination standing firm in the midst of a chaos of doubt and difficulty—the determination to persevere, and to become a writer at any cost.

He therefore, to his father's consternation, announced his objection to following a legal career, and begged to be allowed an opportunity of proving his literary powers. Thereupon there were lively discussions in the family; but at last the kindly M. de Balzac, apparently against his wife's wishes, yielded to his son's earnest entreaties, and allowed him two years in which to try his fortune as a writer. The friends of the family were loud in their exclamations of disapproval at the folly of this proceeding, which would, they said, waste two of the best years of Honore's life. As far as they could see, he possessed no genius; and even if he *were* to succeed in a literary career, he would certainly not gain a fortune, which after all was the principal thing to be considered. However, either the strenuousness and force of Honor's arguments, or the softness of his father's heart, prevailed in his favour; and in spite of the opposition of the whole of his little world, he was allowed to have his own way, and to make trial of his powers. The rest of the family retired to Villeparisis, about sixteen miles from Paris, and he was established in a small attic at No. 9, Rue Lesdiguieres, which was chosen by him for its nearness to the Bibliotheque de l'Arsenal, the only public library of which the contents were unknown to him. At the same time, appearances, always all-important in the Balzac family, were observed, by the fiction that Honore was at Alby, on a visit to a cousin; and in this way his literary venture was kept secret, in case it proved unsuccessful.

Having arranged this, and asserted himself to the extent of insisting that his son should be allowed a certain amount of freedom in choosing his career, even if he fixed on a course which seemed suicidal, old M. de Balzac appears to have retired from the direction of affairs, and to have left his energetic wife to follow her own will about details. There was no doubt in that lady's mind as to the methods to be pursued. Her husband had been culpably weak, and had allowed himself to be swayed by the freak of a boy who hated work and wanted an excuse for idleness. Honore must be brought to reason, and be taught that "the way of transgressors is hard," and that people who refuse to take their fair share of life's labour must of necessity suffer from deprivation of their butter, if not of their bread. Her husband was an old man, and had lost money, and it was most exasperating that Honore should refuse a splendid chance of securing his own future, and one which would most probably never occur again. To a good business woman, who did not naturally share in the boundless optimistic views of M. de Balzac for the future, the crass folly of yielding to the wishes of a boy who could not possibly know what was best for him, was glaringly apparent. However, being a practical woman, when she had done her duty in making the household—except the placid M. de Balzac—thoroughly uncomfortable, and had most probably driven Honore almost wild with suppressed irritation, she embarked on the plan of campaign which was to bring the culprit back, repentant and submissive, to the lawyer's desk.

To accomplish this as quickly as possible, it was necessary to make him extremely uncomfortable; so having furnished his attic with the barest necessities—a bed, a table, and a few chairs—she gave him such a scanty allowance that he would have starved if an old woman, *la mere Comin*, whom he termed his Iris, had not been told to go occasionally to look after him. In spite of the gaiety of Balzac's letters from his garret, the hardships he went through were terrible, and in later years he could not speak of his sufferings at this time without tears coming to his eyes. Apparently he could not even afford to have a fire; and the attic was extremely draughty, blasts coming from the door and window; so that in a letter to his sister he begs her, when sending the coverlet for which he has already asked, to let him have a *very* old shawl, which he can wear at night. His legs, where he feels the cold most, are wrapped in an ancient coat made by a small tailor of Tours, who to his disgust used to alter his father's garments to fit him, and was a dreadful bungler; but the upper half of his body is only protected by the roof and a flannel waistcoat from the frost, and he needs a shawl badly. He also hopes for a Dantesque cap, the kind his mother always makes for him; and this pattern of cap from the hands of Madame de Balzac figures in the accounts of his attire later on in his life. It is not surprising that he has a cold, and later on a terrible toothache; but it *is* astonishing that, in spite of cold, hunger, and discomfort, he preserves his gaiety, pluck, and power of making light of hardships, traits of character which were to be strikingly salient all through his hard, fatiguing career. In spite of the misery of his surroundings, he had many compensations. He had gained the wish of his heart, life was before him, beautiful dreams of future fame floated in the air, and at present he had no hateful burden of debt to weigh him down. Therefore he managed to ignore to a great extent the physical pain and discomfort he went through, as he ignored them all through his life, except when ill health interfered with the accomplishment of his work.

Another characteristic which might also be amazing, did we not meet it constantly in Balzac's life, is his longing for luxury and beauty, and his extraordinary faculty for embarking in a perfectly business-like way on wildly unreasonable schemes. With hardly enough money to provide himself with scanty meals, he intends to economise, in order to buy a piano. "The garret is not big enough to hold one," as he casually remarks; but this fact, which, apart from the starving process necessary in order to obtain funds, would appear to the ordinary mind an insurmountable obstacle to the project, does not daunt the ever-hopeful Honore.

He has taken the dimensions, he says; and if the landlord objects to the expense of moving back the wall, he will pay the money himself, and add it to the price of the piano. Here we recognise exactly the same Balzac whose vagrant schemes later on were listened to by his friends with a mixture of fascination and bewilderment, and who, in utter despair about his pecuniary circumstances at the beginning of a letter, talks airily towards the end of buying a costly picture, or acquiring an estate in the country.

There is a curious and striking contrast in Balzac between the backwardness in the expression of his literary genius, and the early development and crystallisation of his character and powers of mind in other directions. Even when he realised his vocation, forsook verse, and began to write novels, he for long gave no indication of his future powers; while, on the other hand, at the age of twenty, his views on most points were formed, and his judgments matured. Therefore, unlike most men, in whom, even if there be no violent changes, age gradually and imperceptibly modifies the point of view, Balzac, a youth in his garret, differed little in essentials from Balzac at forty-five or fifty, a man of world-wide celebrity. He never appears to have passed through those phases of belief and unbelief —those wild enthusiasms, to be rejected later in life—which generally fall to the lot of young men of talent. Perhaps his reasoning and reflective powers were developed unusually early, so that he sowed his mental wild oats in his boyhood. At any rate, in his garret in 1819 he was the same Balzac that we know in later life. Large-minded and far-seeing—except about his business concerns—he was from his youth a *voyant*, who discerned with extraordinary acuteness the trend of political events; and with an intense respect for authority, he was yet independent, and essentially a strong man.

This absolute stability—a fact Balzac often comments on—is very remarkable, especially as his was a life full of variety, during which he was brought into contact with many influences. He studied the men around him, and gauged their characters—though it must be allowed that he did not make very good practical use of his knowledge; but owing to his strength and breadth of vision, he was himself in all essentials immovable.

The same ambitions, desires, and opinions can be traced all through his career. The wish to enter political life, which haunted him always, was already beginning to stir in 1819, when he wrote at the time of the elections to a friend, M. Theodore Dablin, that he dreamt of nothing but him and the deputies; and his last book, "L'Envers de l'Histoire contemporaine," accentuated, if possible more than any work that had preceded it, the extreme Royalist principles which he showed in his garret play, the ill-fated "Cromwell."

He never swerved from the two great ambitions of his life—to be loved, and to be famous. He was faithful in his friendships; and when once he had found the woman whom he felt might be all in all to him, and who possessed besides personal advantages the qualifications of birth and money—for which he had always craved—no difficulties were allowed to stand in the way, and no length of weary waiting could tire out his patience. He was constant even to his failures. He began his literary career by writing a play, and all through his life the idea of making his fortune by means of a successful drama recurred to him constantly. Several times he went through that most trying of experiences, a failure which only just missed being a brilliant success, and once this affected him so much that he became seriously ill; but, with his usual spirit and courage, he tried again and again. His friend Theophile Gautier, writing of him in *La Presse* of September 30th, 1843, after the failure of "Pamela Giraud," said truly that Balzac intended to go on writing plays, even if he had to get through a hundred acts before he could find his proper form.

One part of Balzac never grew up—he was all his life the "child-man" his sister calls him. After nights without sleep he would come out of his solitude with laughter, joy, and excitement to show a new masterpiece; and this was always more wonderful than anything which had preceded it. He was more of a child than his nieces, Madame Surville tells us: "laughed at puns, envied the lucky being who had the 'gift' of making them, tried to do so himself, and failed, saying regretfully, 'No, that doesn't make a pun.' He used to cite with satisfaction the only two he had ever made, 'and not much of a success either,' he avowed in all humility, 'for I didn't know I was making them,' and we even suspected him of embellishing them afterwards."[*] He was delightfully simple, even to the end of his life. In 1849 he wrote from Russia, where he was confined to his room with illness, to describe minutely a beautiful new dressing-gown in which he marched about the room like a sultan, and was possessed with one of those delightful joys which we only have at eighteen. "I am writing to you now in my termolana,"[+] he adds for the satisfaction of his correspondent.

[*] "Balzac, sa Vie et ses Oeuvres, d'apres sa Correspondance," by Madame L. Surville (nee de Balzac).

[+] "H. de Balzac—Correspondance," vol. ii. P. 418.

We must now return to Honore in his attic, where, as in later years, he drank much coffee, and was unable to resist the passion for fruit which was always his one gourmandise. He records one day that he has eaten two melons, and must pay for the extravagance with a diet of dry bread and nuts, but contemplates further starvation to pay for a seat to see Talma in "Cinna."

He writes to his sister: "I feel to-day that riches do not make happiness, and that the time I shall pass here will be to me a source of pleasant memories. To live according to my fancy; to work as I wish and in my own way; to do nothing if I wish it; to dream of a beautiful future; to think of you and to know you are happy; to have as ladylove the Julie of Rousseau; to have La Fontaine and Moliere as friends, Racine for a master, and Pere-Lachaise to walk to,—oh! if it would only last always."[*]

[*] "Correspondance," vol. i.

Pere-Lachaise was a favourite resort when he was not working very hard; and it was from there that he obtained his finest inspirations, and decided that, of all the feelings of the soul, sorrow is the most difficult to express, because of its simplicity. Curiously enough, he abandoned the Jardin des Plantes because he thought it melancholy, and apparently found his reflections among the tombs more cheerful. He decided that the only beautiful epitaphs are single names—such as La Fontaine, Massena, Moliere, "which tell all, and make one dream." When he returned home to his garret, fresh interests awaited him. Sometimes, he tells us in the "Peau de Chagrin," he would "study the mosses, with their colours revived by showers, or transformed by the sun into a brown velvet that fitfully caught the light. Such things as these formed my recreations: the passing poetic moods of daylight, the melancholy mists, sudden gleams of sunlight, the silence and the magic of night, the mysteries of dawn, the smoke-wreaths from each chimney; every chance event, in fact, in my curious world became familiar to me."

Occasionally on Sundays he would go to a friend's house, ostensibly to play cards—a pastime which he hated. He generally, however, managed to escape from the eye of his hostess; and comfortably ensconced in a window behind thick curtains, or hidden behind a high armchair, he would pour into the ear of a congenial companion some of the thoughts which surged through his impetuous brain. All his life he needed this outlet after concentrated mental labour; and sometimes in a friend's drawing-room, if he knew himself to be surrounded only by intimates, he would give full vent to his conversational powers. On these occasions he would carry his hearers away with him, often against their better judgment, by his eloquence and verve; would send them into fits of hearty laughter by his sallies; his store of droll anecdotes, his jollity and gaiety; and would display his consummate gifts as a dramatic raconteur. Later in life, after he had raised the enmity of a large section of the writing world, and knew that there were many watching eagerly to immortalise in print—with gay malice and wit on the surface, and bitter spite and hatred below—the heedless and possibly arrogant words their enemy had uttered in moments of excitement and expansion, he grew cautious; and sometimes because of this, and sometimes because he was collecting material for his work, he would often be silent in general society. To the end, however, he loved a tete-a-tete with a sympathetic listener— one, it must be conceded, who would be content, except for the occasional comment, to remain himself in the background, as the great man wanted a safety-valve for his own impetuous thoughts, and did not generally care to hear the paler, less interesting impressions of his companion.

With what longing, in the midst of his harassing life in Paris, he would look back to the charming long fireside chats he had had with Madame Hanska; and as the time to meet her again came nearer, with what satisfaction special tit-bits of gossip were reserved to be talked over and explained during the long evenings at Wierzchownia! How he loved to rush in to his sister with the latest news of the personages of his novels, as well as with brilliant plans to improve his general prospects; and with what enthusiasm he poured out to Theophile Gautier, or even to Leon Gozlan, his confidences of all sorts! Plans, absurd and impossible, but worked out with a business-like arrangement of detail which, when mingled with somnambulists and magnetisers, had a weird yet apparently fascinating effect on his hearers; magnificent diatribes against the wickedness of his special enemies, journalists, editors, and the Press in general; strange fancies to do with the world where Eugenie Grandet or Le Pere Goriot had their dwelling,—all these ideas, opinions, and feelings came from his lips with an eloquence, a force, and a life which were all convincing. Yet by a strange anomaly, which is sometimes seen in talkative and apparently unreserved people, Balzac in reality revealed very little of himself—in fact, we may often suspect him of using a flow of apparently spontaneous words as a screen to mask some hidden feeling. Therefore, when people who had considered themselves his intimate friends tried to write about him after his death, they found that they really knew little of the essentials of the man, and could only string together amusing anecdotes, proving him to have been eccentric, amusing, and essentially *bon camarade*, but giving little idea of his real personality and genius.

Even in these early days at the card-parties—where sometimes the hostess noticed the defection of the two young guests, and, holding a card in each delicate hand, would beckon them to take their place at the game, which they would do with humble and discomfited faces, like schoolboys surprised at a forbidden amusement—M. de Petigny, Balzac's companion, must have been struck by his openness in some respects and the absolute mystery with which he surrounded himself in others. Where he lived, what he was doing, what his life was like—all these facts were hidden from his companion, till he revealed himself at last, on the verge of his hoped-for triumph. But, on the other hand, the sentiments and impressions of which M. de Petigny read afterwards in Balzac's books seemed to him only a pale, distant echo of the rich and vivid expressions which fell from his lips in these intimate talks. Magnetism, in which he had a strong faith all his life, was exercising his thoughts greatly. It was "the irresistible ascendency of mind over matter, of a strong and immovable will over a soul open to all impressions."[*] Before long he would have mastered its secrets, and would be able to compel every man to obey him and every woman to love him. He had already, he announced, begun to occupy his fixed position in life, and was on the threshold of a millennium.

[*] Article by M. Jules de Petigny.

Balzac's glimpses of society were, however, rare, and ceased altogether during the last few months of his stay in the Rue Lesdiguieres. However, other more satisfying pleasures were his: "Unspeakable joys are showered on us by the exertion of our mental faculties; the quest of ideas, and the tranquil contemplation of knowledge; delights indescribable, because purely intellectual and impalpable to our senses. So we are obliged to use material terms to express the mysteries of the soul. The pleasure of striking out in some lonely lake of clear water, with forests, rocks, and flowers around, and the soft stirring of the warm breeze—all this would give to those who knew them not a very faint idea of the exultation with which my soul bathed itself in the beams of an unknown light, hearkened to the awful and uncertain voice of inspiration, as vision upon vision poured from some unknown source through my throbbing brain."[*]

[*] "La Peau de Chagrin," by Honore de Balzac.

There was another side to the picture, and perhaps in this description, written in 1830, Balzac has slightly antedated his joy in his creative powers, and describes more correctly his feelings when he wrote "Les Chouans," "La Maison du Chat-qui-pelote," and the "Peau de Chagrin" itself, than those of this earlier period of his life, when the difficulties of expressing himself often seemed insurmountable, and the hiatus between his ideas and the form in which to clothe them was almost impossible to bridge over.

Writing did not at any time come easily to him, and "Stella" and "Coqsigrue," his first novels, were never finished; while a comedy, "Les Deux Philosophes," was also abandoned in despair. Next he set to work at "Cromwell," a tragedy in five acts, which was to be his passport to fame. At this play he laboured for months, shutting himself up completely, and loving his self-imposed slavery—though his want of faculty for versification, and the intense difficulty he experienced in finding words for the ideas which crowded into his imaginative brain were decided drawbacks. While engaged on this work, he may indeed have experienced some of the feelings he describes in the "Peau de Chagrin," quoted above; for, curiously enough, "Cromwell," his first finished production, was the only one of his early works about which he was deceived, and which he imagined to be a *chef d'oeuvre*. It was well he had this happy faith to sustain him, as, according to the account of M. Jules de Petigny, the circumstances under which the play was composed must, to put the matter mildly, have been distinctly depressing.

This gentleman says: "I entered a narrow garret, furnished with a bottomless chair, a rickety table and a miserable pallet bed, with two dirty curtains half drawn round it. On the table were an inkstand, a big copybook scribbled all over, a jug of lemonade, a glass, and a morsel of bread. The heat in this wretched hole was stifling, and one breathed a mephitic air which would have given cholera, if cholera had then been invented!" Balzac was in bed, with a cotton cap of problematic colour on his head. "You see," he said, "the abode I have not left except once for two months—the evening when you met me. During all this time I have not got up from the bed where I work at the great work, for the sake of which I have condemned myself to this hermit's life, and which happily I have just finished, for my powers have come to an end." It must have been during these last months in his garret, when he neglected everything for his projected masterpiece, that, covered with vermin from the dirt of his room, he would creep out in the evening to buy a candle, which, as he possessed no candlestick, he would put in an empty bottle.

The almost insane ardour for and absorption in his work, which were his salient characteristics, had already possession of him; and we see that he laboured as passionately now for fame and for love of his art, as he did later on, when the struggle to free himself from debt, and to gain a home and womanly companionship were additional incentives to effort. At the time of which M. de Petigny speaks, however, his troubles appeared to be over, as the masterpiece for which he had suffered so much was completed; and joyfully confident that triumph awaited him, Honore took it home with him to Villeparisis at the end of April, 1820. He was so certain, poor fellow, of success, that he had specially begged that among those invited to the reading of the tragedy, should be the insulting person who told his father fifteen months before, that he was fit for nothing but a post as copying clerk.

CHAPTER IV

1820 - 1828

Evidently Balzac's happy faith in the beauty of "Cromwell" had impressed his parents, as, apparently without having seen the play, they had assembled a large concourse of friends for the reading; and between happy pride in his boy's genius, and satisfaction at his own acuteness in discerning it, old M. de Balzac was no doubt nearly as joyous as Honore himself. The Balzac family were prepared for triumph, the friends were amused or incredulous, and the solemn trial began.[*] The tragedy, strongly Royalist in principles, opens, according to the plot as given by Balzac in a letter to his sister,[+] with the entrance of Queen Henrietta Maria into Westminster. She is utterly exhausted, and, disguised in humble garments, has returned from taking her children for safety into Holland, and from begging for the help of the King of France. Strafford, in tears, tells her of late events, and of the King's imprisonment and future trial; but during this conversation Cromwell and Ireton enter, and the Queen, in terror, hides behind a tomb, till, horrified at the discussion as to whether or not the King shall be put to death, she comes out, and, as Balzac remarks, "makes them a famous discourse." Act II. sounds a little dull, though no doubt it is highly instructive, as a great part of it is taken up with a monologue by the King detailing the events of his past reign. Later on Charles, instead of keeping Cromwell's son who has fallen into his hands, as a hostage for his own life, gives him up to his father without condition; but Cromwell, unmoved by this generosity, still plots for his King's death. The fifth Act, which Balzac remarks is the most difficult of all, opens with a scene in which the King tells the Queen his last wishes, which Balzac interpolates with (Quelle scene!); then Strafford informs the King of his condemnation (Quelle scene!); the King and Queen say good-bye —(Quelle scene!) again; and the play ends with the Queen vowing eternal vengeance upon England, declaring that enemies will rise everywhere against her, and that one day France will fight against her, conquer her, and crush her.

[*] The original MS., beautifully written out, and tied with faded blue ribbon, is in the possession of the Vicomte de Spoelberch de Lovenjoul.

[+] "Honore de Balzac—Correspondance," vol. i, p. 28.

Honore began his reading with the utmost enthusiasm, modulating his sonorous voice to suit the different characters, and even contriving for a time to impart by his expressive reading a fictitious interest to the dull, tedious tragedy. Gradually, however, the feeling of disappointment and boredom among his audience communicated itself to him. He lost confidence; his beautiful reading began to decline in pathos and interest; and when at last he finished, and, glancing at the downcast faces round him, found that even Laure could not look up at him with a smile of congratulation, he felt a chill at his heart, and knew that he had not triumphed after all. Nevertheless, he very naturally rebelled against the strongly expressed adverse judgment of his enemy of the copying-clerk proposal, and begged to be allowed to appeal to a competent and impartial critic. To this request his father assented, and M. Surville, who was now engaged to Laure, proposed that M. Andrieux, of the Academie Francaise, formerly his own master at the Ecole Polytechnique, should be asked to give an opinion. Honore, his sister says, "accepted this literary elder as sovereign judge," no doubt hoping against hope that a really cultured man would see the beauties which were unfortunately hidden from the eyes of the unintellectual inhabitants of Villeparisis. However, the verdict of M. Andrieux was, if possible, more crushing than any of the events which had preceded it. In the honest opinion of this expert, the author of "Cromwell" ought to do anything, no matter what, *except literature.*

Honore had asked for an impartial judgment, and had promised to abide by it. His discomfiture and sense of failure ought therefore to have been complete. Genius does not, however, follow the ordinary road; and with a mixture of pluck, confidence in himself, and pride which always characterised him, Honore did not allow that he was beaten, and would not show the feelings of grief and disappointment which must have filled his heart. "Tragedies are not my line"—that is all he said; and if he had been allowed to follow his own bent, he would at once have returned to his garret, and have begun to write again with unabated ardour.

Naturally, however, the Balzac family refused to allow him to continue the course of senseless folly which was already beginning to ruin his health. Madame de Balzac was specially strong on this point; and though he had only been allowed fifteen months, instead of the two years promised for his trial, she insisted that he should come home at once, and remain under the maternal eye. Indeed, this seemed quite necessary, after the privations he had gone through. His sufferings never made him thin at any period of his life; but now his face was pale and his eyes hollow, and his lifelong friend, Dr. Nacquart, sent him at once to recruit in the air of his native Touraine.

After this followed a time of bitter trial for poor Honore. His sister Laure married M. Surville in May, 1820, about a month after his return home, and went to live at Bayeux, so that he was deprived of her congenial companionship; and, in spite of his fun and buoyancy, his letters to her show his extreme wretchedness. Years afterwards he told the Duchesse d'Abrantes that the cruel weight of compulsion under which he was crushed till 1822 made his struggles for existence, when once he was free, seem comparatively light. Continually worried by his nervous, irritable mother, deprived of independence, of leisure, of quiet, he saw his dreams of future fame vanish like smoke, and the hated lawyer's office become a certainty, if he failed to make money by writing. In deadly fear of this, and with the paralysing consciousness that his present circumstances were peculiarly unpropitious as a literary education, he rebelled against the hard fate which denied him opportunity to work for fame. "Laure, Laure," he cries at this time, "my two only and immense desires—to be loved and to be celebrated—will they ever be satisfied?"

Whatever his aspirations might be, it was necessary that he should do something to support himself, as his parents firmly refused to grant him the 1,500 francs—about sixty pounds—a year for which he begged, to enable him to live in Paris and to carry out his vocation. He was therefore obliged to write at his home at Villeparisis in the midst of distractions and discouragements. In these unpropitious circumstances he produced in five years—with different collaborators, whose names are now rescued from absolute oblivion by their transitory connection with him—eight novels in thirty-one volumes. That he managed to find a publisher for most of his novels, and to make forty pounds, sixty pounds, or eighty pounds out of each, is according to his sister, a remarkable proof of his strength of will, and also of his power of fascination. The payment generally took the form of a bill payable at some distant period—a form of receiving money which does not seem very satisfying; but at any rate Balzac could prove to his family that he was earning something, and was himself cheered by his small successes. We can imagine his feverish anxiety, and the cunning with which he would exert every wile to induce the publisher—himself a struggling man—to accept his wares, when he knew that a refusal would mean mingled scoffs and lamentations at home, and possibly a menace that not much longer leisure would be allowed him for idling. There is pathos in the fate of one whose genius is unrecognised till his day on earth is over, but far harder seems the lot of the man who longs and struggles, feeling that the power is in him, and who yet, by some strange gulf between thought and expression, can only produce what he knows to be worthless. It speaks much for Balzac's courage, patience, and determination, or perhaps for the intuitive force of a genius which refused to be denied outlet, that he struggled through this weary time, and in spite of opposition kept to his fixed purpose of becoming a writer.

These early works—"L'Heritiere de Birague," "Jean-Louis," "Le Centenaire," "Le Vicaire des Ardennes," "La Derniere Fee," "Wann Chlore," and others, published in 1822 and the three following years —were written under the pseudonyms of Lord R'hoone, Viellergle, and Horace de Saint-Aubin, and are generally wild tales of adventure in the style of Mrs. Radcliffe. Though occasionally the reader comes across a paragraph faintly reminiscent of the Balzac of later years, these youthful attempts are certainly not worthy of the great man who wrote them, and he consistently refused to acknowledge their authorship. The two first, "L'Heritiere de Birague" and "Jean-Louis," were written with the collaboration of M. Auguste le Poitevin de l'Egreville, who took the name of Viellergle, while Balzac adopted that of Lord R'hoone, an anagram of Honore, so that these two novels are signed with both pseudonyms.[*] It is amusing to find that the sage Honore, in 1820, prudently discourages a passing fancy on the part of his sister Laurence for his collaborator, by remarking that writers are very bad *partis*, though he hastens to add that he only means this from a pecuniary point of view! Laure, at Bayeux, is made useful as an amateur advertising agent, and is carefully told that, though she is to talk about the novels a great deal, she is never to lend her copies to any one, because people must buy the books to read them. "L'Heritiere" brought in about thirty-two pounds, and "Jean-Louis" fifty-three pounds, unfortunately both in bills at long date; but it was the first money Honore had ever earned, and he was naturally excited. However, with "La Derniere Fee" he was not so fortunate, as both versions—one of which appeared in 1823 and the other in 1824— were published at his own cost. Nevertheless, he has no illusions about the worth of his books, "L'Heritiere" being, he says, a "veritable cochonnerie litteraire," while "Jean-Louis" has "several rather funny jokes, and some not bad attempts at character, but a detestable plot."

[*] See "Une Page perdue de Honore de Balzac," by the Vicomte de Spoelberch de Lovenjoul.

In the same year, 1822, he writes one of his droll, beseeching letters to beg M. and Mme. Surville to help him out of a great difficulty, and to write one volume of "Le Vicaire des Ardennes" while he writes the other, and afterwards fits the two together. The matter is most important, as he has promised Pollet to have two novels, "Le Vicaire" and "Le Savant"—the latter we never hear of again—ready by October 1st. It is necessary to be specially quick about "Le Vicaire," partly because Auguste, his collaborator, is writing a novel of the same name, and Balzac's production *must* come out first, and also for the joyful reason that he will actually receive twenty-four pounds in ready money for the two books, the further fifty-six pounds following in bills payable at eight months. What do the Survilles think about it? He throws himself on their generosity, though he is afraid Laure will never manage to write sixty pages of a novel every day. Apparently the Survilles, or at least M. Surville—for it is certain that the devoted Laure would have worked herself to death to help Honore—did not see their way to proceeding at this rate of composition, as the next letter from Balzac, written on August 20th, is full of reproaches because the manuscript has not been at once returned to him, that he may go on with it himself. Perhaps this want of help prevented the carrying out of the contract, and was the reason that the world has not been enriched by the appearance of "Le Savant." Honore, however, judging by his next letter, did not bear malice: he was accustomed to make continual requests, reasonable and sometimes *very* unreasonable, to his family; and the large good-humour which was one of the foundations of his robust character, prevented him from showing any irritation when they were refused.

From 1821 to 1824 he wrote thirty-one volumes, and it is an extraordinary proof of his versatility, that in 1824, in the midst of the production of these romantic novels, he published a pamphlet entitled "Du Droit d'Ainesse" which argues with singular force, logic, and erudition against the revolutionary and Napoleonic theories on the division of property; and a small volume entitled "Histoire impartiale des Jesuites," which is an impassioned defence of religion and the monarchy. "The Bourbons are the preservers of the sublime religion of Christ, and they have never betrayed the trust which confided Christianity to them," he cries. No one reading these political essays would think it likely that they were the work of the romantic writer of "La Derniere Fee" or "Argow the Pirate," which were employing Balzac's pen at the same time.

Young men are often very severe critics of the doings of their family; and Balzac, cursed with the sensitiveness of genius, and smarting under the bitter disappointment of disillusionment and of thwarted and compressed powers, was not likely to be an indulgent critic; but making due allowance for these facts, it does not appear that his home was a particularly comfortable place at this time. Old M. de Balzac was as placid as an Egyptian pyramid and perennially cheerful; but the restless Madame de Balzac was now following in the footsteps of her nervous mother and becoming a *malade imaginaire*. This did not add to the comfort of her family, while the small excitements she roused perpetually were peculiarly trying to her eldest son, who was himself not of a placid nature.

However, there were compensations, though the discreet Honore does not mention these in his letters to Laure, as in 1821 his friendship with Madame de Berny began, and only ceased in 1836 with her death, which in spite of his affection for Madame Hanska, was a lifelong sorrow to him. One of Honore's home duties was to act as tutor to his younger brother Henry— the spoilt child of the family—who, owing to supposed delicacy, was educated at home; and as the Bernys lived near Villeparisis, it was arranged that he should at the same time give lessons to one of M. and Madame de Berny's boys. This may have helped to bring about the intimacy between the two houses, and Honore was struck by Madame de Berny's patience and sweetness to a morose husband many years older than herself. Later on, the Bernys left the neighbourhood of Villeparisis, and divided their time between the village of Saint-Firmin, near Chantilly, and Paris; and Balzac occasionally paid them visits in the country, and saw Madame de Berny continually in Paris. She was twenty-two years older than Honore, and no doubt supplied the element of motherliness which was conspicuously absent in Madame de Balzac.

She was a gentle and pathetic figure, the woman who understood Balzac as Madame Hanska did not; who made light of her troubles and sufferings for fear of grieving him in the midst of his own struggles; and who, while performing her duties conscientiously as devoted wife and mother, for twelve years gave up two hours every day to his society. She lent him money, interceded with his parents on his behalf, corrected his proofs, acted as a severe and candid though sympathetic critic, and above all cheered and encouraged him, and prevented him from committing suicide in his dark days of distress. On the other hand, the friendship of a man like Balzac must have been of absorbing interest to a woman of great delicacy of feeling, and evidently considerable literary powers, whose surroundings were uncongenial; and his warm and enduring affection helped her to tide over many of the troubles of a sad life.

Recent researches have discovered several interesting facts about the origin of the woman to whom may be ascribed the merit of "creating" the writer who was destined to exercise so great an influence on his own and succeeding generations.[*] Curiously enough, Louise Antoinette Laure Hinner, destined at the age of fifteen years and ten months to become Madame de Berny, was, like Madame Hanska, a foreigner, being the daughter of Joseph Hinner, a German musician, who was brought by Turgot to France. Here he became harpist to Marie Antoinette, and married Madame Quelpee de Laborde, one of the Queen's ladies in waiting. Two years later, on May 23rd, 1777, the future Madame de Berny came into the world, and made her debut with a great flourish of trumpets, Louis XVI. and Marie Antoinette, represented by the Duc de Fronsac and Laure Auguste de Fitz-James, Princesse de Chimay, being her god-parents. When in 1784 her father died, her mother married the Chevalier de Jarjayes, one of Marie Antoinette's most loyal adherents during the Revolution. It was he who conceived the project of carrying off Louis XVII. from the Temple, and who was entrusted with the precious duty of carrying the seal, ring, and hair belonging to the Royal Family to the exiled Monsieur and Comte d'Artois.[*]

[*] See "Balzac, Imprimeur," in "La Jeunesse de Balzac," by MM. Hanotaux et Vicaire.

We can easily see whence Balzac derived his strong Royalist principles —how from boyhood the lessons taught him by his masters, M. Lepitre and M. Guillonnet de Merville, would be insisted on, only with much greater effect and insistence, by this charming woman of the world. Her mother, still living, had passed her time in the disturbed and exciting atmosphere of plots and counterplots; and she herself could tell him story after story of heartrending tragedies and of hairbreadth escapes, which had happened to her own relations and friends. From her he acquired those aristocratic longings which always characterised him, and through her influence he made acquaintance with several people of high position and importance, and thus was enabled to make an occasional appearance in the *beau-monde* of Paris.

Her portrait gives the idea of an elegant rather than pretty woman, with a long neck, sloping shoulders, black curls on the temples, at each side of a high forehead, and large, languishing dark eyes, under pencilled eyebrows. The oval face has a character of gentle melancholy, and there is something subdued and suffering in the whole expression which invites our pity. She wears in the portrait an Empire dress, confined under the arms by a yellow ribbon.

"La dilecta," as Balzac calls her, cannot have been a very happy woman. Of her nine children, watched with the most tender solicitude, only four lived to grow up; and of these her favourite son, "beautiful as the day, like her tender and spiritual, like her full of noble sentiments," as Balzac says, died the year before her; and only an insane daughter and a wild, unsatisfactory son survived her. This terrible blow broke her heart, and she shut herself up and refused to see even Balzac during the last year of her life. The end must at any rate have been peaceful, as, in order to prolong her existence as much as possible, it had been found necessary to separate her from the irritable husband with whose vagaries she had borne patiently during thirty tedious years; but perhaps she was sorry in the end that this was necessary. Madame de Mortsauf, in the "Lys dans la Vallee," is intended to be a portrait of her, though Balzac says that he has only managed to give a faint reflection of her perfections. However this may be, Henriette de Mortsauf is a charming and ethereal creation, and from her we can understand the fascination Madame de Berny exerted over Balzac, and can realise that, as he says to Madame Hanska, her loss can never be made up to him. It is possible also to sympathise with the feeling, perhaps unacknowledged even to himself, which peeps out in a letter to Madame Hanska in 1840.[*] In this he reproaches his correspondent for her littleness in not writing to him because he cannot answer her letters quickly, and tells her that he has lately been in such straits that he has not been able to pay for franking his letters, and has several times eaten a roll on the Boulevards for his dinner. He goes on: "Ah! I implore you, do not make comparisons between yourself and Madame de Berny. She was of infinite goodness and of absolute devotion; she was what she was. You are complete on your side as she on hers. One never compares two great things. They are what they are." Certainly Balzac never found a second Madame de Berny.

[*] "Lettres a L'Etrangere."

From 1822 to 1824 we know little of Balzac's history, except that he passed the time at home, and was presumably working hard at his romantic novels; but in 1824 a change came, one no doubt hailed at the time with eager delight, though it proved unfortunately to be the foundation of all his subsequent misfortunes.

When he went up to Paris to make arrangements for publishing his novels, he stayed in the old lodgings of his family in the Rue du Roi Dore, and here he often met a friend, M. d'Assonvillez, to whom he confided his fear of being forced into an occupation distasteful to him. M. d'Assonvillez was sympathetic, advised him to seek for a business which would make him independent, and, carried away by Honore's powers of persuasion and eloquence, actually promised to proved the necessary funds. We can imagine Balzac's joy at this offer, and the enthusiasm with which he would take up his abode in Paris, and feel that he was about to earn his living, nay, more, that he would no doubt become enormously rich, and would then have leisure to give up his time to literature. What however decided him to become first publisher and then printer we do not know. He started his publishing campaign with the idea of bringing out compact editions of the complete works of different authors in one volume, and began with Moliere and La Fontaine, carrying on the two publications at the same time, for fear of competition if his secret should be discovered. The idea, which had already been thought of by Urbain Canel, was a good one; but unfortunately Balzac was not able to obtain support from the trade, and had not sufficient capital for advertising. Therefore by the end of the year not twenty copies were sold, and he lost 15,000 francs on this affair alone. Consequently, in order to save the rent of the warehouse in which the books were stored, he was obliged to part with all the precious compact editions for the price by the weight of the paper on which they were printed.

Matters now looked very black, as Balzac owed about 70,000 francs; but M. d'Assonvillez was evidently much impressed by his business capacity, and was naturally anxious to be repaid the money he had lent. He therefore introduced Honore to a relation who was making a large fortune by his printing-press; and Balzac, full of enthusiasm, dreamt of becoming a second Richardson, and of combining the occupations of author and printer. His father was persuaded to provide the necessary funds, and handed him over 30,000 francs—about 1,200 pounds—with which to start the enterprise. In August, 1826, Balzac began again joyously, first by himself and afterwards with a partner named Barbier, whom he had noticed as foreman in one of the printing-offices to which he had taken his novels. Unfortunately a printing-licence cost 15,000 francs in the time of Charles X.; and when this had been paid, Barbier had received a bonus of 12,000 francs, and 15,000 francs had been spent on the necessary materials, there remained very little capital with which to meet the current expenses of the undertaking. Nevertheless, the young partners started full of hope, having bought from Laurent for 30,000 francs the premises at No. 7, Rue des Marais Saint-Germain, now the Rue Visconti, a street so narrow that two vehicles cannot pass in it. A wooden staircase with an iron handrail led from a dark passage to the large barrack-like hall they occupied: an abode which Balzac tried to beautify, possibly for Madame de Berny's visits, by hangings of blue calico.

There Balzac developed quickly. He learnt the struggle of a business life, the duel between man and man, through which thousands pass without gaining anything except business acuteness, but which introduced the great psychologist to hundreds of new types, and showed to his keen, observant eyes man, not in society or domesticity, but in undress, fighting for life itself, or for all that makes life worth living. In the Rue de Lesdiguieres he had struggled with himself, striving in cold and hunger to gain the mastery of his art. Here he battled with others; and since, except on paper, he never possessed business capacity, he failed and went under; but by his defeat he paved the way to future triumph. He passed through an experience possibly unique in the career of a man of letters, one which imparts the peculiar flavour of business, money, and affairs to his books, and which fixed on him for all his days the impression of restless, passionate, thronging humanity which he pictures in his books. The abyss between his early romantic novels and such a book as the "Peau de Chagrin" is immeasurable, and cannot be altogether accounted for by any teaching, however valuable, or even by the strong influence which intercourse with Madame de Berny exercised. Something else definite must have happened to him—some great opening out and development, which caused a sudden appearance on the surface of hitherto latent, unworkable powers. This forcing-process took place at his first contact with the war of life; and though he bore the scars of the encounter as long as he lived, he grew by its clash, ferment, and disaster to his full stature. In "La Maison du Chat-qui-pelote," "Illusions Perdues," and "Cesar Birotteau" he gives different phases of this life, spent partly in the printer's office and partly in the streets, rushing anxiously from place to place and from person to person, trying vainly by interviews to avert the impending ruin.

Matters seemed, however, quite hopeless; but when, towards the end of 1827, an opportunity occurred of becoming possessed of a type-foundry, the partners, perhaps with the desperation of despair, did not hesitate to avail themselves of it. This new acquisition naturally only appeared likely to precipitate the catastrophe, and Barbier prepared to leave the sinking ship. At this juncture Madame de Berny came forward with substantial help, and allowed her name to appear as partner in his place. However, even this assistance did not long avert disaster—bankruptcy was impending, and Madame de Berny and Laure implored Madame de Balzac to prevent this. The latter, wishing at all costs to keep the matter from the ears of her husband, now a very old man and failing in health, begged a cousin, M. Sedillot, to come forward, and at least to save the honour of the family. M. Sedillot, who appears to have been a good man of business, at once set gallantly to work to disentangle the embroglio, and to free Honore from its meshes. As a result of his efforts, the printing-press was sold to M. Laurent, and the type-foundry became the property of the De Bernys, under whom it was highly successful. At the same time, to save Honore from disgrace, Madame de Balzac lent 37,000 francs and Madame de Berny 45,000, the latter sum being paid back in full by Balzac in 1836, the year of Madame de Berny's death. "Without her I should be dead," he tells Madame Hanska. He was most anxious not to sell the type-foundry, and his parents have been severely criticised for their refusal to provide further funds for the purpose of carrying on that and the printing-office.

This blame seems a little unfair. It is true that, after Balzac had been obliged, to his intense grief, to part with both businesses at a loss, a fortune was made out of the type-foundry alone. But the Balzacs had lost money, and had their other children to provide for; while Honore, though well equipped with hope, enthusiasm, and belief in himself, had hitherto failed to justify a trust in his business capacities. In fact, if his parents had been endowed with prophetic eyesight, and had been enabled to take a bird's-eye view of their celebrated son's future enterprises, which were always, according to his own account, destined to fail only by some unfortunate slip at the last, it seems doubtful whether they would have been wise to alter the course they adopted.

CHAPTER V

1828 - 1829

In September, 1828, before the final winding up of affairs, Balzac had fled from Paris, and had gone to spend three weeks with his friends the Pommereuls in Brittany. There he began to write "Les Chouans," the first novel to which he signed his name. With his usual hopefulness, dreams of future fame filled his brain; and in spite of his misfortunes, his relief at having obtained temporary escape from his difficulties and freedom to pursue his literary career was so great, that his jolly laugh often resounded in the old chateau of Fougeres. It was certainly a remarkable case of buoyancy of temperament, as the circumstances in which he found himself were distinctly discouraging. He was now twenty-nine years old; he owed about 100,000 francs, and was utterly penniless; while his reputation for commercial capacity had been completely destroyed. His most pressing liabilities had been paid by his mother, who was all his life one of his principal creditors; and he was now firmly under the yoke of that heavy burden of debt which was destined never again to be lifted from his shoulders. Once again, as they had done nine years before, his parents cast off all responsibility for their unsatisfactory son. They had saved the family honour, which would have been compromised by his bankruptcy; but they felt that whether he lived or starved was his own affair. His position was infinitely worse than it had been in those early days in the Rue Lesdiguieres, when submission would have led to reinstatement in favour. He was now, as he graphically expressed it, "thrown into" the Rue de Tournon,[*] and apparently no provision was made for his wants. His parents, who had moved from Villeparisis to Versailles the year before, in order to be near Madame Surville, limited their interference in his affairs to severe criticism on his want of respect in not coming to see his family, and righteous wrath at his extravagance in hanging his room with blue calico. These reproaches he parried with the defence that he had no money to pay omnibus fares, and could not even write often because of the expense of postage; while anent the muslin, he stated that he possessed it before his failure, as La Touche and he had nailed it up to hide the frightful paper on the walls of the printing-office. Uncrushed by the scathing comments on his attempts at decoration, curious though characteristic efforts on the part of a starving man, he writes to his sister a few days later: "Ah, Laure, if you did but know how passionately I desire (but, hush! keep the secret) two blue screens embroidered in black (silence ever!)."[+] He reopens his letter about the screens to answer one from Madame Surville, written evidently at the instigation of M. and Mme. de Balzac, to blame his supposed idleness; and the poor fellow, to whom *this* fault at least could at no time be justly imputed, asks her if he is not already unhappy enough, and tells her pathetically how he suffers from these unjust suspicions, and that he can never be happy till he is dead. In the end, however, he returns with childlike persistence to the screens as a panacea for all his ills, and finishes with: "But my screens—I want them more than ever, for a little joy in the midst of torment!"

[*] He says himself "Rue Cassini," but this is a mistake.

[+] "Correspondance," vol. i. p. 82.

He had now apparently completely gone under, like many another promising young man of whom great things are expected; and he had in his pride and misery hidden himself from every one, except a few intimate friends. With the death on June 19, 1829, of his father, whose last days were saddened by the knowledge of his son's disaster, the world was poorer by one castle in the air the less; for besides his natural sorrow at the death of the kind old man, who was so much softer than his wife, the dream of becoming a millionaire by means of the Tontine capital faded way, like all poor Honore's other visions. Even Balzac's buoyancy was not always proof against the depressing influence of two or three days of starvation, and he sometimes descended to the lowest depths, and groped in those dark places from which death seems the only escape. When he tells us in "La Peau de Chagrin" that Raphael walked with an uncertain step in the Tuileries Gardens, "as if he were in some desert, elbowed by men whom he did not see, hearing, through all the voices of the crowd, one voice alone, the voice of Death," it is Balzac himself, who, after glorious aspirations, after being in imagination raised to heights to which only a great nature can aspire, now lay bruised and worsted, a complete failure, and thought that by suicide he would at least obtain peace and oblivion. He knew to the full the truth of his words: "Between a self-sought death and the abundant hopes whose voices call a young man to Paris, God only knows what may intervene, what contending ideas have striven within the soul, what poems have been set aside, what moans and what despair have been repressed, what abortive masterpieces and vain endeavours."[*]

[*] Honore de Balzac, "La Peau de Chagrin."

Looking back years afterwards at this terrible time, he can find only one reason why he did not put an end to himself, and that was the existence of Madame de Berny: "She was a mother, a woman friend, a family, a man friend, an adviser," he cries enthusiastically; "she made the writer, she consoled the young man, she formed his taste, she cried like a sister, she laughed, she came every day, like a merciful slumber, to send sorrow to sleep."[*] Certainly there was no woman on earth to whom Balzac owed so deep a debt of gratitude, and certainly also he joyfully acknowledged his obligations. "Every day with her was a fete," he said to Madame Hanska long afterwards.

[*] "Lettres a l'Etrangere."

About this time another friendship was beginning, which, though slower in growth and not so passionate in character, was as faithful, and was only terminated by Balzac's death. When Madame Surville went to live at Versailles, she was delighted to find that an old schoolfellow, Madame Carraud, was settled there, her husband holding the post of director of the military school at Saint-Cyr. Honore had known Madame Carraud since 1819; but he first became intimate with her and her husband in 1826, and later he was their constant guest at Angouleme, where Commandant Carraud was in charge of the Government powder-works, or at Frapesle in Berry, where Madame Carraud had a country house. She was a woman of much intelligence and ambition, high-principled and possessing much common sense. Balzac occasionally complained that she was a little wanting in softness; but, nevertheless, he invariably turned to her for comfort in the vicissitudes of his more passionate attachments. He was also much attached to M. Carraud, a man of great scientific attainments and a good husband, but, to his wife's despair, utterly lacking in energy and ambition; so that instead of taking the position to which by his abilities he was entitled, he soon retired altogether from public life, and Madame Carraud, who should, according to Balzac, have found scope for her talents in Paris, was buried in the country. Nevertheless, the Carrauds were a happy couple, genuinely devoted to each other; and Madame Carraud cited the instance of their affection, in spite of the difference of their point of view on many subjects, when in 1833 she wrote to Honore urging him to marry.[*] "There is no need to tell you that my husband and I are not sympathetic in everything. We are so unlike each other that the same objects appear quite differently to us. Yet I know the happiness about which I speak. We both feel it in the same degree, though in a different way. I would not give it up for the fullest existence, according to generally received ideas. I have not an empty moment."

[*] Letter from Madame Carraud in the Vicomte de Spoelberch de Lovenjoul's collection, published in *La Revue Bleue*, November 21st, 1903.

She was an ardent politician, and we gain much of our knowledge of Balzac's political views from his letters to her when he wished to become a deputy; while she also possessed the faculty which he valued most in his women friends, that of intelligent literary criticism. She could be critical on other points as well; and, like Madame Hanska, blamed Balzac for mobility of ideas and inconstancy of resolution, which she said wasted his intellect. She complained that, in the time that he might have used to bring one plan successfully to completion, he generally started ten or twelve new ones, all of which vanished into smoke, and brought him no advantage.[*]

[*] "L'Ecole des Menages" in "Autour de Honore de Balzac," by the Vicomte de Spoelberch de Lovenjoul.

Hardly a year passed without Balzac spending some time at the hospitable house at Frapesle, the doors of which were always open to him; and there, away from creditors, publishers, journalists, and all his other enemies, he was able to write in peace and quietness. There, too, he made many pleasant acquaintances, among them M. Armand Pereme, the distinguished antiquary, and M. Periollas, who was at one time under M. Carraud at Saint-Cyr, and afterwards became chief of a squadron of artillery. To Madame Carraud he also owed an introduction to his most intimate male friend, Auguste Borget, a genre painter who travelled in China, and drew many pictures of the scenery there. Borget lodged in the same house with Balzac in the Rue Cassini, and is mentioned by him in a letter to Madame Hanska, in 1833, as one of his three real friends beside her and his sister, Madame de Berny and Madame Carraud being the other two. It was a very real grief to Balzac when Borget was away; and he says that even when the painter is travelling, sketching, and never writes to him, he is constantly in his remembrance; while in another letter he speaks of his friend's nobility of soul and beauty of sentiment. To Borget was dedicated the touching story of "La Messe de l'Athee"; and in case of Balzac's sudden death it was to this "good, old, and true friend" that the duty of burning Madame Hanska's letters were entrusted, though eventually their recipient performed this painful task himself in 1847.

A still older friend was M. Dablin, a rich, retired ironmonger with artistic tastes, who left his valuable collection of artistic objects to the Louvre. He was known to Balzac before 1817; and in 1830 the successful writer remembers with gratitude that M. Dablin used to be his only visitor during his martyrdom in the Rue Lesdiguieres in 1819. At that time and later he was most generous in lending Honore money; and the only cloud that came between them for a long time was his indignation when Balzac wished to find him further security than his own life for a loan he had promised. Later on, in 1845, when M. Dablin, rather hurt by some heedless words from

Balzac, and evidently jealous of his former protege's grand acquaintances, complained that honours and fortune changed people's hearts—the great novelist found time, after his daily sixteen hours of work, to write a long letter to his old benefactor.[*] In this he tells him that nothing will alter his affection for him, that all his real friends are equal in his sight; and he makes the true boast that, though he may have the egotism of the hard worker, he has never yet forsaken any one for whom he feels affection, and is the same now in heart as when he was a boy.

[*] "Correspondance," vol. ii. p. 115.

Other early and lifelong friendships were with Madame Delannoy, who lent him money, and was in all ways kind to him, and with M. de Margonne, who lived at Sache, a chateau on the Indre, in the beautiful Touraine valley described in "Le Lys dans la Vallee," and who had held Balzac on his knees when a child. Balzac often paid him visits, especially when he wanted to meditate over some serious work, as he found the solitude and pure air, and the fact that he was treated in the neighbourhood simply as a native of the country and not as a celebrity, peculiarly stimulating to his imagination and powers of creation. He wrote "Louis Lambert," among other novels at the house of this hospitable friend. Madame de Margonne he did not care for: she was, according to his unflattering portrait of her, intolerant and devout, deformed, and not at all *spirituelle*. But she did not count for much; Balzac went to the house for the sake of her husband.

An intimacy was formed about this time between Balzac and La Touche, the editor of the *Figaro*, who, as has been already mentioned, helped him in the prosaic task of nailing up draperies. This intimacy must have been of great value to Balzac's education in the art of literature, and is remarkable for that reason in the history of a man in whose writings small trace of outside influence can be descried, and who, except in the case of Theophile Gautier, seemed little affected by the thought of his contemporaries. Therefore, though a long way behind Madame de Berny—without whom Balzac, as we know him, would hardly have existed—La Touche deserves recognition for his work, however small, in moulding the literary ideals and forming the taste of the great writer. Besides this, his friendship with Balzac is almost unique in the history of the latter, in the fact that, for some reason we do not know, it was suddenly broken off; and that almost the only occasion when Balzac showed personal dislike almost amounting to hatred, in criticism, was when, in 1840, in the *Revue Parisienne*, he published an article on "Leo," a novel by La Touche. He became, George Sand says, completely indifferent to his old master, while the latter —a pathetic, yet thorny and uncomfortable figure, as portrayed by his contemporaries— continued to belittle and revile his former pupil, while all the time he loved him, and longed for a reconciliation which never took place. La Touche had a quick instinct for discovering genius: he introduced Andre Chenier's posthumous poems to the public, and launched Jules Sandeau and George Sand. But he was soured by seeing his pupils enter the promised land only open to genius, while he was left outside himself. Sooner or later, the eager, affected little hypochondriacal man with the bright eyes quarrelled with all his friends, and a rupture would naturally soon take place between the ultra-sensitive teacher, ready to take offence on the smallest pretext, and the hearty, robust Tourainean, who, whatever his troubles might be, faced the world with a laugh, who insisted on his genius with cheery egotism, and who, in spite of real goodheartedness and depth of affection, was too full of himself to be always careful about the feelings of others. How much Balzac owed to La Touche we do not know; but though, as we have already seen, there were other reasons for his sudden stride in literature between 1825 and 1828, it is significant that "Les Chouans," the first book to which he affixed his name, and in which his genius really shows itself, was written directly after his intercourse with this literary teacher. No doubt La Touche, who was cursed with the miserable fate of possessing the temperament of genius without the electric spark itself, magnified the help he had given, and felt extreme bitterness at the shortness of memory shown by the great writer, whom he vainly strove to sting into feeling by the acerbity of his attacks.

Never at any time did Balzac go out much into society, but his anonymous novels, though they did not bring him fame, had opened to him the doors of several literary and artistic salons, and he was a frequenter of that of Madame Sophie Gay, the author of several novels, one of which, "Anatole," is said to have been read by Napoleon during the last night spent at Fontainebleau in 1814. Hers was essentially an Empire salon, antagonistic to the government of the Bourbons, and Balzac's feelings were perhaps occasionally ruffled by the talk that went on around him, though more probably the interest he found in the study of different phases of opinion outweighed his party prepossessions. Those evenings must have been an anxious pleasure; for, with no money to pay a cab fare, there was always the agonising question as to whether on arrival his boots would be of spotless cleanliness, while the extravagance of a pair of white gloves meant a diminution in food which it was not pleasant to contemplate. Then, too, he felt savage disgust at the elegant costumes and smart cabriolets owned by empty-headed fops with insufferable airs of conquest, who looked at him askance, and to whom he could not prove the genius that was in him, or give voice to his belief that some day he would dominate them all. The restlessness and discomfort, and at the same time the sense of unknown and fascinating possibilities which are the birthright of talented youth, and in the portrayal of which Balzac is supreme, must have been well known to him by experience; and his almost Oriental love of beauty and luxury made his life of grinding poverty peculiarly galling.

Conspicuous in her mother's salon, queen of conversationalists, reciting verses in honour of the independence of Greece, exciting peals of laughter by her wit and her power to draw out that of others, was a brilliant figure — that of the beautiful Delphine Gay, who was, in 1831, to become Madame de Girardin. She is a charming figure, a woman with unfailing tact and a singular lack of literary jealousy, so that all her contemporaries speak of her with affection. She made strenuous efforts to keep the peace between Balzac and her husband, the autocratic editor of *La Presse*; and till 1847, when the final rupture took place, Balzac's real liking for her conquered his resentment at what he considered unjustifiable proceedings on the part of her husband. Once indeed there was a complete cessation of friendly relations, and even dark hints about a duel; but usually Madame de Girardin prevailed; and though there were many recriminations on both sides, and several times nearly an explosion, Balzac wrote for *La Presse*, visited her salon, and was generally on terms of politeness with her husband. She was proud of her beautiful complexion, and had a drawing-room hung with pale green satin to show it to the best advantage; while, like her mother, she wrote novels, one of which she called "La Canne de M. de Balzac," after the novelist's famous cane adorned with turquoises.

One of the habituees of Madame Gay's salon was the Duchesse d'Abrantes; and between her and Balzac there existed a literary comradeship, possibly cemented by the impecunious condition which was common to both. In 1827 she lived at Versailles; and whenever Balzac went to see his parents, he also paid her a visit; when long talks took place about their mutual struggles, misfortunes and hopes of gaining money by writing. The poor woman was always in monetary difficulties. After the fall of the Empire and the death of her husband, whom she courageously followed throughout his campaign in Spain, she continued to live in the same luxury that had surrounded her during her days of splendour; and as the Bourbon Government refused to help her, she was soon reduced to a state of destitution, and turned to her pen to pay off her creditors. She wrote several novels, which at this time are completely forgotten; but in 1831 she began to bring out her Memoirs, and these give a graphic account of the social life under the Empire, and have become a classic. These Memoirs were first published in sixteen volumes, and it must have been a relief to the public when a second edition, consisting of only twelve volumes, was brought out three years later.

In 1829, the time of which we are now writing, Balzac could only sympathise when the poor Duchess, formerly raised to great heights and now fallen very low, felt depressed at her reverses, and took a gloomy view of life. He would assure her that happiness could not possibly be over for ever, and would predict a bright dawn some future day; while as soon as he began to prosper himself, he did his best to lend her a helping hand. He effected an introduction to Charles Rabou, so that her articles were received by the *Revue de Paris*, and he assisted as intermediary between her and the publishers, taking infinite trouble on her behalf, and in the end gaining most advantageous terms for her. No assistance, however, was of permanent use. She, who knew so much, had never learnt to manage money, and, helped by her eldest son, Napoleon d'Abrantes, she spent every penny she earned. On July 7th, 1838, she died in the utmost poverty in a miserable room in the Rue des Batailles, having been turned out of the hospital, where she had hoped to end her days in peace, because she could not pay her expenses in advance. Balzac writes to Madame Hanska: "The papers will have told you about the Duchesse d'Abrantes' deplorable death. She ended as the Empire ended. Some day I will explain this woman to you; it will be a nice evening's occupation at Wierzchownia."[*]

[*] "Lettres a l'Etrangere."

Another of Balzac's friendships, rather different in character from those already mentioned, was that with George Sand, "his brother George" he used to call her. He first made her acquaintance in 1831, and would often go puffing up the stairs of the five-storied house on the Quai Saint-Michel, at the top of which she lived. His ostensible object was to give advice about her writing, but in reality he would leave this comparatively uninteresting subject very quickly, and pour out floods of talk about his own novels. "Ah, I have found something else! You will see! You will see! A splendid idea! A situation! A dialogue! No one has ever seen anything like it!" "It was joy, laughter, and a superabundance of enthusiasm, of which one cannot give any idea. And this after nights without slumber and days without repose,"[*] remarks George Sand.

[*] "Autour de la Table," by George Sand.

There were limitations in his view of her, as he never fully realised the scope of her genius, and looked on her as half a man, so that he would sometimes shock her by the breadth of his conversation. After her rupture with Jules Sandeau, whose side in the affair he espoused vehemently, he disapproved of her for some time, and contrasted rather contemptuously the versatility of her affairs of the heart with the ideal of passionate, enduring love portrayed in her novels. However, later on, when he himself had been disappointed in Sandeau, and when the latter had further roused his indignation by writing a novel called "Marianna," which was intended to drag George Sand's name through the mud, Balzac defended her energetically. About the same time (1839) he brought out his novel "Beatrix," in which she is portrayed as Mlle. de Touches, with "the beauty of Isis, more serious than gracious, and as if struck with the sadness of constant meditation." Her eyes, according to Balzac, were her great beauty, and all her expression was in them, otherwise her face was stupid; but with her splendid black hair and her complexion—olive by day and white in artificial light—she must have been a striking and picturesque figure. Later on Balzac appears to have partly reconciled himself to her moral irregularities, on the convenient ground that she, like himself, was an exceptional being; and we hear of several visits he paid to Nohant, where he delighted in long hours of talk on social questions with a comrade to whom he need not show the *galanteries d'epiderme* necessary in intercourse with ordinary women. He says of her: "She had no littleness of soul, and none of those low jealousies which obscure so much contemporary talent. Dumas is like her on this point. George Sand is a very noble friend."[*]

[*] "Lettres a l'Etrangere."

This is all anticipation; we must now go back to 1828 and 1829, and picture Balzac's existence first in the Rue de Tournon and then in one room at the Rue Cassini. Insufficiently clad and wretchedly fed, he occasionally went to evening parties to collect material for his writing; at other times he visited some sympathising friend, and poured out his troubles to her; but he had only one real support—the sympathy and affection of Madame de Berny. It was a frightfully hard life. He took coffee to keep himself awake, and he wrote and wrote till he was exhausted; all the time being in the condition of a "tracked hare," harassed and pursued by his creditors, and knowing that all his gains must go to them.

His only relaxations were little visits. He went to Tours, where he danced at a ball with a girl with red hair, and with another so little "that a man would only marry her that she might act as a pin for his shirt."[*] He travelled to Sache, to see M. de Margonne; to Champrosay, where he met his sister; and to Fougeres in Brittany, at the invitation of the Baron de Pommereul. During the last-named visit, as we have already seen, he not only collected the material, but also wrote the greater part of his novel "Les Chouans," which proved the turning-point of his career.

[*] "Correspondance," vol. i. p. 82.

This novel, the first signed with his name, Honore Balzac, was published by Canel and Levavasseur in March, 1829, and in December of the same year the "Physiologie du Mariage by a Celibataire," appeared, and excited general attention; though many people, Madame Carraud among the number, were much shocked by it. Each of these books brought in about fifty pounds—not a large sum, especially when we think that Balzac must at this time have owed about two thousand pounds; but he had now his foot upon the first rung of the ladder of fame, and editors and publishers began to apply to him for novels and articles.

It is a curious fact that Balzac, who answered a question put to him during his lawsuit against the *Revue de Paris* on the subject of his right to the prefix "de," with the rather grandiloquent words, "My name is on my certificate of birth, as that of the Duke of Fitz-James is on his,"[*] should on the title-page of "Les Chouans" have called himself simply M. H. Balzac, and on that of the "Scenes de la Vie Privee," which appeared in April, 1830, M. Balzac, still without the "de." In 1826 he gives his designation and title as "H. Balzac, imprimeur, Rue des Marais, St.-Germain, 31," and we have already seen that he was entered on the school register as Honore Balzac, and that his parents at that time called themselves M. and Mme. Balzac. Occasionally, however, as early as 1822, in letters to his sister Honore insists on the particle "de," and all his life he claimed to be a member of a very old Gaulish family—a pretension which gave his enemies a famous opportunity for deriding him.

[*] First Preface to the "Lys dans la Vallee," p 482, vol. xxii. of "Oeuvres Completes de H. de Balzac," Edition definitive.

In 1836, during his lawsuit with the *Revue de Paris*, he certainly spoke on the subject with no doubtful voice:

"Even if my name sounds too well in certain ears, even if it is envied by those who are not pleased with their own, I cannot give it up. My father was quite within his rights on this subject, having consulted the records in the Archive Office. He was proud of being one of the conquered race, of a family which in Auvergne had resisted the invasion, and from which the D'Entragues took their origin. He discovered in the Archive Office the notice of a grant of land made by the Balzacs to establish a monastery in the environs of the little town of Balzac, and a copy of this was, he told me, registered by his care at the Parliament of Paris."[*]

[*] See First Preface to the "Lys dans la Vallee."

Balzac continues for some time in this strain, giving his enemies a fresh handle for ridicule. After the loss of the lawsuit, the *Revue de Paris*, raging with indignation, answered him with "Un dernier mot a M. de Balzac," an article which the writer, after a reflection full of venom, must have dashed off with set teeth and a sardonic smile, and in which there is a most scathing paragraph on the vexed question of the "de":

"He [Balzac] tells us that he *is of an old Gaulish family* (You understand, 'Gaulish'—one of Charlemagne's peers! A French family, what is that? Gaulish!) It is not his own fault, poor man! Further, M. de Balzac will prove to you that the Bourbons and the Montmorencies and other French gentlemen must lower their armorial bearings before him, who is a Gaul, and more—a Gaul of an old family! In fact, this name 'De Balzac' is a patronymic name (patronymically ridiculous and Gaulish). He has always been De Balzac, only that! while the Montmorencies—those unfortunate Montmorencies— were formerly called Bouchard; and the Bourbons—a secondary family who are neither patronymic nor Gaulish (of old Gaulish family is of course understood) were called Capet. M. de Balzac is therefore more noble than the King!"

Towards the end, rage renders the talented writer slightly incoherent, and we can imagine a blotted and illegible manuscript; but the question raised is an interesting one, and Balzac attached great importance to it. A favourite form of spite with his enemies was to adopt the same measures as did this writer, who, except in the title, calls him throughout "M. Balzac," a form of insult which possessed the double advantage of imposing no strain on the mind of the attacking party, and yet of hitting the victim on a peculiarly tender spot.

Balzac's statement that he was entered "De Balzac" on the register of his birth is on the face of it untrue, as he was born on the 2nd Prairial of the year VII., a time when all titles were proscribed; so that the omission of the "de" means nothing, while his contention that he dropped the "de" in 1826, because he would not soil his noble name by associating it with trade, might very easily be correct. Unfortunately, however, for Balzac's argument, when old M. Balzac died, on June 19th, 1829, he was described in the register as Bernard Francois Balzac, without the "de." He does not even seem to have stood on his rights during his lifetime, as in 1826, after the death of Laurence, who had become Madame de Montzaigle—it must have been a satisfaction to the Balzac family to have one indisputable "de" among them—cards were sent out in the names of M. and Madame Balzac, M. and Madame Surville, and MM. Honore and Henri Balzac.

Still, it might be possible for us to maintain, if it so pleased us, that, in spite of certain evidence to the contrary, the Balzacs were simple, unpretentious people, who, having dropped the "de" at the time of the Revolution, did not care to resume it; but here M. Edmond Bire, who furnishes us with the information already given, completely cuts the ground away from under our feet. It appears that M. Charles Portal, the well-known antiquary, has in his researches discovered the birth register of old M. Balzac. He was born on July 22nd, 1746, at La Nougarie, in the parish of Saint-Martin de Canezac, and is described in this document, not as Balzac at all, but as Bernard Francois Balssa, the son of a labourer! At what date he took the name of Balzac, and whether his celebrated son knew of the harmless deception, we do not know; but possibly his change of name was another of the little reserves which the clever old gentleman thought it necessary to maintain about his past life, and Honore really considered himself a member of an old family.

At any rate, as M. Bire says, he certainly earned by his pen the right to nobility, and in this account of him he will be known by his usual appellation of "De Balzac."

CHAPTER VI

1829 - 1832

The record of the next few years of Balzac's life is a difficult one, so many and varied were the interests crowded into them, so short the hours of sleep, and so long the nights of work, followed without rest by an eight hours' day of continual rush. Visits to printers, publishers, and editors, worrying interviews with creditors, and letters on business, politics, and literature, followed each other in bewilderingly quick succession, and the only respite was to be found in occasional talks with such friends as Madame de Berny, Madame Carraud, or the Duchesse d'Abrantes.

Success was arriving. But success with Balzac never meant leisure, or relief from a heavy burden of debt; it merely gave scope for enormous prodigies of labour. His passion for work amounted to a disease; and who can measure the gamut of emotion, ranging from rapture down to straining effort, which was gone through in those silent hours of darkness, when the man, the best part of whom lived only in solitude and night, sat in his monk's habit, before a writing-table littered with papers? Then, impelled by the genius of creation, he would allow his imagination full sway, and would turn to account the material collected by his keen powers of observation and his unparalleled intuition. It was strenuous labour, with the attendant joy of calling every faculty, including the highest of all—that of creation— into activity, and the hours no doubt often passed like moments. But the fierce battling with expression, the effort to tax super-abundant powers to the utmost, left their mark; and in the morning Balzac would drag himself to the printer or publisher, with his hair in disorder, his lips dry, and his forehead lined.

Jules Sandeau, who had been taken by Balzac to live with him, and who remarked that he would rather die than work as he did, says that sometimes, when the passion and inspiration for writing were strong on him, he would shut himself up for three weeks in his closely curtained room, never breathing the outside air or knowing night from day. When utterly exhausted, he would throw himself on his pallet-bed for a few hours, and slumber heavily and feverishly; and when he could fast no longer, he would call for a meal, which must, however, be scanty, because digestion would divert the blood from his brain. Otherwise, hour after hour, he sat before his square table, and concentrated his powerful mind on his work, utterly oblivious of the fact that there was anything in the world save the elbowing, crushing throng of phantom—yet to him absolutely real—personages, whom he took into his being, and in whose life he lived. For the time he felt with their feelings, saw with their eyes, became possessed by them, as the great actor becomes possessed by the personality he represents. "C'etait un voyant, non un observateur," as Philarete Chasles said with truth.

In 1829 Balzac was introduced by the publisher M. Levavasseur to Emile de Girardin, who became—and the connection was life-long—what Mme. de Girardin called La Touche,—an "intimate enemy." At first all was harmony. Emile de Girardin's letters, beginning in 1830 with "Mon tres-cher Monsieur," are addressed in 1831 to "Mon cher Balzac"; but it is doubtful whether the finish of one written in October, 1830, and ending with "Amitie d'ambition!!!"[*] is exactly flattering to the recipient—it savours rather strongly of what is termed in vulgar parlance "cupboard love." However, Girardin was the first to recognise the great writer's talents, and at the end of 1829, or the beginning of 1830, after having inserted an article by Balzac in *La Mode*, of which he was editor, he invited his collaboration, as well as that of Victor Varaigne, Hippolyte Auger, and Bois le Comte, in forming a bibliographical supplement to the daily papers, which was to be entitled "Le feuilleton des journaux politiques." This was a failure, but Balzac was associated with Emile de Girardin in several other literary enterprises; and it was through the agency of this energetic editor that he wrote his letters on Paris in the *Voleur*, which, extending from September 26th, 1830, to March 29th, 1831, would form a volume in themselves. After the Revolution of 1830 stories went out of fashion, the reviews and magazines being completely occupied with the task of discussing the political situation; and Balzac wrote numberless articles in the *Silhouette*, which was edited by Victor Ratier, and in the *Caricature*, edited by M. Philippon. A few years later, the latter journal became violently political; but at this time it consisted merely of witty and amusing articles, ridiculing all parties impartially.

[*] "La Genese d'un Roman de Balzac," p. 105, by the Vicomte de Spoelberch de Lovenjoul.

With Victor Ratier, Balzac contemplated a partnership in writing for the theatre, though he thought Ratier hardly sufficiently industrious to make a satisfactory collaborator. However, he threatened him in case of laziness with a poor and honest young man as a rival, and, to rouse Ratier to energy, remarked that the unnamed prodigy was, like himself, full of courage, whereas Ratier resembled "an Indian on his mat."[*] Balzac's imaginative brain was to supply the plot and characters of each drama; but he was careful, as in the case of his early novels, that his name should not appear, as the plays were to be mere vaudevilles written to gain money, and would certainly not increase their author's reputation. Ratier was therefore to pose as their sole author, and was to undertake the actual writing of the play, unless he were too lazy for the effort, when the honest and unfortunate young man would take his place. The pecuniary part of the bargain was not mentioned, except the fact that both partners would become enormously rich; and that result is so invariable a characteristic of Balzac's schemes that it need hardly be noticed. However, this brilliant plan came to nothing, not, as we may suppose, from any failure on the part of the indolent Ratier—as there was in this case his unnamed rival to fall back upon—but most probably because its promoter had not a moment's leisure in which to think of it again.

[*] "Correspondance," vol. i. p. 115.

Towards the end of 1830 he began to write for the *Revue de Paris*, a journal with which his relations, generally inharmonious, culminated in the celebrated lawsuit of 1836. The review was at this time the property of a company; and the sole object of the shareholders being to obtain large dividends, they adopted the short-sighted policy of cutting down their payment to authors, a course which led to continual recriminations, and naturally made the office of chief editor very difficult. When Balzac first wrote for the review, Charles Rabou held this post, following Dr. Veron; but he resigned in a few months, and was succeeded in his turn by Amedee Pichot. With him Balzac waged continual war, finally dealing a heavy blow to the review by deserting it altogether in 1833.

The cause of the dispute, in the first instance, was one which often reappears in the history of Balzac's relations with different editors. Being happily possessed of devoted friends, who allowed him complete freedom while he stayed with them, he found it easier to write in the quiet of the country than amidst the worries and distractions of Paris. In 1830, after travelling in Brittany, he spent four months, from July to November, at La Grenadiere, that pretty little house near to Saint-Cyr-sur-Loire, which he coveted continually, but never succeeded in acquiring. In 1834 he thought the arrangements for its purchase were at last settled. After three years of continual refusals, the owners had consented to sell, and he already imagined himself surrounded with books, and established for six months at a time at this studious retreat. However, pecuniary difficulties came as usual in the way, and except as a visitor, Balzac never tasted the joys of a country life.

From La Grenadiere he wrote a remarkable letter to Ratier,[*] full of love for the beauty of nature, a feeling which filled him with a sense of the littleness of man, and expressing also that uncomfortable doubt which must occasionally assail the mind of any man possessed of powerful physique as well as imagination—the doubt whether the existence of the thinker is not after all a poor thing compared with that of the active worker, who is tossed about, risks his life, and himself creates a living drama. He finishes with the words: "And it seems to me that the sea, a man-of-war, and an English boat to destroy, with a chance of drowning, are better than an inkpot, and a pen, and the Rue Saint-Denis."

[*] "Correspondance," vol. i. p 98.

In May, 1831, Balzac was again away from Paris, this time taking up his abode in Nemours, where he describes himself as living alone in a tent in the depths of the earth, subsisting on coffee, and working day and night at "La Peau de Chagrin," with "L'Auberge Rouge," which he was writing for the *Revue de Paris*, as his only distraction.

These absences did not apparently cause any friction; but when, in November, 1831, Balzac went to Sache to stay with M. de Margonne, and then moved on to the Carrauds, he left "Le Maitre Cornelius," which he was writing for the *Revue de Paris*, in an unfinished and uncorrected condition. Thereupon, Amedee Pichot, who naturally wanted consecutive numbers of the story for his magazine, committed what was in Balzac's eyes an unpardonable breach of trust, by publishing the uncorrected proofs, leaving out or altering what he did not understand. Balzac was furious at his signature being appended to what he considered unfinished work. Amedee Pichot was also very angry, because Balzac had unduly lengthened the first part of the story, and had kept him two months waiting for the finish. Therefore, as diligence was the only mode of transit, and it was necessary that "Le Maitre Cornelius" should end with the year, it was impossible to send the proofs before printing for correction to Angouleme. Nevertheless, as he had undoubtedly exceeded his rights as editor, he thought it wise to temporise, and wrote an explanatory and conciliatory letter; and as this did not pacify Balzac, he dispatched a second of similar tenor. However, a few days later, on January 9th, 1832, he felt compelled by the tone of Balzac's correspondence to send a third beginning: "Sir, I find from the tone of your letter that I am guilty of doing you a great wrong. I have treated on an equality and as a comrade a superior person, whom I should have been contented to admire. I therefore beg your pardon humbly for the 'My dear Balzac' of my preceding letters. I will preserve the distance of 'Monsieur' between you and me."[*]

[*] "Une Page Perdue de Honore de Balzac," by the Vicomte de Spoelberch de Lovenjoul; from which the whole account of the dispute between Balzac and Pichot is taken.

However, Balzac was furious. His respect for his own name and his intense literary conscientiousness were stronger even than his desire for money, and it was a very black crime in his eyes for any one to produce one of his works before the public until it had been brought to the highest possible pitch of perfection. This intense anxiety to do his best, which caused him the most painstaking labour, often pressed very hardly on managers of magazines. He was generally paid in advance, so that his money was safe; and though he could be absolutely trusted to finish sooner or later what he had undertaken, he showed a lofty indifference to the exigencies of monthly publication. Moreover, as is shown in the evidence given later on during his lawsuit with the *Revue de Paris*, he would sometimes, in his haste for money, accept new engagements when he already had a plethora of work in hand. Nevertheless, whatever the failures to fulfil a contract on his part might be, he was implacable towards those who did not rightly discharge their obligations to him; and Pichot was never forgiven. In September, 1832, after endless disputes about the rate and terms of payment, the most fertile source of recriminations between Balzac and his various publishers and editors, a formal treaty was drawn up between the great writer, who was at Sache, and Amedee Pichot, as director of the *Revue de Paris*. By this, with the option of breaking the connection after six months, Balzac undertook to write for the *Revue* for a year, being still entitled during that time to furnish articles to the *Renovateur*, the *Journal Quotidienne Politique*, and *L'Artiste*. In spite of this legal document, there were many disputed points; and the letters which passed between the two men, and which now began with the formal "Monsieur," were full of bickerings about money matters, about Balzac's delay in furnishing copy, and about the length of his contributions. On one occasion Pichot is severe in his rebukes, because Balzac has prevented the Duchesse d'Abrantes from providing a promised article, by telling her that his own writing will fill two whole numbers of the *Revue*. On another, it is curious to find that Balzac, who was rather ashamed of the immoral reputation of his works, thanks M. Pichot quite humbly for suppressing a passage in the "Voyage de Paris a Java," which the director considered unfit for family perusal, and excuses himself on the subject with the naive explanation that he was at the same time writing the "Contes Drolatiques"![*] Finally, in March, 1833, after six months of the treaty had expired, Balzac withdrew altogether from the *Revue de Paris*. He gave no explicit explanation for this step; but in 1836, at the time of his lawsuit with the *Revue de Paris*, he stated as the reason for his desertion that he considered Pichot to be the author, under different pseudonyms, of the adverse criticism of his novels which appeared in its pages. In the *Revue* he had, among other novels, brought out the beginning of "L'Histoire des Treize," and the parsimonious shareholders now had the mortification of seeing the great man carry his wares to *L'Europe Litteraire*; while the *Revue de Paris*, in consequence of his desertion, declined in popularity.

[*] "Autour de Honore de Balzac," by the Vicomte de Spoelberch de Lovenjoul.

Balzac was now fairly launched on the road of literary fame, and some of his writings at this time had a momentous influence on his life. In April, 1830, Madame Hanska, his future wife, read with delight, in her far-off chateau in Ukraine, the "Scenes de la Vie Privee," containing the "Vendetta," "Les Dangers de l'Inconduite," "Le Bal de Sceaux, ou Le Pair de France," "Gloire et Malheur," "La Femme Vertueuse" and "La Paix de Menage"—two volumes which Balzac had published as quickly as he could, to counteract the alienation of his women-readers by the "Physiologie du Mariage." In August, 1831, appeared "La Peau de Chagrin," which so disappointed Madame Hanska by its cynical tone, that she was impelled to write the first letter from L'Etrangere, which reached Balzac on February 28th, 1832, a date never to be forgotten in the annals of his life. He was not, however, very exact in remembering it himself, and in later life sometimes became confused in his calculations between the number of years since he had received this letter, and the time which had elapsed since he first had the joy of meeting her. "La Peau de Chagrin" greatly increased Balzac's fame, and in October, 1831, another anonymous correspondent, Madame la Marquise de Castries, also destined to exercise a strong, though perhaps transitory, influence over Balzac, had written to deprecate its moral tone, as well as that of the "Physiologie du Mariage." Balzac answered her that "La Peau de Chagrin" was only intended to be part of a whole, and must not be judged alone; and the same idea is enlarged upon in a letter to the Comte de Montalembert,[*] written in August, 1831, which shows Balzac's extreme anxiety not to dissociate his writings from the cause of religion. In it he explains, with much insistence, that, in site of the apparent scepticism of

"La Peau de Chagrin," the idea of God is really the mainspring of the whole book, and on these grounds he begs for a review in *L'Avenir*. The letter also contains an announcement which is interesting as a proof that two years before the date given by his sister, the idea of his great systematic work was already formulated, and that in his imagination it had assumed colossal proportions. He says: "'La Peau de Chagrin' is the formula of human life, an abstraction made from individualities, and, as M. Ballanche says, everything in it is myth and allegory. It is therefore the point of departure for my work. Afterwards individualities and particular existences, from the most humble to those of the King and of the Priest, the highest expressions of our society, will group themselves according to their rank. In these pictures I shall follow the effect of Thought on Life. Then another work, entitled 'History of the Succession of the Marquis of Carabas,' will formulate the life of nations, the phases of their governments, and will show decidedly that politics turn in one circle, and are evidently stationary; and that repose can only be found in the strong government of a hierarchy."

[*] Letters sent by the Vicomte de Spoelberch de Lovenjoul to the *Revue Bleue*, November 14th, 1903.

The "Peau de Chagrin," which is a powerful satire on the vice and selfishness of the day, suffers in its allegorical, though not in its humanly interesting side, by the vivid picture it gives of Balzac's youth; as, in spite of the introduction of the influence of the magic Ass Skin, the account of Raphael in the early part of the book, as the frugal, determined genius with high intellectual aspirations, does not harmonise with his weak, despicable character as it unfolds itself subsequently. The critics exercised their minds greatly about the identity of the heroines, the beautiful and heartless Fedora—in whom apparently many ladies recognised their own portrait—and the humble and exquisite Pauline, type of devoted and self-forgetting love. Mademoiselle Pelissier, who possessed an income of twenty-five thousand francs, and had a house in the Rue Neuve-du-Luxembourg, where she held a salon much frequented by political personalities of the day, was identified by popular gossip as the model of Fedora. It was said by Parisian society that Balzac was anxious to marry her, but that the lady, who afterwards became Madame Rossini, refused to listen to his suit, though she confessed to a great admiration for his fascinating black eyes.

The original of Pauline has never been discovered, but, possibly with a few traits borrowed from Madame de Berny, she is what Balzac describes in the last pages of "La Peau de Chagrin" as an "ideal, as a visionary face in the fire, a face with unimaginable delicate outlines, a floating apparition, which no chance will ever bring back again."

Since the year 1830 Balzac had lodged in the Rue Cassini, a little, unfrequented street near the Observatory, with a wall running along one side, on which was written "L'Absolu, marchand de briques," a name which Theophile Gautier fancies may have suggested to him the title of his novel "La Recherche de l'Absolu." Borget, Balzac's great friend and confidant, had rooms in the same house; and later on, when Borget was on one of his frequent journeys, these rooms were occupied by Jules Sandeau, after his parting with George Sand. In despair at her desertion, he tried to commit suicide; and Balzac, touched with pity at his forlorn condition, proposed that he should come to Borget's rooms, and took complete and kindly charge of him—a generosity which Sandeau, after having lived at Balzac's expense for two years, repaid in 1836, by deserting his benefactor when he was in difficulties.

Balzac was now in the full swing of work. He writes to the Duchesse d'Abrantes in 1831:[*] "Write, I cannot! The fatigue is too great. You do not know that I owed in 1828, above what I possessed. I had only my pen with which to earn my living, and to pay a hundred and twenty thousand francs. In several months I shall have paid everything, and I shall have arranged my poor little household; but for six months I have all the troubles of poverty, I enjoy my last miseries. I have begged from nobody, I have not held out my hand for a penny; I have hidden my sorrows, and my wounds."

[*] "Correspondance," vol. i. p. 131.

Poor Balzac! over and over again we hear the same story about the beautiful time in the future, which he saw coming nearer and nearer, but which always evaded his grasp at the last. Very often, when he appears grasping and dictatorial in his business dealings, we may trace his want of urbanity to some pressing pecuniary anxiety, which he was too proud to reveal. No doubt these difficulties often sprang from his extraordinary want of reflection and prudence, as his desire to make a dashing appearance before the world led him frequently into the most senseless extravagance. For instance, when he went out of Paris in June, 1832, intending to travel for several months, he left behind him two horses with nothing to do, but naturally requiring a groom, food, and stabling; and it was not till the end of July that, on his mother's recommendation, he sent orders that they were to be sold. His money affairs are so complicated, and his own accounts of them so conflicting, that it is impossible to understand them thoroughly. Apparently, however, from 1827 to 1836 he could not support himself and satisfy his creditors without drawing bills. These he often could not meet, and had to renew; and the accumulated interest on these obligations formed a floating debt, which was from time to time increased by some new extravagance.

In his vain struggles to escape, he worked as surely no man has ever worked before or since. In 1830 he brought out about seventy, and in 1831 about seventy-five publications, including novels, and articles serious and satirical, on politics and general topics; and in twelve years, from 1830 to 1842, he wrote seventy-nine novels alone, not counting his shorter compositions. Werdet, who became his publisher in 1834, gives a curious account of his doings; and this may, with slight modifications, be accepted as a picture of his usual mode of life when in the full swing of composition.

He usually went to bed at eight o'clock, after a light dinner, accompanied by a glass or two of Vouvray, his favourite wine; and he was seated at his desk by two o'clock in the morning. He wrote from that time till six, only occasionally refreshing himself with coffee from a coffee-pot which was permanently in the fireplace. At six he had his bath, in which he remained for an hour, and his servant afterwards brought him more coffee. Werdet was then admitted to bring proofs, take away the corrected ones, and wrest, if possible, fresh manuscript from him. From nine he wrote till noon, when he breakfasted on two boiled eggs and some bread, and from one till six the labour of correction went on again. This unnatural life lasted for six weeks or two months, during which time he refused to see even his most intimate friends; and then he plunged again into the ordinary affairs of life, or mysteriously and suddenly disappeared—to be next heard of in some distant part of France, or perhaps in Corsica, Sardinia, or Italy. It is not surprising that even in these early days, and in spite of Balzac's exuberant vitality, there are frequent mentions of terrible fatigue and lassitude, and that the services of his lifelong friend, Dr. Nacquart, were often in requisition, though his warnings about the dangers of overwork were generally unheeded.

Even with Balzac's extraordinary power of work, the number of his writings is remarkable, when we consider the labour their composition cost him. Sometimes, according to Theophile Gautier, he bestowed a whole night's labour on one phrase, and wrote it over and over again a hundred times, the exact words that he wanted only coming to him after he had exhausted all the possible approximate forms. When he intended to begin a novel, and had thought of and lived in a subject for some time, he wrote a plan of his proposed work in several pages, and dispatched this to the printer, who separated the different headings, and sent them back, each on a large sheet of blank paper. Balzac read these headings attentively, and applied to them his critical faculty. Some he rejected altogether, others he corrected, but everywhere he made additions. Lines were drawn from the beginning, the middle, and the end of each sentence towards the margin of the paper; each line leading to an interpolation, a development, an added epithet or an adverb. At the end of several hours the sheet of paper looked like a plan of fireworks, and later on the confusion was further complicated by signs of all sorts crossing the lines, while scraps of paper covered with amplifications were pinned or stuck with sealing-wax to the margin. This sheet of hieroglyphics was sent to the printing-office, and was the despair of the typographers; who, as Balzac overheard, stipulated for only an hour each in turn at the correction of his proofs. Next day the amplified placards came back, and Balzac added further details, and laboured to fit the expression exactly to the idea, and to attain perfection of outline and symmetry of proportion. Sometimes one episode dwarfed the rest, or a secondary figure usurped the central position on his canvas, and then he would heroically efface the results of four or five nights' labour. Six, seven, even ten times, were the proofs sent backwards and forwards, before the great writer was satisfied.

In the *Figaro* of December 15th, 1837, Edouard Ourliac gives a burlesque account of the confusion caused in the printing-offices by Balzac's peculiar methods of composition. This is an extract from the article:

"Let us sing, drink and embrace, like the chorus of an *opera comique*. Let us stretch our calves, and turn on our toes like ballet-dancers. Let us at last rejoice: the *Figaro*, without getting the credit of it, has overcome the elements and all sublunary cataclysms.

"Hercules is only a rascal, the apples of Hesperides only turnips, the siege of Troy but a revolt of the national guard. The *Figaro* has just conquered 'Cesar Birotteau'!

"Never have the angry gods, never have Juno, Neptune, M. de Rambuteau, or the Prefect of Police, opposed to Jason, Theseus, or walkers in Paris, more obstacles, monsters, ruins, dragons, demolitions, than these two unfortunate octavos have fought against.

"We have them at last, and we know what they have cost. The public will only have the trouble of reading them. That will be a pleasure. As to M. de Balzac—twenty days' work, two handfuls of paper, one more beautiful book: that counts for nothing.

"However it may be, it is a typographical exploit, a literary and industrial *tour de force* worthy to be remembered. Writer, editor, and printer have deserved more or less from their country. Posterity will talk of the compositors, and our descendants will regret that they do not know the names of the apprentices. I already, like them, regret it; otherwise I would mention them.

"The *Figaro* had promised the book on December 15th, and M. de Balzac began it on November 17th. M. de Balzac and the *Figaro* both have the strange habit of keeping their word. The printing-office was ready, and stamping its foot like a restive charger.

"M. de Balzac sends two hundred pages pencilled in five nights of fever. One knows his way. It was a sketch, a chaos, an apocalypse, a Hindoo poem.

"The printing-office paled. The delay is short, the writing unheard of. They transform the monster; they translate it as much as possible into known signs. The cleverest still understand nothing. They take it to the author.

"The author sends back the first proofs, glued on to enormous pages, posters, screens. It is now that you may shiver and feel pity. The appearance of these sheets is monstrous. From each sign, from each printed word, go pen lines, which radiate and meander like a Congreve rocket, and spread themselves out at the margin in a luminous rain of phrases, epithets, and substantives, underlined, crossed, mixed, erased, superposed: the effect is dazzling.

"Imagine four or five hundred arabesques of this sort, interlaced, knotted, climbing and sliding from one margin to another, and from the south to the north. Imagine twelve maps on the top of each other, entangling towns, rivers, and mountains—a skein tangled by a cat, all the hieroglyphics of the dynasty of Pharaoh, or the fireworks of twenty festivities.

"At this sight the printing-office does not rejoice. The compositors strike their breasts, the printing-presses groan, the foremen tear their hair, their apprentices lose their heads. The most intelligent attack the proofs, and recognise Persian, others Malagash, some the symbolic characters of Vishnu. They work by chance and by the grace of God.

"Next day M. de Balzac returns two pages of pure Chinese. The delay is only fifteen days. A generous foreman offers to blow out his brains.

"Two new sheets arrive, written very legibly in Siamese. Two workmen lose their sight and the small command of language they possessed.

"The proofs are thus sent backwards and forwards seven times.

"Several symptoms of excellent French begin to be recognised, even some connection between the phrases is observed."

So the article proceeds; always in a tone of comic good-temper, but pointing to a very real grievance and point of dispute; and helping the reader to realise the long friction which went on, and finally resulted in the unanimity with which publishers and editors turned against Balzac after his famous lawsuit, and showed a vindictive hate which at first sight is surprising. However, in this case the matter ends happily, as the article closes with:

"It ['Cesar Birotteau'] is now merely a work in two volumes, an immense picture, a whole poem, composed, written, and corrected fifteen times in the same number of days—composed in twenty days by M. de Balzac in spite of the printer's office, composed in twenty days by the printer's office in spite of M. de Balzac.

"It is true that at the same time M. de Balzac was employing forty printers at another printing-office. We do not examine here the value of the book. It was made marvellously and marvellously quickly. Whatever it is, it can only be a *chef d'oeuvre!*"

CHAPTER VII

1832

The year 1832 was a crisis and a turning-point in the history of Balzac's private life.

Old relations changed their aspect; he received a terrible and mortifying wound to his heart and to his vanity; and while he staggered under this blow, a new interest, not in the beginning absorbing, but destined in time to engulf all others, crept at first almost unnoticed into his life.

He was now thirty-three years old; it was time that he should perform the duty of a French citizen and should settle down and marry; and as a preliminary, it seemed necessary that Madame de Berny should no longer continue to occupy her predominant place in his life. She was, as we know twenty-two years older than he, and was a woman capable not only of romantic attachment, but also of the most disinterested conduct where her affections were concerned. She saw clearly that, having formed Balzac, helped him practically, taught him, given him useful introductions—in short, made him—the time had now come when it would be for his good that she should retire partially into the background; and she had the courage to conceive, and the power to make, the sacrifice. He, on his side, felt the idea of the proposed separation keenly, and never forgot all his life what he owed to the "dilecta," or ceased to feel a deep and faithful affection for her. Still, for him there were compensations, which did not exist for the woman who was growing old. He was famous, on the way to attain his goal; and he was regarded as the champion of misunderstood and misused women. Therefore, as the species has always been a large one, letters poured in upon him from all parts of Europe—England being the exception—letters telling him how exactly he had gauged the circumstances, sentiments, and misfortunes of his unknown correspondents, asking his advice, expressing intense admiration for his writings, and pouring out the inmost feelings and experiences of the writers. The position was intoxicating for the man who, a few years before, had been unknown and disregarded; and the fact that Balzac never forgot his old friendships in the excitement of the adulation lavished upon him, is a proof that his own belief in the real steadfastness of his character was not mistaken.

Among these unknown correspondents, there were two who specially interested him. One of these was the Marquise de Castries, who, though rather under a cloud at this time, was one of the most aristocratic stars of the Faubourg Saint-Germain, and sister-in-law to the Duc de Fitz-James, with whom Balzac was already connected in several literary undertakings.

As we have already seen, she wrote anonymously towards the end of September, 1831 to complain of the moral tone of the "Physiologie du Mariage" and of "La Peau de Chagrin." In Balzac's reply, which was despatched on February 28th, 1832, he thanked her for the proof of confidence she had shown in making herself known to him, and in wishing for his acquaintance; and said that he looked forward to many hours spent in her society, hours during which he would not need to pose as an artist or literary man, but could simply be himself.[*]

[*] "Correspondance," vol. i., p. 141.

Separated from her husband, and a most accomplished coquette, the Marquise was recovering from a serious love-affair, when she summoned Balzac to afford her amusement and distraction. Delicate and fragile, her face was rather too long for perfect beauty, but there was something spiritual and slender about it, which recalled the faces of the Middle Ages. Her health had been shattered by a hunting accident, and her expression was habitually one of smiling melancholy and of hidden suffering. Her beautiful Venetian red hair grew above a high white forehead; and in addition to the attractiveness of her elegant *svelte* figure, she possessed in the highest degree the all-powerful seductive influence which we call "charm."

Reclining gracefully in a long chair, she received her intimates in a small simple drawing-room furnished in old-fashioned style, with cushions of ancient velvet and eighteenth-century screens—a room instinct with the aristocratic aroma of the Faubourg Saint-Germain. There Balzac went eagerly during the spring of 1832, and imbibed the strange old-world atmosphere of the exclusive Faubourg, of which he has given a masterly picture in the "Duchesse de Langeais." In this he shows that by reason of its selfishness, its divisions, and want of patriotism and large-mindedness, the Faubourg Saint-Germain had abrogated the proud position it might have held, and was now an obsolete institution, aloof and cornered, wasting its powers on frivolity and the worship of etiquette. At first, gratified vanity at his selection as an intimate by so great a lady, and pleasure at the opportunity given him for the study of what was separated from the ordinary world by an impassable barrier, were Balzac's chief inducements for frequent visits to the Rue de Varenne. Gradually, however, the caressing tones of Madame de Castries' voice, the quiet grace of her language, and her infinite variety, found their way to his heart, and he fell madly in love.

Speaking of her afterwards in the "Duchesse de Langeais," which was written in the utmost bitterness, when he had been, according to his own view, led on, played with and deceived by the fascinating Marquise, Balzac describes her thus: She was "eminently a woman, and essentially a coquette, Parisian to the core, loving the brilliancy of the world and its amusements, reflecting not at all, or reflecting too late; of a natural imprudence which rose at times almost to poetic heights, deliciously insolent, yet humble in the depths of her heart, asserting strength like a reed erect, but, like the reed, ready to bend beneath a firm hand; talking much of religion, not loving it, and yet prepared to accept it as a possible finality."

In the same book are several interesting remarks about Armand de Montriveau, the lover of the Duchesse de Langeais, who is, in many points, Balzac under another name. On one page we read: "He seemed to have reached some crisis in his life, but all took place within his own breast, and he confided nothing to the world without." In another place is a description of Montriveau's appearance. "His head, which was large and square, had the characteristic trait of an abundant mass of black hair, which surrounded his face in a way that recalled General Kleber, whom indeed he also resembled in the vigour of his bearing, the shape of his face, the tranquil courage of his eye, and the expression of inward ardour which shone out through his strong features. He was of medium height, broad in the chest, and muscular as a lion. When he walked, his carriage, his step, his least gesture, bespoke a consciousness of power which was imposing; there was something even despotic about it. He seemed aware that nothing could oppose his will; possibly because he willed only that which was right. Nevertheless, he was, like all really strong men, gentle in speech, simple in manner, and naturally kind." Certainly Balzac, as usual, did not err on the side of modesty!

Curiously enough, the very day—February 28th, 1832—on which Balzac wrote to accept the offer of the Marquise de Castries' friendship, was the day that the first letter from L'Etrangere reached him. At first sight there was nothing to distinguish this most momentous letter from others which came to him by almost every post, or to indicate that it was destined to change the whole current of his life. It was sent by an unknown woman, and the object of the writer was, while expressing intense admiration for Balzac's work, to criticise the view of the feminine sex taken by him in "La Peau de Chagrin." His correspondent begged him to renounce ironical portrayals of woman, which denied the pure and noble role destined for her by Heaven, and to return to the lofty ideal of the sex depicted in "Scenes de la Vie Privee."

This letter, which was addressed to Balzac to the care of Gosselin, the publisher of "La Peau de Chagrin," has never been found. There must have been something remarkable about the wording and tone of it; as Balzac received many such effusions, but was so much impressed by this one, and by the communications which followed, that he decided to dedicate "L'Expiation" to his unknown correspondent. This story he was writing when he received her first letter, and it formed part of the enlarged edition of the "Scenes de la Vie Privee" which was published in May, 1832. On communicating this project, however, to Madame de Berny, she strongly objected to the offer of this extraordinary honour to "L'Etrangere"; and now doubly obedient to her wishes, and anxious not to hurt her feelings, he abandoned the idea after the book had been printed. In January, 1833, in his first letter to Madame Hanska, he explained the matter at length, and sent her a copy which had not been altered, and which had her seal on the title-page. The book sent her has disappeared; but examining some copies of the second edition of the "Scenes," the Vicomte de Spoelberch de Lovenjoul found that a page had been glued against the binding, and, detaching this carefully, discovered the design of the wax seal, and the dedication "Diis ignotis, 28th February, 1832,"[*] the date on which Balzac received the first letter from "L'Etrangere."

[*] I have seen this.

This letter gave Balzac many delightful hours, as, when he was able to write to her, he explained to Madame Hanska. In his pride and satisfaction, he showed it to many friends, Madame Carraud being among the number; but she, with her usual rather provoking common-sense, refused to share his enthusiasm, and suggested that it might have been written as a practical joke. To this insinuation Balzac gave no credence; he naturally found it easy to believe in one more enthusiastic foreign admirer, and he was seriously troubled by the fact that the first dizain of the "Contes Drolatiques," which certainly would not satisfy his correspondent's views on the lofty mission of womanhood, was likely to appear shortly. However, whether she did not read the first dizain of the "Contes," which appeared in April, 1832, or whether the perusal of them showed her more strongly than before that Balzac was really in need of good advice, Madame Hanska did not show her displeasure by breaking off her correspondence with him. Balzac had much to occupy his mind in 1832, as he was conscientiously, though not successfully, trying to make himself agreeable to the lady selected as his wife by his family. At the same time, while with regret and trouble in his heart he tried to relegate Madame de Berny to the position of an ordinary friend, and felt the delightful agitation, followed by bitter mortification, of his intercourse with Madame de Castries, we must remember that from time to time he received a flowery epistle from Russia, written in the turgid and rather bombastic style peculiar to Madame Hanska.

On the other hand, we can imagine the interest and excitement felt by the Chatelaine of Wierzchownia as she wrote, and secretly dispatched to the well-known author, the sentimental outpourings of her soul. The composition of these letters must certainly have supplied a savour to a rather flavourless life; for it was dull in that far-off chateau in Ukraine, which, as Balzac described it afterwards, was as large as the Louvre, and was surrounded by territories as extensive as a French Department. There were actually a carcel lamp and a hospital—which seem a curious conjunction—on the estate, and there were looking-glasses ten feet high in the rooms, but no hangings on the walls. Possibly Madame Hanska did not miss these, but what she did miss was society. She, M. de Hanski,[*] Anna's governess, Mlle. Henriette Borel, and last, but not least, the beloved Anna herself, the only child, on whom Madame Hanska lavished the most passionate love, were a small party in the chateau; and besides two Polish relations, Mlles Denise and Severine Wylezynska, who generally inhabited the summer-house, christened by Balzac "La Demoiselliere," they were the only civilised people in the midst of a huge waste populated by peasants. M. de Hanski often suffered from "blue devils," which did not make him a cheerful companion; and when Madame Hanska had performed a few graceful duties, as chatelaine to the poor of the neighbourhood, there was no occupation left except reading or writing letters. She was an intelligent and intellectual woman; and Balzac's novels, not at first fully appreciated in France because of their deficiencies in style, were eagerly seized on in Germany, Austria, and Russia. She read them with delight; and her natural desire for action, her longing also to pour out, herself unknown, the secret aspirations and yearnings of her heart to some one who would understand her, prompted the first letter; which, according to M. de Spoelberch de Lovenjoul, was dictated by her to Anna's governess, Mlle. Henriette Borel. So she started lightly on the road which was to lead her, the leisured and elegant great lady suffering only from ennui, to the period of her life during which she would toil hour after hour at writing, would be overwhelmed by business, pestered by duns and creditors, overworked, overburdened, and over-worried. She was certainly not very fortunate, for she seems never to have experienced the passionate love which might have made up for everything.

Till the time when she first put herself into communication with Balzac, her life had not been cheerful. A member of a Polish great family, the Countess Eve Rzewuska was born at the Chateau of Pohrbyszcze on January 25, 1804 or 1806. She was one of a large family, having three brothers and three sisters, nearly all of whom played distinguished parts in France or Russia; and her eldest brother, Count Henry Rzewuski, was one of the most popular writers of Poland. In 1818 or 1822 she married the rich M. Vencelas de Hanski, who was twenty-five years her senior, an old gentleman of limited mind; pompous, unsociable, and often depressed; but apparently fond of his wife, and willing to allow her the travelling and society which he did not himself care for. Madame Hanska had many troubles in her married life, as she lost four out of her five children; and being an intensely maternal woman, the deepest feelings of her heart were henceforward devoted to Anna, her only surviving child, whom she never left for a day till the marriage of her darling in 1846, and of whom, after the separation, she could not think without tears.

She was a distinctly different type from the gentle, devoted Madame de Berny, whose French attributes were modified by the sentiment and romance she inherited from her Teutonic ancestors; or from Madame de Castries, the fragile and brilliant coquette. Mentally and physically there was a certain massiveness in Madame Hanska which was absent in her rivals. She was characterised by an egoism and self-assertiveness unknown to the "dilecta"; while, on the other hand, her principles were too strong to allow her to use a man as her plaything, as Madame de Castries had no scruple in doing. Side by side with her tendency to mysticism, she possessed much practical ability, a capacity for taking the initiative in the affairs of life, as well as considerable literary and critical power. Balzac had enormous respect for her intellect, and references to the splendid "analytical" forehead, which must have been a striking feature in her face, occur as often in his letters as admiring allusions to her pretty dimpled hands, or playful jokes about her droll French pronunciation. Her miniature by Daffinger,[*] taken in the prime of her beauty, gives an idea of great energy, strength of will, and intelligence. She is dark, with a decided mouth, and rather thick lips as red as a child's. Her hair is black, and is plainly braided at each side of her forehead; her eyes are dark and profound, though with the vague look of short sight; and her arms and shoulders are beautiful. Altogether she is a handsome woman, though there are indications of that tendency to *embonpoint* about which she was always troubled, and which Balzac, with his usual love of prescribing for his friends, advised her to combat by daily exercise.

However, in the spring of 1832, the time which we are considering, Madame Hanska was not even a name to Balzac; she was merely "L'Etrangere," an unknown woman who might be pretty or ugly, young or old; but who at any rate possessed the knack—or perhaps the author of "Seraphita" or of "Louis Lambert" would have said the power by transmutation of thought and sympathy—of interesting him in the highest degree.

In June, with the hope that absence would loosen the bonds of affection which united him and Madame de Berny, and with an *arriere pensee* about another charming personality whom he might meet on his travels, Balzac left Paris for six months, and began his tour by paying a visit to M. de Margonne at Sache. There he wrote "Louis Lambert" as a last farewell to Madame de Berny; and in memory of his ten years' intimacy with her, on the title-page were the dates 1822 and 1832, and underneath the words "Et nunc et semper." The manuscript was sent to her for criticism, and she wrote a charming letter[*] on receipt of it to Angouleme, where Balzac was staying with Madame Carraud. In this she shows the utmost tenderness and gentle playfulness; but while modestly deprecating her power to perform the task he demands from her, which she says should be entrusted to Madame Carraud, she has the noble disinterestedness to point out to him where she considers he has erred. She tells him that, after reading the book through twice, and endeavouring to see it as a whole, she *thinks* he has undertaken an impossible task, and that, trying to represent absolute truth in its action, he has attempted what is the province of God alone. Then, with the utmost tact and delicacy, she touches on a difficult point, and says that when Goethe and Byron attempt to paint the aspirations of a superior being, we admire their breadth of view, and wish we could aid them with our minds to reach the unattainable; but that an author who announces that he has swept to the utmost range of thought shocks us by his vanity, and she begs Balzac to eliminate certain phrases in his book which sound as though he had this belief. She finished thus: "Manage, my dear one, that every one shall see you from everywhere by the height at which you have placed yourself, but do not claim their admiration, for from all parts strong magnifying-glasses will be turned on you; and what becomes of the most delightful object when seen through the microscope?" Loving Balzac so tenderly, growing old so quickly, with Madame de Castries and the unknown Russian ready to seize the empire which she had abdicated willingly, though at bitter cost, what a temptation it must have been to leave these words unsaid, and now that she was parting from Balzac to accord him the unstinted admiration for which he yearned! That Madame de Berny thought of him only, of herself not at all, speaks volumes for the nobility and purity of her love, and we again feel that the "predilecta" never rose to her heights, and that to his first love belongs the credit of "creating" Balzac.

[*] See "La Jeunesse de Balzac," by MM. Hanotaux and Vicaire, p. 74.

During Balzac's absence from Paris, Madame de Balzac, who was installed in his rooms in the Rue Cassini, appears in quite a new light, and one which leads to the suspicion that the much-abused lady was not quite as black as she had been painted. The hard and heartless mother is now transmogrified into the patient and indefatigable runner of errands; and we must admire the business capacity, as well as bodily strength, which Madame de Balzac showed in carrying out her son's various behests. In one letter alone she was enjoined to carry out the following directions[*]: (1) She was to copy out an article in the *Silhouette*, which she would find on the second shelf for quartos near the door in Balzac's room. (2) She was to send him her copy of "Contes Drolatiques," and also "Les Chouans," which she would receive corrected from Madame de Berny. Furthermore, she was told to dress in her best and go to the library, taking with her the third and fourth volumes of "Scenes de la Vie Privee," as a present to M. de Manne, the librarian. She was then to hunt in the "Biographie Universelle" under B or P for Bernard Palissy, read the article, make a note of all books mentioned in it as written *by* him or *about* him, and ask M. de Manne for them. Next, Laure was to be visited, as the "Biographie," which had formerly belonged to old M. de Balzac, was at her house; and the works on Palissy mentioned in that must be compared carefully with those already noted down; and if fresh names were found, another visit must be paid to the librarian. If he did not possess all the books and they were not very dear, they were to be bought. A visit to Gosselin was to be the next excursion for poor Madame de Balzac, who apparently walked everywhere to save hackney carriage fares; and as minor matters she must send a letter he enclosed to its destination, and see that the groom exercised the horses every day.

[*] "Correspondance," vol. i. p. 153.

Certainly, if Balzac worked like a galley slave himself, he also kept his relations well employed; but Madame de Balzac apparently did everything contentedly, in the hope, as a good business woman, that the debts would at last be paid off; and though there were occasional breezes, the relations between her and her son were cordial at this time. Possibly she was pleased at his removal from the influence of Madame de Berny, of whom she was always jealous; and certainly she was delighted at the idea of his marriage. The intended daughter-in-law, whose name is never mentioned, was evidently a widow with a fortune, so the affair was highly satisfactory. The lady was expected to pay a visit to Mere, near Sache; and Balzac felt obliged to go there three times a week to see whether she had arrived—a duty which interfered sadly with his work. If he seemed likely to prosper in his suit, she was to be impressed by the sight of his groom and horses. However, this matrimonial business transaction was not successful, as we hear nothing more of it, and the next direction his mother receives is to the effect that she had better sell all his stable equipage.

Whether Madame de Balzac resented these demands on her, or whether she was disgusted at Balzac's failure to secure a rich wife, and thus put an end to the family troubles, we do not know; but when he returned to Paris at the end of the year, to his great disappointment she refused to live with him, and left him alone when he sorely needed sympathy and consolation.

It is curiously characteristic of Balzac, that at this very time, when in secret he contemplates marriage, he writes to Madame Carraud that he is going to Aix to run after some one who will perhaps laugh at him —one of those aristocratic women she would no doubt hold in abhorrence: "An angel beauty in whom one imagines a beautiful soul, a true duchess, very disdainful, very loving, delicate, witty, a coquette, a novelty to me! One of those phenomena who efface themselves from time to time, and who says she loves me, who wishes to keep me with her in a palace at Venice (for I tell you everything) —who wishes that I shall in future write only for her, one of those women one must worship on one's knees if she desires it, and whom one has the utmost pleasure in conquering—a dream woman! Jealous of everything! Ah, it would be better to be at Angouleme at the Poudrerie, very sensible, very quiet, listening to the mills working, making oneself sticky with truffles, learning from you how to pocket a billiard-ball, laughing and talking, than to lose both time and life!"[*]

[*] "Correspondance," vol. i. p. 161.

After his stay at Sache, Balzac went on to the Poudrerie, where he became ill from overwork, and wrote to his sister that a journey was quite necessary for his health. On August 22nd he started from Angouleme, having borrowed 150 francs from M. Carraud to take him as far as Lyons. He had already spent the 100 francs sent him by his mother, and he expected to find 300 francs more awaiting him at Lyons. There he arrived on the 25th, having unfortunately fallen in mounting the imperial of the diligence, and grazed his shin against the footboard thus making a small hole in the bone. However, we can appreciate the excellent reasons which led him to the conclusion that, in spite of the inflammation in his leg, it would be wise to press on at once to Aix. When he arrived there, on August 26th, he was evidently rewarded by a very cordial greeting from the Marquise; as, the day after, he wrote a most affectionate and joyful letter to his mother, thanking her in the warmest terms for all she had done, and for the pleasure she had procured him by enabling him to take this journey.

He was now established in a simple little room, with a view over the lovely valley of the Lac du Bourget; he got up each morning at half-past five, and worked from then till half-past five in the evening, his *dejeuner* being sent in from the club, and Madame de Castries providing him with excellent coffee, that primary necessity of his existence. At six he dined with her, and they spent the evening till eleven o'clock together. It was an exciting drama that went on during those long *tete-a-tetes*. On one side was the accomplished coquette, possibly only determined to make a plaything of the man of genius, to charm him and keep him at her feet; or perhaps with a lurking hope that her skilful game would turn to earnestness, and that in the course of it she would manage to forget that charming young Metternich who died at Florence and left her inconsolable. On the other was Balzac, his senses bewildered by passionate love, but his acuteness and knowledge of human nature not allowing him to be altogether deceived; so that he writes to Madame Carraud: "She is the most delicate type of woman—Madame de Beauseant, only better; but are not all these pretty manners exercised at the expense of the heart?"[*] Nevertheless, these were only passing doubts: he could not really believe that she would behave as she was doing if there were no love for him in her heart, and he pursued his suit with the intense ardour natural to him. Occasionally she became alarmed, and tried to rebuff him by a cold, irritable manner; but he continued to treat her with the utmost gentleness. No doubt, she was not altogether without feeling: an absolutely cold woman could not have exercised dominion over a man of the stamp of Balzac; and though she is always represented as playing a game, probably there were agitations, doubts, questionings, and possibly real trouble, on her side, as well as on that of Balzac. At any rate, the admirer of his novels may give her the benefit of the doubt, and remember in gratitude that she undoubtedly added to the gamut of the great psychologist's emotions, and therefore increased his knowledge of the human heart, and the truth and vividness of his books. Balzac, who spoke of the "doleurs qui font trop vivre," plunged very deeply into the learning of the school of life at this time.

[*] "Correspondance," vol. i. p. 195.

At last came a final rupture, of which we can only conjecture the cause, as no satisfactory explanation is forthcoming. The original "Confession" in the "Medecin de Campagne," which is the history of Balzac's relations and parting with Madame de Castries, is in the possession of the Vicomte de Spoelberch de Lovenjoul. The present Confession was substituted in its place, because the first revealed too much of Balzac's private life. However, even in the original Confession, we learn no reason for Madame de Castries' sudden resolve to dismiss her adorer, as Balzac declares with indignant despair that he can give no explanation of it. Apparently she parted from him one evening with her usual warmth of affection, and next morning everything was changed, and she treated him with the utmost coldness.

Madame de Castries, with her brother-in-law, the Duc de Fitz-James and his family, had settled to leave Aix on October 10th, and to travel in Italy, visiting Rome and Naples; and they had been anxious that Balzac should be one of the party. At first Balzac only spoke of this vaguely, because of the question of money; but as pecuniary matters were never allowed to interfere with anything he really wanted to do, his mother cannot have been surprised to receive a letter written on September 23rd, telling her that the matter was settled, and that he was going to Italy.[*] As she would naturally ask how this was to be managed, he explains that he will put off paying a debt of 500 francs, and that, being only responsible for a fourth share in the hire of Madame de Castries' carriage, this money would suffice for his expenses as far as Rome. There he will require 500 francs, and the same amount again at Naples; but this money will be gained by the "Medecin de Campagne," and he will only ask Madame de Balzac for 500 francs — without which he will perhaps, after all, manage — to bring him back from Naples in March. On September 30th he writes to M. Mame, the publisher, to tell him about the nearly-finished "Medecin de Campagne," and still talks of his projected journey; but on October 9th, as a result of Madame de Castries' behaviour towards him, he has left her at Aix, and is himself at Annecy, and on October 16th he has travelled on to Geneva. His only explanation for his sudden change of plan is a vague remark to his mother about the 1,000 francs required for the journey,[+] and about the difficulty of publishing books while he is away from France; while on the real reason of his change of plan he is absolutely silent. Before the end of 1832 he is back in Paris, and in spite of his success and celebrity is probably passing through the bitterest months of his life.

[*] "Correspondance," vol. i. p. 202.

[+] "Correspondance," vol. i. p. 220.

CHAPTER VIII

1832 - 1835

Meanwhile, during the tragic drama of the downfall of poor Balzac's high hopes, Madame Hanska continued to write steadily; but she was becoming tired of receiving no answer to her letters, and of not even knowing whether or no they had reached their destination. Therefore she wrote on November 7th, 1832, to ask Balzac for a little message in the *Quotidienne*, which she took in regularly, to say that he had received her letters; and Balzac, in reply, inserted the following notice in the *Quotidienne* of December 9th, 1832. "M. de B. has received the message sent him; he can only to-day give information of this through a newspaper, and regrets that he does not know where to address his answer. To. L'E.—H. de B."[*]

[*] A copy of the *Quotidienne* with this advertisement is in the possession of the Vicomte de Spoelberch de Lovenjoul, and I have seen it.

After this, it is amusing to see that Balzac was most particular in impressing on his publishers the necessity of advertising his forthcoming works in the *Quotidienne*, one of the few French papers allowed admission into Russia. On the other hand, the receipt of the *Quotidienne* with this announcement made Madame Hanska so bold, that in a letter dated January 9th, 1833, she gave Balzac the welcome information that she and M. de Hanski were leaving Ukraine for a time, and coming nearer France; and that she would indicate to him some way of corresponding with her secretly. As this is the last of her letters that can be found, we do not know what method she pointed out to Balzac; and his first letter to her is dated January, 1833, and after their meeting at Neufchatel in September, he wrote a short account of his day every evening to his beloved one, and once in eight days he despatched this journal to its destination. As he kept to this plan with only occasional interruptions whenever he was absent from her, till his marriage four months before his death, these letters, some of which are published in a volume called "Lettres a l'Etrangere," form a most valuable record of his life. In one of the first, it is interesting to see that he is obliged to soothe her uneasiness at the strange variety of his handwritings, as Madame Carraud had answered one of her letters in his name; and to allay her suspicions, he makes the rather unlikely explanation, that he has as many writings as there are days in the year. In the future, however, her letters are sacred, no eye but his own being permitted to gaze on them; and with his usual reticence where his feelings are seriously involved, he ceases to mention to his friends his correspondent in far Ukraine.

A little later he comments with joy on the fact that Madame Hanska has sent him a copy of the "Imitation of Christ,"[*] which represents our Lord on the cross, just as he is writing "Le Medecin de Campagne," which portrays the bearing of the cross by resignation, and love, faith in the future, and the spreading around of the perfume of good deeds. To Balzac, believer in the power of the transmission of thought, this coincidence was of good augury.

[*] "Lettres a l'Etrangere."

All this time he had not forgotten Madame de Berny, or the faithless Madame de Castries; and is profoundly miserable. On January 1st, 1833, he writes to his faithful friend, Madame Carraud, to pour out his troubles, and says: "In vain I try to transfer my life to my brain; nature has given me too much heart, and in spite of everything, more than enough for ten men is left. Therefore I suffer. All the more because chance made me know happiness in all its moral extent, while depriving me of sensual beauty. She" (Madame de Berny) "gave me a true love which must finish. This is horrible! I go through troubles and tempests which no one knows of. I have no distractions. Nothing refreshes this heat, which spreads and will perhaps devour me." He then passes on to Madame de Castries, and continues: "An unheard-of coldness has succeeded gradually to what I thought was passion, in a woman who came to me rather nobly."[*] In a letter to Madame Hanska, speaking of Madame de Castries, though he does not name her, he says: "She causes me suffering, but I do not judge her. Only I think that if you loved some one, if you had drawn him every day towards you into heaven, and you were free, you would not leave him alone in the depths of an abyss of cold, after having warmed him with the fire of your soul."[+]

[*] Letters sent by the Vicomte de Spoelberch de Lovenjoul to the *Revue Bleue* of November 21st, 1903.

[+] "Lettres a l'Etrangere."

Gradually, however, the new love gained ground; though at first Balzac showed that nervous dread of repetition of pain which was, in a man of his buoyancy and self-confidence, the last expression of depression and disillusionment. "I trembled in writing to you. I said to myself: 'Will this be only a new bitterness? Will the skies open to me again, for me only to be driven from them?'"[*] Nevertheless, passages such as the following, even taking into account the sentimental tone Balzac always adopted to his female correspondents, show that he was not destined to remain permanently inconsolable. "I love you, unknown, and this strange thing is the natural effect of an empty and unhappy life, only filled with ideas, and the misfortunes of which I have diminished by chimerical pleasures."[*]

[*] "Lettres a l'Etrangere."

In these words he gives himself the explanation of his overmastering love for Madame Hanska, a love which seems to have puzzled his contemporaries and some of his subsequent biographers. The man with the passionate nature, who cried in his youth for the satisfaction of his two immense desires—to be celebrated and to be loved—soon found the emptiness of the life of fame alone; and Madame Hanska, dowered with all that he longed for, came into his life at the psychological moment when he had broken with the old love, born into the world too soon, and had suffered bitterly at the cruel hands of the new. He turned to her with a rapture of new hope in the glories that might rise for him; and through trouble, disappointment and delay, he never once wavered in his allegiance.

In the early spring of 1833, the Hanski family, after no doubt many preparations, and surrounded by a great paraphernalia—for travelling in those days was a serious matter—started on the journey about which Madame Hanska had already told Balzac. Neufchatel was their destination; and through Mlle Henriette Borel, Anna's governess, who was a native of the place, and Madame Hanska's confidante, the Villa Andrie, in the Faubourg, just opposite the Hotel du Faubourg, was secured for them. Mlle Borel was a most useful person, as she always went to the post to claim Balzac's letters, and through Madame Hanska he sends her many directions, and specially enjoins great caution. We are told[*] that she was so much struck by the solemnities at M. de Hanski's funeral—the lights, the songs, and the national costumes —that she decided to abjure the Protestant faith, and that in 1843 she took the veil. We may wonder however, whether tardy remorse for her deceit towards the dead man, who had treated her with kindness, had not its influence in causing this sudden religious enthusiasm, and whether the Sister in the Convent of the Visitation in Paris gave herself extra penance for her sins of connivance.

[*] "Balzac a Neufchatel," by M. Bachelin.

From Neufchatel, Madame Hanska sent Balzac her exact address; and as he had really settled to go to Besancon in his search for inexpensive paper to enable him to carry out his grand scheme for an universal cheap library, it was settled that, travelling ostensibly for this purpose, he should go for a few days to Neufchatel, and meet Madame Hanska. He therefore wrote to Charles de Bernard, at Besancon, to ask him to take a place for him in the diligence to Neufchatel, on September 25th, 1833; and it is easy to imagine his qualms of anxiety, and yet joyful excitement, when he left Paris on the 22nd, and started on his fateful journey. At Neufchatel, he went to the Hotel du Faucon,[*] in the centre of the town, but found a note begging him to be on the Promenade du Faubourg next day from one to four; and he at once removed to the Hotel du Faubourg, so that he might be near the Villa Andrie. Madame Hanska no doubt shared to a certain extent his tremors of anticipation; but as a beauty and great lady she would naturally feel more confident than Balzac—especially when she had donned with care her most elegant and becoming toilette, and felt armed at every point for the encounter.

[*] "Un Roman d'Amour," by the Vicomte de Spoelberch de Lovenjoul, p. 75.

The Promenade du Faubourg at Neufchatel overlooks the lake, and is terminated by a promontory known as the Cret, a splendid point of vantage, whence there is a view of the Villa Andrie and over the gardens of the Hotel du Faubourg. Here, on the afternoon of September 26th, 1833, among others strollers, were two who might have seemed to an observant eye to be waiting for somebody: one was a stout, inelegant little man, with something bizarre about his costume, and the other a dark, handsome lady, dressed in the height of fashion, and perhaps known to some of the loungers as the rich Russian Countess. The manner of their meeting is uncertain; but whether Madame Hanska, with one of Balzac's novels in her hand, recognised him at once and rushed towards him joyously, or whether, as another story goes, she was at first disenchanted by his unromantic appearance and drew back, matters little.[*] In either case, according to Balzac's letter to his sister written on his return to Paris, they exchanged their first kiss under the shade of a great oak in the Val de Travers, and swore to wait for each other; and he speaks rapturously of Madame Hanska's beautiful black hair, of her fine dark skin and her pretty little hands. He mentions, too, her colossal riches, though these do not of course count beside her personal charms; but the remark is characteristic, and Balzac's pride and exultation are very apparent.[+] At last he has found his "grande dame," endowed with youth, beauty and riches, one who would not be ashamed to live with him in a garret, and yet would, by her birth, be able to hold her own in the most exclusive society in the world.

[*] "Un Roman d'Amour," by the Vicomte de Spoelberch de Lovenjoul, p. 75.

[+] I have seen in M. de Spoelberch de Lovenjoul's collection, the autograph of the whole of this letter as quoted in the "Roman d'Amour."

He is specially pleased, too, that he has succeeded in charming Madame Hanska's husband, to whom he was apparently introduced at once, though we do not know by what means. Certainly M. de Hanski appears to have felt a warm liking for the great writer, who charmed him and made him laugh by his amusing talk, kept his blue devils at bay, sent him first copies of his books, and sympathised with his views on political matters. M. de Hanski was also much flattered by Balzac's friendship for his wife, and would finish a polite and stilted epistle by saying that he need trouble Balzac no more, as he knows his wife is at the same time writing him one of her long chattering letters. Even when, by sad mischance, two of Balzac's love-letters fell into M. de Hanski's hands, and the great writer was forced to stoop to the pretence that they were written in jest, the husband seems to have accepted the explanation, and not to have troubled further about the matter. Later on, he sent Balzac a magnificent inkstand as a present, which the recipient rather ungratefully remarked required palatial surroundings, and was too grand for his use.

On October 1st, the happy time at Neufchatel came to an end, as the Hanskis were leaving that day, and Balzac's work awaited him in Paris. He got up at five o'clock on the morning of his departure, and went on to the promontory, whence he could gaze at the Villa Andrie, in the vain hope of a last meeting with Madame Hanska; but to his disappointment the Villa was absolutely quiet, no one was stirring. He had a most uncomfortable journey back, for everything was so crowded that fifteen or sixteen intending passengers were refused at each town; and as Charles de Bernard had not been able to secure a place for him in the mail coach, he was obliged to travel in the imperial of the diligence with five Swiss, who treated him as though he were an animal going to the market, and he arrived in Paris bruised all over.

In Balzac's letters after his return to Paris there is much mention of his enjoyment of the Swiss scenery, which is after all only Madame Hanska under another name; but he is absolutely discreet, and never speaks of the lady herself. He is redoubling his work, on the chance of managing to pay her another visit. "For a month longer, prodigies of work, to enable me to see you. You are in all my thoughts, in all the lines that I shall trace, in all the moments of my life, in all my being, in my hair which grows for you."[*]

[*] "Lettres a l'Etrangere."

Fortunately the long years of waiting, the anxieties, the hope constantly deferred, the pangs of unequally matched affection, and at last the short and imperfect fruition, were hidden from him. Henceforward everything in his life refers to Madame Hanska, and he waits patiently for his hoped-for union with her. His deference to his absent friend, his fear of her disapproval, his admiration for her perfections, are half pathetic and half comical.

Though she does not appear to have been strait-laced in her reading, he is terribly afraid of falling in her estimation by what he writes, and he explains anxiously that such books as "Le Medecin de Campagne" or "Seraphita" show him in his true light, and that the "Physiologie du Mariage" is really written in defence of women. The "Contes Drolatiques" he is also nervous about, and he is much agitated when he hears that she has read some of them without his permission.

He is not always *quite* candid, and the reader of "Lettres a l'Etrangere" may safely surmise that there is a little picturesque exaggeration in his account of the solitary life he leads; and that Madame Hanska had occasionally good reason for her reproaches at the reports she heard, though Balzac always replies to these complaints with a most touching display of injured innocence. Nevertheless, the "Lettres a l'Etrangere" are the record of a faithful and ever-growing love, and there is much in them which must increase the reader's admiration for Balzac.

The year 1833 was a prosperous one with him, as in October he sold to the publisher, Madame Charles Bechet, for 27,000 francs, an edition of "Etudes de Moeurs au XIXieme Siecle" in twelve octavo volumes, consisting of the third edition of "Scenes de la Vie Privee," the first of "Scenes de la Vie de Province," and the first part of the "Scenes de la Vie Parisienne." The last volume of this edition did not appear till 1837, and before that time Balzac had taken further strides towards his grand conception of the Comedie Humaine. In October, 1834,[*] he writes to Madame Hanska that the "Etudes de Moeurs," in which is traced thread by thread the history of the human heart, is only to be the base of the structure; and that next, in the "Etudes Philosophiques," he will go back from effect to cause, from the feelings, their life and way of working, to the conditions behind them on which life, society, and man have their being; and that having described society, he will in the "Etudes Philosophiques" judge it. In the "Etudes de Moeurs" types will be formed from individuals, in the "Etudes Philosophiques" individuals from types. Then, after effects and causes, will come principles, in the "Etudes Analytiques." "Les moeurs sont le spectacle, les causes son les coulisses et les machines, et les principes c'est l'auteur." When this great palace is at last completed, he will write the science of it in "L'Essai sur les Forces Humaines"; and on the base, he, a child and a laugher, will trace the immense arabesque of the "Contes Drolatiques," those Rabelaisian stories in old French tracing the progress of the language, which he often declared would be his principal claim to fame. In 1842 the name "La Comedie Humaine" was after much consideration given to the whole structure, and in the preface he explains this title by saying: "The vastness of a plan which includes Society's history and criticism, the analysis of its evils, the discussion of its principles, justifies me, I think, in giving to my work the name under which it is appearing to-day—'The Human Comedy.' Pretentious, is it? Is it not rather true? That is a question for the public to decide when the work is finished."

[*] "Lettres a l'Etrangere."

Unfortunately, in spite of the fact that in twelve years, from 1830 to 1842, Balzac wrote seventy-nine novels—an enormous number, especially remembering the fact that during the same time he published tales and numberless articles—the great work was never finished; and the last philosophical study, which was entitled "The Marquis of Carabbas," and was to treat of the life of nations, was not even begun.

However, in 1833, when he really started the germ of his life-work, he, like his father, had the idea that he would live to an enormous age; and he was in high spirits about the pecuniary side of his transaction with Madame Bechet.

Except for what he owes his mother, in seven months he will be free of debt, he cries rapturously; but it is hardly necessary to mention that this happy time of deliverance never did arrive. Indeed, we are scarcely surprised, when he writes on November 20th, to say that his affairs are in the most deplorable condition; that he has just sent four thousand francs, his last resource, to Mame, the publisher, and is as poor as Job; with one lawsuit going on, and another beginning for which he requires twelve hundred francs. His chronic state of disagreement with Emile de Girardin, editor of *La Presse*, had at this time, in spite of Madame de Girardin's attempts at mediation, become acute; so that they nearly fought a duel. The year before, as we have already seen, he had quarrelled with his former friend, Amedee Pichot, and had deserted the *Revue de Paris*, so his business relations were, as usual, not very happy.

However, he was at first much pleased with Madame Bechet, who, with unexpected liberality, herself paid 4000 francs for corrections; and in July, 1834, he got rid of publisher Gosselin, whom he politely designates as a "nightmare of silliness," and a "rost-beaf ambulant," and started business with Werdet, not yet the "vulture who fed on Prometheus," but an excellent young man, somewhat resembling "l'illustre Gaudissart," full of devotion and energy.

The year 1833 was rich in masterpieces. In September appeared "Le Medecin de Campagne," with its motto, "For wounded souls, shade and silence"; and though, like "Louis Lambert," it was not at first a success, later on its true value was realised; and the hero, the good Dr. Benassis, is one of Balzac's purest and most noble creations. It was followed in December by "Eugenie Grandet," a masterpiece of Dutch genre, immortalised by the vivid vitality of old Grandet, that type of modern miser who, in contradistinction to Moliere's Harpagon, enjoyed universal respect and admiration, his fortune being to some people in his province "the object of patriotic pride." The book raised such a storm of enthusiasm, that Balzac became jealous for the fame of his other works, and would cry indignantly: "Those who call me the father of Eugenie Grandet wish to belittle me. It is a masterpiece, I know; but it is a little masterpiece; they are very careful not to mention the great ones."[*] This, which is the best known and most generally admired of Balzac's novels, is dedicated by a strange irony of fate to Maria, whose identity has never been discovered; the only fact really known about her being her pathetic request to Balzac, that he would love her just for a year, and she would love him for all eternity. She did not, however, have undisputed possession of even the short time she longed for, as Madame Hanska's all-conquering influence was in the ascendant; but, as Balzac was always discreet, perhaps poor Maria was not aware of this.

[*] "Balzac, sa Vie et ses Oeuvres d'apres sa Correspondance," by Madame L. Surville.

In the midst of the acclamations and congratulations on the appearance of "Eugenie Grandet," Balzac again left Paris, and went to Geneva, where he arrived on December 25th, 1833. He left for Paris on February 8th, having spent six weeks with the Hanski family. During this time a definite promise was made by Madame Hanska, that she would marry him if she became a widow. "Adoremus in aeternum" was their motto; he was her humble "moujik," and she was his "predilecta, his love, his life, his only thought."[*]

[*] "Lettres a l'Etrangere."

Curiously enough, his occupation in Geneva, in the rapture of his newly-found happiness, was to write the "Duchesse de Langeais," by which he intended to revenge himself on Madame de Castries, though he could not help, in his book, making her turn to him at last, when it was too late. The wound was still smarting. He detests and despises her, he says; and the only words of spitefulness recorded in his generous, large-minded life, are when he mentions, with pretended pity, that owing to ill-health she has completely lost her beauty. In spite of this outburst, however, we find that he came forward later on, and helped her with much energy when she was in difficulties. He never had the satisfaction of knowing whether she were punished or not; as when he showed her the book before it was published, with the ostensible reason of wishing her to disarm the Faubourg St. Germain, which is severely criticised in its pages, she professed much admiration for it.

Meanwhile, Madame de Berny was beginning the slow process of dying; and Balzac speaks constantly with trouble of her failing health, and of the heart disease from which she suffered, and which, with her usual unselfishness, she tried to conceal from him. She was too ill now to correct his proofs, and her family circumstances were, as we have already seen, very miserable; so that her life was closing sadly. In January, 1835, Balzac spent eight days with her at La Boulonniere, near Nemours, working hard all the time; and was horrified to find her so ill, that even the pleasure of reading his books brought on severe heart attacks.

His life at this time was enormously busy; the passion for work had him in its grip, and even *his* robust constitution suffered from the enormous strain to which he subjected it by his constant abuse of coffee, which caused intense nervous irritation; and by the short hours of sleep he allowed himself. He never rested for a moment, he was never indifferent for a moment, his faculties were constantly on the stretch, and Dr. Nacquart remonstrated in vain. In August, 1834, he was attacked by slight congestion of the brain, and imperatively ordered two months' rest; which, of course, he did not take; and now from time to time, in his letters, occur entries of sinister omen, about symptoms of illness, and doctor's neglected advice. In October "La Recherche de l'Absolu" appeared, and instead of greeting it with the enthusiasm he usually accorded to his books, he remarked to Madame Hanska that he hoped it was good, but that he was too tired to judge. However, by December of the same year, when "Le Pere Goriot" was published, he had to a certain extent recovered his elasticity, and said that it was a beautiful work, though terribly sad, and showed the moral corruption of Paris like a disgusting wound. A few days later he became more enthusiastic, and wrote: "You will be very proud of 'Le Pere Goriot.' My friends insist that nothing is comparable to it, and that it is above all my other compositions."[*] Certainly the vivid portrait of old Goriot, that ignoble King Lear, who in his extraordinary passion of paternal love rouses our sympathy, in spite of his many absurdities and shortcomings, is a striking instance of Balzac's power in the creation of type.

[*] "Lettres a l'Etrangere."

He was straining every nerve to be able to meet Madame Hanska in Vienna; but with all his efforts his journey was put off month after month, and it was not till May 9th, 1835, that he was at last able to start. He arrived at Vienna on the 16th; having hired a post carriage for the journey, a little extravagance which cost him 15,000 francs. His stay there was not a rest, as, to Madame Hanska's annoyance, he worked twelve hours a day at "Le Lys dans la Vallee," and explained to her that he was doing a good deal in thus sacrificing three hours a day for her sake—fifteen hours out of the twenty-four being his usual time for labour. He visited Munich on his way back, and arrived in Paris on June 11th, to find a crowd of creditors awaiting his arrival, and his pecuniary affairs in terrible confusion. Owing, he considered, to the machinations of his enemies, articles had appeared in different papers announcing that he had been imprisoned for debt—a report which naturally ruined his credit, and caused a general gathering of those to whom he owed money. It was not a pleasant home-coming; as Werdet and Madame Bechet were in utter despair, and reproached Balzac bitterly for his absence, while all his silver had been pawned by his sister to pay his most pressing liabilities.

It is curious about this time to notice the reappearance of the early romantic novels, "Jane la Pale," "La Derniere Fee," and their fellows.[*] Balzac, as we have seen was in terrible straits for money, and he knew that the Belgians, who at this time practised the most shameless piracy, would reprint the books for their own advantage, if he did not. Therefore, in self-defence, he determined to bring out an edition himself; though, as he consistently refused to acknowledge the authorship of these despised productions, the treaty was drawn up in the name of friends. Nevertheless, with his usual caution, he drew up a secret document which was signed by M. Regnault, one of those in whose name the sale to the publisher was arranged, to the effect that the works of the late Horace de Saint-Aubin were really the property of M. de Balzac. "L'Heritiere de Birague" and "Jean Louis" did not appear in this edition, probably owing to the intervention of M. Le Poitevin, who considered them partly his property; but they were published with the others in an edition printed in 1853, after a lawsuit between Balzac's widow and his early collaborator.

[*] "Une Page Perdue de Honore de Balzac," by the Vicomte de Spoelberch de Lovenjoul.

The condition of the whole Balzac family at the close of 1835 was tragic, M. Henri, back from abroad, and utterly incapable, as Balzac says, of doing anything, talked of blowing out his brains; Madame Surville was ill, Madame Balzac's reason or life was despaired of; and Balzac chose this time to consult a somnambulist about Madame Hanska, and was told the distressing news that she was in anxiety of some sort, and that her heart was enlarged! Fortunately, in October, 1835, the Hanski family returned to Wierzchownia, and the constant worry to Balzac of their proximity to France was removed for the time.

In December another misfortune befell Balzac. A fire broke out at the printing office in the Rue du Pot-de-Fer, and burnt the first hundred and sixty pages of the third dizain of the "Contes Drolatiques," as well as five hundred volumes of the first and second dizain, which had cost him four francs each. He thus lost 3,500 francs, and to add to the calamity, did not receive the sum of 6,000 francs which in the ordinary course of events would have been due to him at the end of the year, when but for this disaster he would have handed over the third dizain to Werdet and an associate.

Figures and sums of money occur constantly in Balzac's letters; but his accounts of his pecuniary affairs are so conflicting and so complicated that it is impossible to understand them; indeed it is doubtful whether he ever mastered them himself, as he continually expected to be out of debt in a few months. According to his own story to Madame Hanska, he left the printing office owing 100,000 francs, had to find 6,000 francs a year for interest on this debt, and required 3,000 francs to live on; while in 1828, 1829, and 1830, he only made 3,000 francs each year, so that in three years he had increased his debt by 24,000 francs. In 1830 the Revolution caused general disaster among the publishers, and "La Peau de Chagrin" only made 700 francs, so that in 1830 and 1831 Balzac had an income of only 10,000 francs a year, and had to pay out 18,000 francs. From 1833 to 1836 he received 10,000 francs a year by his treaty with Madame Bechet; 6,000 of this he paid in interest on his debt, while 4,000 apparently remained to live on. However, between the fire in the Rue du Pot-de-Fer, Werdet's delinquencies, the failure of the *Chronique*, and the sums paid back to publishers who had advanced money on arrangements Balzac cancelled to fulfil this new agreement, hardly anything was left; and in 1837 he owed 162,000 francs.

In August, 1835, he describes his life thus[*]: "Work, always work! Heated nights succeed heated nights, days of meditation days of meditation; from execution to conception, from conception to execution! Little money compared with what I want, much money compared with production. If each of my books were paid like those of Walter Scott, I should manage; but although well paid, I do not attain my goal. I received 8,000 francs for the 'Lys'; half of this came from the publisher, half from the *Revue de Paris*. The article in the *Conservateur* will pay me 3,000 francs. I shall have finished 'Seraphita,' begun 'Les Memoires de Deux Jeunes Mariees,' and finished Mme. Bechet's edition. I do not know whether a brain, pen, and hand will ever before have accomplished such a 'tour de force' with the help of a bottle of ink."

[*] "Lettres a l'Etrangere."

As it is impossible for even a Balzac to live without relaxation, even if he goes without rest, what, may we ask, were his recreations at this time? In the first place he often went to the theatre; and he was passionately fond of music, occupying a place in the box at the Italian Opera, which was reserved specially for dandies. One of his extravagances was a dinner at which he entertained the five other "tigres," as the occupants of this box were nicknamed, and Rossini, Olympe Pelissier, Nodier, Sandeau, and Bohain. At this banquet, the most sumptuous fare and the most exquisite wines were provided for the guests, and the table was decked with the rarest flowers. Balzac enjoyed the festivity immensely, as well as the *eclat* which followed it; and relates with delight that all Paris was talking of it, and that Rossini said he had not seen more magnificence when he dined at royal tables.

However busy he was, he never completely deprived himself of the pleasure of listening to music; though on one occasion he remarks regretfully, that he has been obliged to limit his attendance at the Opera to two visits each month; and on another, that he has been so overwhelmed with business that he has not been able even to have a bath, or go to the Italian Opera, two things that are more necessary to him than bread. His works abound in references to his beloved art, and when he was writing "Massimilla Doni" he employed a professional musician to instruct him about it. Beethoven, in particular, he speaks of with the utmost enthusiasm, and after hearing his "Symphony in Ut mineur," he says that the great musician is the only person who makes him feel jealous, and that he prefers him even to Rossini and Mozart. "The spirit of the writer," he says, "cannot give such enjoyment, because what *we* print is finished and determined, whereas Beethoven wafts his audience to the infinite."[*]

[*] "Lettres a l'Etrangere."

The other amusements of this great thinker and seer would strike the reader as strange, if he did not perhaps, by this time, realise that no anomaly need surprise him in Balzac's extraordinary personality.

He writes to Madame Hanska[*]: "As to my joys, they are innocent. They consist in new furniture for my room, a cane which makes all Paris chatter, a divine opera-glass, which my workers have had made by the optician at the Observatory; also the gold buttons on my new coat, buttons chiselled by the hand of a fairy, for the man who carries a cane worthy of Louis XIV. in the nineteenth century cannot wear ignoble pinchbeck buttons. These are little innocent toys, which make me considered a millionaire. I have created the sect of the 'Cannophiles' in the world of fashion, and every one thinks me utterly frivolous. This amuses me!" Certainly Balzac was not wrong when he told his correspondent that there was much of the child in him.

[*] "Lettres a l'Etrangere."

CHAPTER IX

NO PARTICULAR DATE

In the Salon of 1837 appeared a portrait of Balzac by Boulanger,[*] of which Theophile Gautier gave the following description in *La Presse*: "M. de Balzac is not precisely beautiful. His features are irregular; he is fat and short. Here is a summary which does not seem to lend itself to a painting, but this is only the reverse of the medal. The life and ardour reflected in the whole face give it a special beauty.

[*] See the chapter entitled "Un Portrait" in "Autour de Honore de Balzac," by the Vicomte de Spoelberch de Lovenjoul.

"In this portrait, M. de Balzac, enveloped in the large folds of a monk's habit, sits with his arms crossed, in a calm and strong attitude; the neck is uncovered, the look firm and direct; the light, shining from above, illumines the satin-like smoothness of the upper parts of the forehead, and throws a bright light on the bumps of imagination and humour, which are strongly developed in M. de Balzac; the black hair, also lit up, shining and radiant, comes from the temples in bright waves, and gives singular light to the top of the head; the eyes steeped in a golden penumbra with tawny eyeballs, on a moist and blue crystalline lens like that of a child, send out a glance of astonishing acuteness; the nose, divided into abrupt polished flat places, breathes strongly and passionately, through large red nostrils; the mouth, large and voluptuous, particularly in the lower lip, smiles with a rabelaisian smile under the shade of a moustache much lighter in colour than the hair; and the chin, slightly raised, is attached to the throat by a fold of flesh, ample and strong, which resembles the dewlap of a young bull. The throat itself is of athletic and rare strength, the plump full cheeks are touched with the vermilion of nervous health, and all the flesh tints are resplendent with the most joyful and reassuring brilliancy.

"In this monk's and soldier's head there is a mixture of reflection and of good-humour, of resolution and of high spirits, which is infinitely rare; the thinker and good liver melt into each other with quaint harmony. Put a cuirass on this large breast, and you will have one of those fat German foot-soldiers so jovially painted by Terburg. With the monks' habit, it is

Jean des Entommeurs[*]; nevertheless, do not forget that the eyes throw, through all this embonpoint and good-humour, the yellow look of a lion to counteract this Flemish familiarity. Such a man would be equal to excesses of the table, of pleasure, and of work. We are no longer astonished at the immense quantity of volumes published by him in so short a time. This prodigious labour has left no trace of fatigue on the strong cheeks dappled with red, and on the large white forehead. The enormous work which would have crushed six ordinary authors under its weight is hardly the third of the monument he wishes to raise."

[*] One of the characters in Rabelais.

The original of this portrait was sent to Madame Hanska at Wierzchownia; but a sketch of it belongs to M. Alexandre Dumas the younger, and has often been engraved. From this, it seems as though Theophile Gautier must have read his knowledge of Balzac's character as a whole into his interpretation of the picture. To the ordinary observer, Boulanger's portrait represents Balzac as the thinker, worker, and fighter, stern and strenuous; not the delightful comrade who inspired joy and merriment, and the recollection of whom made Heine smile on his death-bed. The wonderful eyes which had not their equal, and which asked questions like a doctor or a priest, are brilliantly portrayed. Balzac himself allows this, though he complains to Madame Hanska that they have more of the psychological expression of the worker than of the loving soul of the individual—a fact for which we may be grateful to Boulanger. Balzac is much delighted, however, with Boulanger's portrayal of the insistence and intrepid faith in the future, a la Coligny or a la Peter the Great, which are at the base of his character; and he goes on to give an attractive, though rather picturesque account of his career and past misfortunes, which is evidently intended to counteract any misgivings Madame Hanska may feel at his sternness as depicted in the portrait.

"Boulanger has seen the writer only,[*] not the tenderness of the idiot who will always be deceived, not the softness towards other people's troubles which cause all my misfortunes to come from my holding out my hand to weak people who are falling into disaster. In 1827 I help a working printer, and therefore in 1829 find myself crushed by fifty thousand francs of debt, and thrown without bread into a gutter. In 1833, when my pen appears to be likely to bring in enough to pay off my obligations, I attach myself to Werdet. I wish to make him my only publisher, and in my desire to bring him prosperity, I sign engagements, and in 1837 find myself owing a hundred and fifty thousand francs, and liable on this account to be put under arrest, so that I am obliged to hide. During this time I make myself the Don Quixote of the poor. I hope to give courage to Sandeau, and I lose through him four to five thousand francs, which would have saved other people." It would be interesting to hear what Barbier and Werdet would have said, if they had been allowed to read this letter; but on Browning's principle, that a man should show one side to the world, and the other to the woman he loves, no doubt Balzac's account of past events was quite justifiable.

[*] "Lettres a l'Etrangere."

Boulanger's picture gave Balzac a great deal of trouble, as well as delighted yet anxious speculation about Madame Hanska's opinion of it, when it arrived in Wierzchownia. This was naturally an important matter, his meetings with her being so rare that, except his letters, the picture would generally be her only reminder of him; and for this reason it was most necessary that it should show him at his best. It was therefore very trying that Boulanger should have exaggerated the character of his quiet strength, and made him look like a bully and a soldier; and we can enter thoroughly into his feelings, and sympathise heartily with his uneasiness, because Boulanger has not quite caught the fineness of contour under the fatness of the face. Undoubtedly, the picture does not give the idea of a person of extreme refinement, or distinction of appearance. Nevertheless, judging from stories told by his contemporaries, and also from some of the books written by the great novelist, it seems likely that Boulanger's powerful and strongly coloured portrait, though only redeemed from coarseness by the intense concentration of expression and the intellectual light in the wonderful eyes, was strikingly true to nature, and caught one very real aspect of the man. Perhaps, however, it was not the one calculated to work most strongly on the feelings of his absent lady-love; who, no doubt, poor Balzac hoped, would often make her way to the spot in the picture gallery where his picture hung in its quaint frame of black velvet, and would refresh herself with the sight of her absent friend. When her miniature by Daffinger was sent him, he was stupefied all day with joy; and he always carried it about with him, considering it an amulet which brought him good fortune.

He believed in talismans, and had pretty fanciful ideas about being present to his friends in the sudden flicker of the fire, or the brightening of a candle-flame. Balzac, the Seer, the believer in animal magnetism, in somnambulism, in telepathy, the weaver of strange fancies and impossible daydreams—Balzac with philosophical theories on the function of thought, and faith in the mystical creed of Swedenborg—in short, the Balzac of "Louis Lambert" and "Seraphita," is not, however, depicted by Boulanger: *he* can only be found in M. Rodin's wonderful statue. There the great *voyant*, who, in the beautiful vision entitled "L'Assomption," saw man and woman perfected and brought to their highest development, stands in rapt contemplation and concentration, his head slightly raised, as if listening for the voice of inspiration, or hearing murmurs of mysteries still unfathomed.

Somnambulism, in particular, occupied much of Balzac's attention. He wrote in 1832 to a doctor, M. Chapelain, who evidently shared his interest in the subject, to ask why medical men had not made use of it to discover the cause of cholera[*]; and on another occasion, after an accident to his leg, he sent M. Chapelain, from Aix, two pieces of flannel which he had worn, and wanted to know from them what caused the mischief, and why the doctors at their last consultation advised a blister. Unluckily, we hear no more of this matter, and never have the satisfaction of learning how much the learned doctor deduced from the fragments submitted to his inspection. Time after time Balzac mentions in his correspondence that he has consulted somnambulists when he has been anxious about the health of the Hanski family; and it is curious that a few months before he received the letter from Madame Hanska, telling of her husband's death, he had visited a sorcerer, who by means of cards, told him many extraordinary things about his past career, and said that in six weeks he would receive news which would change his whole life.

[*] "Correspondance," vol. i. p. 147.

The portrait was still destined to cause Balzac much anxiety. After the close of the Salon, the painter had promised to take a copy of it for Madame de Balzac, who, "between ourselves," Balzac remarked to Madame Hanska, would not care much about it, and certainly would not know the difference between the replica and the original, in which the soul of the model was searched for, examined and depicted,[*] and which was, of course, to belong to the beloved friend.

[*] "Lettres a l'Etrangere."

However, there were still many delays. Boulanger showed "horrible ingratitude," and did not appreciate sufficiently the honour done him by his illustrious sitter in allowing his portrait to be taken. He refused at first to begin the copy; but this difficulty was at last arranged, and the original was carefully packed in a wooden crate, instead of going in a roll as Balzac had at first intended. Still there were innumerable stoppages, and doubt where the precious canvas was located; till the impatient Balzac was only deterred from his intention of starting a lawsuit against the authorities, by a fear of bringing the noble name of Hanski into notoriety. It is sad that the last time we hear of this precious picture in Balzac's lifetime was when he went to Wierzchownia, in 1849; and then it had been relegated to a library which few people visited, and he describes it with his usual energy, as the most hideous daub it is possible to see—quite black, from the faulty mixing of the colours; a canvas of which, for the sake of France, he is thoroughly ashamed.

The sketch of the portrait is not disfigured; and the engravings of it give an interesting view of Balzac's personality. With due deference to the great psychologist, we cannot think the painter was wrong in imparting a slightly truculent expression to the face. Balzac was essentially a fighter: he started life with a struggle against his family, against the opinion of his friends, and, harder than all, against his own impotence to give expression to his genius; and, in the course of his career he made countless enemies, and finished by enrolling among their ranks most of the literary men of the day. This alienation was to a great extent caused by his inveterate habit of boasting, of applying the adjectives "sublime" and "magnificent" to his own works: an idiosyncracy which was naturally annoying to his brother authors. It was deprecated even by his devoted and admiring friends; though they knew that, as George Sand says, it was only caused by the *naivete* of an artist, to whom his work was all-important.

His personal charm was so great, that Werdet, his enemy, says that in his presence those who loved him, forgot any real or fancied complaint against him, and only remembered the affection they felt for him. Nevertheless, in the course of his life of fighting, his ever-pressing anxieties and the strain of his work, coupled with his belief in the importance and sacredness of his destiny, made him something of an egotist. Therefore, in spite of his real goodness of heart, he would sometimes shoulder his way through the world, oblivious of the unfortunate people who had come to grief owing to their connection with him, and careless of the lesser, though very real troubles of harassed and exasperated editors, when his promised copy was not forthcoming.

Like Napoleon, to whom, amidst the gibes of his contemporaries, he likened himself, he wanted everything; and those with this aspiration must necessarily be heedless of their neighbours' smaller ambitions. "Without genius, I am undone!" he cried in despair; but when it was proved beyond dispute that this gift of debatable beneficence was his, he was still unsatisfied.

What, after all, was the use of genius except as a stepping-stone to the solid good things of the earth? Where lay the advantage of superiority to ordinary men, if it could not be employed as a lever with which to raise oneself? Reasoning thus, his extraordinary versatility, his power of assimilation, and his varied interests, made his ambitions many and diverse. The man who could enter with the masterly familiarity of an expert into affairs of Church, State, Society, and Finance, who would talk of medicine like a doctor, or of science like a savant, naturally aspired to excellence in many directions.

At times, as we have already seen, strange fancies filled his brain: dreams, for instance, of occupying the highest posts in the land, or of gaining fabulous sums of money by some wildly impossible scheme, such as visiting the Great Mogul with a magical ring, or obtaining rubies and emeralds from a rich Dutchman. The two apparently incompatible sides to Balzac's character are difficult to reconcile. On some occasions he appears as the keen business man, who studies facts in their logical sequence, and has the power of drawing up legal documents with no necessary point omitted. The masterly Code which he composed for the use of the "Societe des Gens-de-Lettres" is an example of this faculty. At other times we are astonished to find that the great writer is a credulous believer in impossibilities, and a follower of strange superstitions. A similar paradox may be found in his books, where, side by side with a truth and occasional brutality which makes him in some respects the forerunner of the realists, we find a wealth of imagination and insistence on the power of the higher emotions, which are completely alien to the school of Flaubert and Zola.

Perhaps in his own dictum, that genius is never quite sane, gives a partial explanation of many of his fantastic schemes. The question of money was his great preoccupation and anxiety, and possibly his pecuniary difficulties, and the strain of the heavy chain of debt he dragged after him, constantly adding to its weight by some fresh extravagance, had affected his mind on this one point. Marriage with poverty he could not conceive; and, as he was intensely affectionate, he longed for a home and womanly companionship. "Is there no woman in the world for me?" he cried despairingly; but in this, as in everything else, he required so much, that it was difficult to find any one who would, in his eyes, be worthy to become Madame Honore de Balzac. His wife must be no ordinary woman; in addition to birth and wealth, she must possess youth, beauty, and high intellectual gifts; and one great difficulty was, that the lady endowed with this combination of excellencies would naturally require some winning, and Balzac had no time to woo. However, it was absolutely necessary that his married life should be one of luxury and magnificence, beautiful surroundings being indispensable to his scheme of existence, "Il faut," he said, "que l'artiste mene une vie splendide." Therefore, till the right lady was found, Balzac toiled unceasingly; and when in Madame Hanska the personification of his ideal at last appeared, he redoubled his efforts, till overwork, and his longing for her, caused the decay of his physical powers, and his strength for labour diminished.

Literature, a rich marriage, a successful play, or a political career, were all incidentally to make his fortune; though it must be said, in justice, that this motive, though it entwines itself with everything in Balzac's life, was not his only, or even his principal incentive to action.

In his desire to become a deputy, for instance, the longing to serve his country and to have a voice in her Councils, which he would use boldly, conscientiously, without fear or favour, to further her true interests, was ever present with him. As early as 1819, he had begun to take the keenest interest in the elections, telling M. Dablin, from whom he wanted a visit, that he dreamed of nothing but him and the deputies, and begging him for a complete list of those chosen in each department, with a short notice of his opinion on each.

By the law of election of 1830, any Frenchman who was thirty years of age, and contributed 500 francs a year directly, in taxes, was eligible as a deputy. When the law was made Balzac was thirty-one, and paid the requisite amount; he therefore determined, in spite of his enormous output of literary work at this time, to add the career of a deputy to his labours; and in April, 1831, he wrote to ask for the assistance of the General Baron de Pommereul, with whom he had been staying at Fougeres, collecting material for "Les Chouans," while at the same time he worked up the country politically. His manifesto, at this period, is found in the "Enquete sur la Politique des Deux Ministeres,"[*] in which he calls the Government a "monarchie tempere par les emeutes," objects to the "juste milieu" observed by the Ministers; and while bringing forward, with apparent impartiality, the advantages of the two courses of peace and war, very evidently longs for France to take the battlefield again, to obtain what he considers her natural frontier, that of the Rhine. He also enters *con amore* into the details of raising a Napoleonic army, and of establishing the system of the Landwehr in France. A very remarkable passage in this manifesto is that on the Press; by which, he says, the Government is terrorised. With extraordinary penetration, he advises that the strength of journalism shall be broken by the sacrifice of the three or four millions gained by the "timbre," and the liberation of the newspapers, which are stronger than the seven ministers—for they upset the Government, and cannot be themselves suppressed—there will be a hundred, and the number will neutralise their power, so that they will become of no account politically.

[*] Another political pamphlet, entitled "Du Gouvernement Moderne," written by Balzac at Aix in 1832, has lately been published in the *North American Review*. The original is in the collection of the Vicomte de Spoelberch de Lovenjoul.

Balzac had no chance at Fougeres, where a rich proprietor of the neighbourhood was chosen as deputy, and no doubt M. de Pommereul advised him not to proceed further in the matter. However, with his usual tenacity, he wrote in September to M. Henri Berthoud, manager of the *Gazette de Cambrai*, who wanted to collaborate with the *Revue de*

Paris, promising to further his wishes by all the means in his power, if M. Berthoud would, on his part, support his candidature at Cambrai. At the same time, he determined to try Angouleme, where he sometimes went to stay with a relation, M. Grand-Besancon, and had met a M. Berges, chief of the Government preparatory school, who was much struck by his talent, and promised to help him. In June, 1831, he wrote to Madame Carraud,[*] who took much interest in his political aspirations, and sent her three copies of the Manifesto for distribution. He told her that he was working day and night to become deputy, was going out into society for this purpose; and was so overwhelmed with business, that he had not touched "La Peau de Chagrin" since he was last at Saint-Cyr.

[*] "Correspondance," vol. i. p. 118.

He was evidently full of hope; but in spite of the powerful support of the *Revue de Paris*, the *Temps*, the *Debats*, and the *Voleur*, the steady-going electors had no mind to be represented by a penniless young author, who was chiefly known to the general public as the writer of the "Physiologie du Mariage," a book distinctly *not* adapted for family reading. Therefore, in this, as in many other hopes of his life, Balzac was doomed to disappointment; though the readers of novels may be grateful to the unkind fate which caused him to turn with renewed ardour to the neglected "Peau de Chagrin." He cherished a slight resentment against Angouleme, as he showed in "Illusions Perdues," where the aristocracy of that town are rather unkindly treated; but he was not discouraged in his political ambitions, and in 1832 he joined with M. Laurentie, the Duc de Noailles, the Duc de Fitz-James (nephew to the Princesse de Chimay, who acted as proxy for Marie Antoinette at Madame de Berny's christening) and others, to found a Legitimist journal, the *Renovateur*. In this appeared an article against the proposed destruction of the monument to the Duc de Berry, in which Balzac indignantly asks: "Why do you not finish the monument, and raise an altar where the priests may pray God to pardon the assassin?"

Having thus shown his principles clearly, he turned his attention in 1832 to Chinon, which was close to Tours, where he and his family had lived for so long, and to Sache, where he was a constant visitor. There, if anywhere, he seemed likely to succeed; and the *Quotidienne*, the paper which afterwards supported him during his lawsuit against the *Revue de Paris*, had promised its voice in his favour. Again cruel Fate dogged his footsteps, as in May he tumbled out of his tilbury, and his head came violently into contact with what he calls the "heroic pavements of July"; the accident being a sad result of his childish delight in driving at a tremendous pace in the Bois, which is rebuked by his sage adviser, Madame Carraud. Certainly carriages, horses, and a stable, seemed hardly prudent acquisitions for a man in debt; but

Balzac always defended his pet extravagances with the specious reasoning that nothing succeeds like success; and that most of his literary friends did not become rich because they lived in garrets, and were on that account trampled on by haughty publishers and editors. He writes to Madame de Girardin on this occasion: "Only think, that I who am so handsome have been cruelly disfigured for several days, and it has seemed curious to be uglier than I really am."[*] As a further and more serious result, he was laid up in bed, and had to undergo a severe regimen of bleeding, during the time that he should have been at Sache, working hard about his election; and when he did arrive there, in June, he recognised that he was too late for success. However, another dissolution, which after all did not take place, was expected in September, and Balzac looked forward to making a determined attempt then. This hope being frustrated, it was not till 1834 that he again came forward as a candidate: this time for Villefranche, where, curiously enough, another M. de Balzac was nominated, and when M. de Hanski wrote to congratulate Balzac, the latter was obliged to explain the mistake. On this occasion he had purposed to present himself as champion of the Bourbon Royal Family, especially of the Duchesse de Berry, for whom he had an immense admiration, while she read his books with much delight during her captivity in the Castle of Blaye. He wrote to M. de Hanski that he considered the exile of Madame and the Comte de Chambord the great blot on France in the nineteenth century, as the French Revolution had been her shame in the eighteenth.

[*] "Correspondance," vol. i. p. 147.

This was Balzac's last serious attempt to stand for Parliament during the Monarchy of July, though he often talked in his letters to Madame Hanska of his political aspirations, looked forward to becoming a deputy in 1839, and hoped till then to dominate European opinion —rather a large ambition—by a political publication. In his letters he is continually on the point of beginning his career as a statesman; and in 1835 his views are even more inflated than usual. He will absorb the *Revue des Deux Mondes* and the *Revue de Paris*, is in treaty to obtain one newspaper, and will start two others himself, so that his power will be irresistible. "Le temps presse, les evenements se compliquent,"[*] he cries impatiently. He is still strangled by want of money—a hundred thousand francs is the modest sum he requires; but he will write a play in the name of his secretary, and the spectre of debt will be laid for ever.

[*] "Lettres a l'Etrangere."

However, in the stress of work, which made his own life like the crowded canvas of one of his own novels, these brilliant schemes came to nothing, and Balzac was never in the proud position of a deputy. He gives his views clearly in a letter to Madame Carraud in 1830.[*] "France ought to be a constitutional monarchy, to have a hereditary royal family, a house of peers of extraordinary strength, which will represent property, etc., with all possible guarantees for heredity, and privileges of which the nature must be discussed; then a second assembly, elective, representing all the interests of the intermediary mass, which separates those of high social position from the classes who are generally termed the people."

[*] "Correspondance," vol. i. p. 108.

"The purport of the laws, and their spirit, should be designed to enlighten the masses as much as possible—those who have nothing, the workmen, the common people, etc., in order that as many as possible should arrive at the intermediary state; but the people should, at the same time, be kept under a most powerful yoke, so that its individuals may find light, help, and protection, and that no idea, no statute, no transaction, may make them turbulent.

"The greatest possible liberty should be allowed to the leisured classes, for they possess something to keep, they have everything to lose, they can never be dissolute.

"As much power as possible should be granted to the Government. Thus the Government, the rich people, and the bourgeoisie have interest in keeping the lowest class happy, and in increasing the number of the middle class, which is the true strength of the state.

"If rich people, the hereditary possessors of fortune in the highest Chamber, are corrupt in their manners, and start abuses, these are inseparable from the existence of all society; they must be accepted, to balance the advantages given."

This extract is taken from a letter which is, Balzac tells his correspondent, strictly private; but, with his usual independence and fearlessness, he did not hesitate to enunciate his opinions in public, and invariably refused to stoop to compromise or to disguise. Consequently, we cannot wonder that he never attained his ambition; particularly as he lacked the aid of money, and had no support, except the politically doubtful one of a literary reputation. His penetration and power of prescience were remarkable, and it is startling to find that he foretells the fall of the Monarchy of July, and the Revolution of 1848.[*] "I do not think," he says, "that in ten years from now the actual form of government will subsist—August, 1830, has forgotten the part played by youth and intelligence. Youth compressed will burst like the boiler of a steam engine." In "Les Paysans," one of his most wonderful novels, he gives a vivid picture of the constant struggle going on under the surface between the peasants and the bourgeoisie, and shows that the triumph of the former class must be the inevitable result.

[*] "Revue Parisienne," p. 26

His was essentially a loyal, reverential nature, with the soldierly respect for constituted authority which is often the characteristic of strong natures; and he was absolutely unswerving in his principles —the courage and tenacity which distinguished him through life, never deserting him in political emergencies. He was patriotic and high-minded; absolutely immovable in all that concerned his duty. On one occasion, when it was proposed at a public meeting that the Legitimists should follow the example of their political opponents and should stoop to evil doings, he refused decidedly, saying: "The cause of the life of man is superhuman. It is God who judges; His judgment does not hinge on our passions."[*] In his eyes, Religion and the Monarchy were twin sisters, and he speaks sadly in "Le Medecin de Campagne" of the downfall of both these powers. "With the monarchy we have lost honour, with our unfruitful attempts at government, patriotism; and with our fathers' religion, Christian virtue. These principles now only exist partially, instead of inspiring the masses, for these ideas never perish altogether. At present, to support society we have nothing but selfishness."[+] Elsewhere, he laments the atheistic government, and the increase of incredulity; and longs for Christian institutions, and a strong hierarchy, united to a religious society.

[*] "Balzac et ses Oeuvres," by Lamartine de Prat.

[+] "Le Medecin de Campagne."

Balzac was not orthodox. There is no doubt, from a letter to Madame Hanska, that the Swedenborgian creed he enunciates in "Seraphita" is to a great extent his own; but he believed in God, in the immortality of the soul, and considered natural religion, of which, in his eyes, the Bourbons were the depositors, absolutely essential to the well-being of a State. He had a great respect for the priesthood, and has left many a charming and sympathetic picture of the parish cure, such as l'Abbe Janvier in "Le Medecin de Campagne," who acts hand in hand with the good doctor Benassis, as an enlightened benefactor to the poor; or l'Abbe Bonnet, the hero of "Le Cure du Village," whose face had "the impress of faith, an impress giving the stamp of the human greatness which approaches most nearly to divine greatness, and of which the undefinable expression beautifies the most ordinary features." In "Les Paysans" we have another fine portrait, L'Abbe Brossette, who is doing his work nobly among debased and cunning peasants. "To serve was his motto, to serve the Church and the Monarchy at the most menaced points; to serve in the last rank, like a soldier who feels destined sooner or later to rise to generalship, by his desire to do well, and by his courage."

There is a beautiful touch in that terrible book "La Cousine Bette," where the infamous Madame Marneffe is dying of a loathsome and infectious disease, so that even Bette, who feels for her the "strongest sentiment known, the affection of a woman for a woman, had not the heroic constancy of the Church," and could not enter the room. Religion alone, in the guise of a Sister of Mercy, watched over her.

CHAPTER X

1836

Balzac opened the first day of the year 1836 by becoming proprietor of the *Chronique de Paris*, an obscure Legitimist publication, which had been founded in 1834 by M. William Duckett. It started under Balzac's management with a great flourish of trumpets, the Comte (afterwards Marquis) de Belloy and the Comte de Gramont taking posts as his sectaries; while Jules Sandeau, Emile Regnault, Gustave Planche, Theophile Gautier, Charles de Bernard, and others, became his collaborators. Balzac's special work was to provide a series of papers on political questions, entitled "La France et l'Etranger," papers which show his extraordinary versatility; and his helpers were to provide novels and poems, satire, drama, and social criticism; so that the scope of the periodical was a wide one.

At first, Balzac was most sanguine about the success of his new enterprise, and was very active and enthusiastic in working for it. On March 27th, he wrote to Madame Hanska about the embarrassment caused him by his plate having been pawned during his unfortunate absence in Vienna, nearly a year ago. It was worth five or six thousand francs, and he required three thousand to redeem it. This sum he had never been able to raise, while, to add to his difficulties, on the 31st of the month he would owe about eight thousand four hundred francs. Nevertheless, he *must* have the silver next day or perish, as he had asked some people to dine who would, he hoped, give sixteen thousand francs for sixteen shares in the *Chronique*. If borrowed plate were on his table he was terribly afraid that the whole transaction would fail; as one of the people invited was a painter, and painters are an "observant, malicious, profound race, who take in everything at a glance."[*] Everything else in his rooms would represent the opulence, ease, and wealth of the happy artist.

[*] "Lettres a l'Etrangere."

Poor Balzac! To add to his difficulties, it was impossible to borrow anywhere in Paris, as he had only purchased the *Chronique* through the exceptional credit he enjoyed, and this would be at once destroyed if he were known to be in difficulties. We do not hear any further particulars about this tragedy, and cannot tell how far the conjunction of the borrowed plate—if it *were* after all borrowed —and the astute painter, contributed to the downfall of the *Chronique*. Werdet, however, attributes the disaster to the laziness of the talented staff, who could not be induced to work together. However that may be, the result was a terrible blow to Balzac; who was now, in addition to all his other liabilities, in debt for forty thousand francs to the shareholders.

It is as a member of the staff of the *Chronique*, that the name of Theophile Gautier first appears in connection with Balzac; and the two men remained close friends till Balzac's death. In 1835 Theophile Gautier published "Mademoiselle de Maupin," in which his incomparable style excited Balzac's intense admiration, painfully conscious as he was of his own deficiencies in this direction. Therefore, in forming the staff of the *Chronique*, he at once thought of Gautier, and despatched Jules Sandeau to arrange matters with the young author, and to give him an invitation to breakfast. Theophile Gautier, much flattered, but at the same time rather alarmed at the idea of an interview with the celebrated Balzac, tells us that he thought over various brilliant discourses on his way to the Rue Cassini, but was so nervous when he arrived that all his preparations came to nothing, and he merely remarked on the fineness of the weather. However, Balzac soon put him at his ease, and evidently took a fancy to him at once, as during breakfast he let him into the secret that for this solemn occasion he had borrowed silver dishes from his publisher!

The friendship between Balzac and Gautier, though not as intimate and confidential as that between Balzac and Borget, was true and steadfast; and was never disturbed by literary jealousy. Gautier supported Balzac's plays in *La Presse*, and helped with many of his writings. Traces of his workmanship, M. de Spoelberch de Lovenjoul tells us, are specially noticeable in the descriptions of the art of painting and of the studio, in the edition of "Un Chef-d'Oeuvre Inconnu" which appeared in 1837.[*] These descriptions are in Gautier's manner, and do not appear in the edition of 1831; so that in all probability they were written, or at any rate inspired by him. Gautier also wrote for Balzac, who had absolutely no faculty for verse, the supposed translation of two Spanish sonnets in the "Memoires de Deux Jeunes Mariees," and the sonnet called "La Tulipe" in "Un Grand Homme de Province a Paris." On his side, Balzac defended Gautier on all occasions, and in 1839 dedicated "Les Secrets de la Princesse de Cadignan," then called "Un Princesse Parisienne," "A Theophile Gautier, son ami, H. de Balzac."

[*] "H. de Balzac and Theophile Gautier" in "Autour de Honore de Balzac," by the Vicomte de Spoelberch de Lovenjoul.

Beyond this friendship, the affair of the *Chronique* brought Balzac nothing but worry and trouble. And it came at a time when misfortune assailed him on all sides. Madame de Berny was approaching her end, and he wrote to his mother on January 1st, 1836, the day he started the *Chronique de Paris*: "Ah! my poor mother, I am broken-hearted. Madame de Berny is dying! It is impossible to doubt it! Only God and I know what is my despair. And I must work! Work weeping."[*]

[*] "Correspondance," vol. i. p. 323.

In the midst of his trouble, a most unfortunate occurrence took place, which besides embittering his life at the time had a decided effect on his subsequent career; and indirectly obscured his reputation even after his death.

In 1833, as we have already seen, Balzac, after long dissensions with Amedee Pichot, had definitely left the *Revue de Paris*. However, in 1834, when Pichot retired from the management, the new directors, MM. Anthoine de Saint-Joseph, Bonnaire, and Achille Brindeau, tried to satisfy their readers by recalling Balzac; and "Seraphita" began to appear in the pages of the *Revue*. Difficulties, as might be expected, soon arose between Balzac and the management; and the undercurrent of irritation which subsisted on both sides only required some slight extra cause of offence, to render an outbreak inevitable. In September, 1835, M. Buloz, already director of the *Revue des Deux Mondes*, an extremely able, but bad-mannered and dictatorial man, took possession also of the much-tossed-about *Revue de Paris*. Balzac had known Buloz since 1831, when the latter bought the *Revue des Deux Mondes*, which was then in very low water, and was working with tremendous energy to make it successful. At that time, Buloz and he often shared a modest dinner, and with the permission of M. Rabou, then manager of the *Revue de Paris*, Balzac contributed "L'Enfant Maudit," "Le Message," and "Le Rendez-Vous" to the *Revue des Deux Mondes*, and only charged a hundred francs for the same quantity of pages for which he was paid a hundred and sixty francs by Rabou. However, on April 15th, 1832, there appeared in the *Revue des Deux Mondes* a scathing, anonymous criticism of the first dizain of the "Contes Drolatiques." This had apparently been written by Gustave Planche; but Balzac considered Buloz responsible for it, and therefore refused to write any longer for his review. In August, 1832, Buloz, who does not appear to have been particularly scrupulous in his business relations, wrote to apologise, saying that though it was not in his power to suppress the offending article, he had done his best to soften it; and that now he was sole master of the Revue, so that not a word or line could pass without his permission. He therefore begged Balzac to resume his old connection with him, and explained that if he had not been confined to his bed and unable to walk, or even to bear the shaking of a cab, he would have come to visit him, and matters would have been quickly arranged. Balzac's answer, which is written from Angouleme, is couched in the uncompromising terms of "no surrender," which he generally adopted when he considered himself aggrieved. He did not absolutely refuse to write for the Review, and referred Buloz to Madame de Balzac for terms; but, by the tone of his letter, he negatived decidedly the idea of resuming friendly relations with his correspondent, and while rather illogically professing a lofty indifference to criticism, remarked that he felt the utmost contempt for those who calumniated his books.[*]

[*] See "Correspondance Inedite—Honore de Balzac," *Revue Bleue*, March 14, 1903.

After this the *Revue des Deux Mondes* became hostile to Balzac; and when Buloz and Brindeau bought the *Revue de Paris*, a proceeding which must have been a shock to him, he believed that Brindeau would be sole director, and drew up his agreement with him alone; having already refused to have business dealings with the ever active Buloz. However, Buloz soon took the principal place, and was so apologetic for his past misdeeds, and so insistent in promising amendment for the future, that Balzac, evidently reflecting that it would be distinctly against his interests to exclude himself from two of the most important reviews in Paris, consented to reconsider his decision. Therefore the following agreement, which is interesting as an example of Balzac's usual conditions when issuing his novels in serial form, was drawn up between the two men.

The Review was only to use Balzac's articles for its subscribers. He was to regain absolute rights over his books three months after their first publication—this was an invariable stipulation in all Balzac's treaties—and was to give up fifty francs out of the two hundred and fifty considered due to him for each "feuille" of fifteen pages, to reimburse Buloz for the number of times the proofs had to be reprinted.[*] On these terms he agreed to finish "Le Pere Goriot," as well as "Seraphita," and to write the "Memoires d'une Jeune Mariee," with the understanding that a separate contract was to be made for each of his contributions, and that he was free to write for other periodicals.

[*] The account of the lawsuit between Balzac and the *Revue de Paris* is taken from his "Historique du Proces auquel a donne lieu 'Le Lys dans la Vallee,'" which formed the second preface of the first edition of "Le Lys dans la Vallee" and is contained in vol. xxii. of the Edition Definitive of Balzac's works; and from "H. de Balzac et 'La Revue de Paris,'" which is the

Review's account of the case, and may be found in "Un dernier chapitre de l'Historie des Oeuvres de H. de Balzac," by the Vicomte de Spoelberche de Lovenjoul.

Almost at once difficulties began, difficulties which are inevitable when a genius of the stamp of Balzac is bound by an unfortunate agreement to provide a specified quantity of copy at stated intervals. Balzac could not write to order. "Seraphita," planned to please Madame Hanska, was intended to be a masterpiece such as the world had never seen. From Balzac's letters there is no doubt that he was conscientiously anxious to finish it, only, as he remarks, "I have perhaps presumed too much of my strength in thinking that I could do so many things in so short a time."[*] When he made the unfortunate journey to Vienna, "Seraphita" still required, at his own computation, eight days' and eight nights' work; but, settled there, he turned his attention at once to "Le Lys dans la Vallee," which he had substituted for the "Memoires d'une Jeune Mariee," and at which he laboured strenuously. The first number of this appeared in the *Revue de Paris*, on November 22, 1835; but in the meantime Balzac's uncorrected proofs had been sold by Buloz to MM. Bellizard and Dufour, proprietors of the *Revue Etrangere de St. Petersbourg*. Therefore, in October, before the authorised version was published in Paris, there appeared in Russia, under the title of "Le Lys dans la Vallee," what Balzac indignantly characterised as the "unformed thoughts which served me as sketch and plan."

[*] "Lettres a l'Etrangere."

This was double treachery on the part of Buloz, as, by the treaty already mentioned, he had bought the right to publish Balzac's novels in the *Revue de Paris* only; and even if this stipulation had not been made, he had no excuse for selling as Balzac's completed work, what he knew to be absolutely unfinished. Balzac, after this, refused to receive him on friendly terms; but a meeting was arranged at the house of Jules Sandeau, at which Balzac and the Comte de Belloy met Buloz and Bonnaire. Sandeau and Emile Regnault, who were friends of both the contending parties, were also present; and they, after this conference, became for a time exclusively Balzac's friends, as he remarks significantly. Balzac owed the Review 2,100 francs; but the remainder of the "Lys" was ready to appear, and he calculated that for this, the payment due to him would be about 2,400 francs. He therefore proposed that the account between him and the journal should be closed with the end of the "Lys"; and that as indemnity for the injury done him by the action of Buloz in publishing his unfinished work in the *Revue Etrangere*, he should be permitted to send the novel in book form to a publisher at once, instead of waiting the three months stipulated in the agreement. MM. Buloz and Bonnaire refused this arrangement, declaring that it would be extortion;

and after giving them twenty-four hours for reflection, Balzac announced his intention of writing no longer for the *Revue de Paris*, and prepared to bring an action against the proprietors.

Buloz and Bonnaire, however, decided that it would be good policy for the first attack to be on their side, and as Balzac could not obtain his proofs from Russia for a month at least, they sued him for breach of contract in not writing "Les Memoires d'une Jeune Mariee," and claimed 10,000 francs damages for his refusal to finish the "Lys dans la Vallee"; as well as fifty francs for each day's delay in his doing this. Balzac brought forward his counter claim, and offered the *Revue de Paris* the 2,100 francs which had been advanced to him; but they refused to be satisfied with the payment of this debt; and in May, 1836, the case opened.

There was a side issue on the subject of "Seraphita," about which the *Revue* certainly had just cause for complaint. In May, 1834, Balzac had been paid 1,700 francs in advance for this, and the first number appeared on June 1st, the second not following till July 20th. Then Balzac disappeared altogether; and when he returned in November, he proposed to begin "Le Pere Goriot" in the *Revue*, and promised after this had come to an end to return to "Seraphita"; but it was not till the middle of August, 1835, that he at last produced another number. After this there were again delays, and, according to Buloz, the whole of "Seraphita" was never offered to the *Revue de Paris*. The truth, however, appears to have been that Buloz at last completely lost his temper at Balzac's continual failures to fulfil his engagements, and declared that "Seraphita" was unintelligible, and was losing subscribers to the Review. Balzac, furious at this insult, paid Buloz 300 francs, to defray the expenses already incurred for the printing of "Seraphita," and took back his work. Buloz's receipt for this money is dated November 21st, 1835, two days before the appearance of the first number of the "Lys dans la Vallee" in Paris, so storms were gathering on all sides. Ten days after this, on December 2nd, Werdet brought out "Seraphita" in book form in "Le Livre Mystique," which contained also "Louis Lambert" and "Les Proscrits," a fact which proved Balzac's contention that in November it was ready for publication in the *Revue de Paris*. The first edition of "Le Livre Mystique" was sold in ten days, and the second followed it a month after, which, as Balzac remarked sardonically, was "good fortune for an unintelligible work." This success on the part of his enemy no doubt did not help to soften the indignant Buloz; and he must have been further exasperated by an article in the *Chronique de Paris*, in which Balzac was styled the "Providence des Revues," and the injury the *Revue de Paris* sustained in the loss of his collaboration was insisted on with irritating emphasis.

The case was carried on with the utmost bitterness by the *Revue de Paris*; Balzac's morals, his honesty, even his prose, being attacked with the greatest violence. Editors and publishers on all sides gave their testimony against him. He must have been amazed and confounded by the deep hatred he had evoked by his want of consideration, which on several occasions certainly amounted to a breach of good faith. All his old sins found him out. Amedee Pichot, former manager of the *Revue de Paris*, Forfellier of the *Echo de la Jeune France*, and Capo de Feuillide of *L'Europe Litteraire*, raised their voices against the high-handed and rapacious author. The smothered enmity and irritation of years at last found vent; and it was in vain that Balzac demonstrated, in the masterly defence of his conduct written in one night, which formed the preface to the "Lys dans la Vallee," that he had always remained technically within his rights, and that as far as money was concerned he owed the publishers nothing. Unwritten conventions had been defied, because it was possible to defy them with impunity; and editors who had gone through many black hours because of the failure of the great man to keep his promises, and who smarted under the recollection of the discourteous refusal of advances it had been an effort to make, did not spare their arrogant enemy now that it was possible to band together against him.

Perhaps, however, the bitterest blow to poor Balzac, was the fact that his brother authors, of whose rights he had been consistently the champion, did not scruple to turn against him. Either terrorised by the all-powerful Buloz, or jealous of one who insisted on his own abilities and literary supremacy with loud-voiced reiteration, Alexandre Dumas, Roger de Beauvoir, Frederic Soulie, Eugene Sue, Mery, and Balzac's future acquaintance Leon Gozlan, signed a declaration at the instance of Buloz, to the effect that it was the general custom that articles written for the *Revue de Paris* should be published also in the *Revue Etrangere*, and should thus avoid Belgian piracy. Jules Janin, whose criticisms on Balzac are peculiarly venomous, and Loeve-Veimars, added riders to this statement, expressing the same views, only with greater insistence. To these assertions, Balzac replied that Buloz had specially paid George Sand 100 francs a sheet over the price arranged, to obtain the right of sending her corrected proofs to Russia; and that arrangements on a similar basis had been made with Gustave Planche and M. Fontaney. The fact that exceptional payments were made on these occasions was conclusive evidence against simultaneous publication in Paris and St. Petersburg being the received practice. Moreover, as Balzac observes with unanswerable justice, even if this custom *did* exist, it would count as nothing against the agreement between him and Buloz. "M. Janin can take a carriage and go himself to carry his manuscripts to Brussels; M.

Sue can get into a boat and sell his books in Greece; M. Loeve-Veimars can oblige his editors if they consent, to make as many printed copies of his future works as there are languages in Europe: all that will be quite right, the *Revue* is to-day like a publisher. My treaties, however, are made and written; they are before the eyes of the judge, they are not denied, and state that I only gave my articles to the *Revue de Paris*, to be inserted solely *in* the *Revue*, and nowhere else."

Balzac won the case. It was decided by the Tribunal of Judges on Friday, June 3rd, 1836, that he was not bound to give the "Memoires d'une Jeune Mariee" to the *Revue de Paris*, as when promised, the story had not been yet written, and the "Lys dans la Vallee" had been substituted for it; also that the 2100 francs which he had already offered to Buloz was all that he owed the Review. The judges left unsettled the question as to whether the proprietors of the *Revue de Paris* were entitled to hand over their contributors' corrected proofs to the *Revue Etrangere*; but decreed that they were certainly in the wrong when they parted with unfinished proofs. They were therefore condemned to pay the costs of the action.

Balzac's was a costly victory. Except the *Quotidienne*, which stood by him consistently, not a paper was on his side. His clumsiness of style, his habit of occasionally coining words to express his meaning, and the coarseness of some of his writings, combined with the prejudice caused by his literary arrogance, had always, to a certain extent, blinded literary and critical France to his consummate merits as a writer. Now, however, want of appreciation had changed to bitter dislike; and in addition to abuse, indiscriminate and often absurd of his writings, his enemies assailed his morals, ridiculed his personal appearance, and made fun of his dress and surroundings. He was not conciliatory; he did not bow to the storm. In June, 1839, appeared the second part of "Illusions Perdues," which was entitled "Un Grand Homme de Province a Paris," and was a violent attack on French journalism; and in March, 1843, Balzac published the "Monographie de la Presse Parisienne," a brilliant piece of work, but certainly not calculated to repair the breach between him and the publishing world. Nevertheless, though his pride and independence prevented him from trying to temporise, there is no doubt that Balzac suffered keenly from the hostility he encountered on all sides. He writes to Madame Hanska directly after the lawsuit: "Ah! you cannot imagine how intense my life has been during this month! I was alone for everything; harassed by the journal people who demanded money of me, harassed by payments to make, without having any money because I was making none, harassed by the lawsuit, harassed by my book, the proofs of which I had to correct day and night. No, I am astonished at having survived this struggle. Life is too heavy; I do not live with pleasure."[*] To add to his difficulties, Madame Bechet had lately become Madame Jacquillard, and possibly urged to action by M. Jacquillard, and alarmed by tales of Balzac's misdemeanours, she became restive, and demanded the last two volumes of the "Etudes de Moeurs" in twenty-four hours, or fifty francs for each day's delay. The affairs of the *Chronique* were at this time causing Balzac much anxiety, and he fled to the Margonnes at Sache; not for rest, but to work fifteen hours a day for "cette odieuse Bechet"; and there, in eight days, he not only invented and composed the "Illusions Perdues," but also wrote a third of it.

[*] "Lettres a l'Etrangere."

However, the strain had been too great even for *his* extraordinary powers, and while walking in the park after dinner with M. and Mme. de Margonne, on the day that letters arrived from Paris with the news that liquidation of the *Chronique* was necessary, he fell down in a fit under one of the trees. Completely stunned for the time, he could write nothing; and thought, in despair, of giving up the hopeless struggle, and of hiding himself at Wierzchownia. Fortunately, his unconquerable courage soon returned; he travelled to Paris, wound up the affairs of the *Chronique*; and as Werdet had allowed him twenty days' liberty, and his tailor and a workman had lent him money to pay his most pressing debts, he obtained a letter of credit from Rothschild, and started for Italy.

His ostensible object was a visit to Turin, to defend the Comte Guidoboni-Visconti in a lawsuit, as the Count, whose acquaintance he had made at the Italian Opera, could not go himself to Italy. In reality, however, in his exhaustion, and the overstrained state of his nerves, he craved for the freedom and distraction which he could only find in travel. Madame Visconti was an Englishwoman—another Etrangere —her name before her marriage had been Frances Sarah Lowell. Later on, she became one of Balzac's closest friends, and Madame Hanska was extremely jealous of her influence.

It is amusing to discover that Balzac did not take this journey alone. He was accompanied by a lady whom he describes in a letter as "charming, *spirituelle*, and virtuous," and who, never having had the chance in her life of breathing the air of Italy, and being able to steal twenty days from the fatigues of housekeeping, had trusted in him for inviolable secrecy and "scipionesque" behaviour. "She knows whom I love, and finds there the strongest safeguard."[*] This lady was Madame Marbouty, known in literature as Claire Brunne, and during her stay in Italy as "Marcel"—a name taken from the devoted servant in Meyerbeer's opera "Les Huguenots," which had just appeared. A few weeks earlier, she had refused to travel in

Touraine with Balzac, as she considered that a journey with him in France would compromise her; but, apparently, in Italy this objection did not apply. She travelled in man's clothes, as Balzac's page, and both he and she were childishly delighted by the mystification they caused. Comte Sclopis, the celebrated Piedmontese statesman, who acted as their cicerone in Turin society, was much fascinated by the charming page. The liking was evidently mutual, as, after the travellers had left Italy, Balzac records that at Vevey, Lausanne, and all the places they visited, Marcel cried: "And no Sclopis!" and it sounds as though the exclamation had been accompanied by a sigh. Several times during the journey the lively Amazon was mistaken for George Sand, whom she resembled in face, as well as in the fancy for donning masculine attire; and the mistake caused her intense satisfaction. At Geneva, haunted to Balzac by happy memories, the travellers stayed at the Hotel de l'Arc, and Balzac's mind was full of his lady-love, whose spirit seemed to him to hallow the place. He saw the house where she stayed, went along the road where they had walked together, and was refreshed in the midst of his troubles and anxieties by the thought of her.

[*] See "L'Ecole des Manages," in "Autour de Honore de Balzac," by the Vicomte de Spoelberch de Lovenjoul.

On August 22nd the travellers returned to Paris on excellent terms with each other, and for some years after this journey friendly relations continued. In 1842, in remembrance of their adventure, Balzac dedicated "La Grenadiere" to Madame Marbouty, under the name of Caroline, and added the words, "A la poesie du voyage, le voyageur reconnaissant." Later on, however, they quarrelled, and she wrote "Une Fausse Position," in which Balzac is represented in a decidedly unflattering light; and after this he naturally withdrew the dedication in "La Grenadiere."

On his return from this amusing trip a terrible trouble awaited Balzac. Among the letters heaped together upon his writing-table was one from Alexandre de Berny, announcing abruptly the death of Madame de Berny, which had taken place on July 27th. Balzac was utterly crushed by this blow. He had not seen Madame de Berny for some time, as since the death of her favourite son she had shut herself up completely, pretending to Balzac that she was not very ill, but saying laughingly that she only wanted to see him when she was beautiful and in good health. Now she was dead, and the news came without preparation in the midst of his other troubles. She was half his life, he cried in despair; and writing to Madame Hanska he said that his sorrow had almost killed him. In the midst of this overwhelming grief other worries added their quota to the weight oppressing Balzac. Henri de Balzac gave his family continual trouble, while Laurence's husband, M. de Montzaigle, refused to support his children; in fact, the only faint relief to the darkness surrounding the Balzac family at this time was M. Surville's hopefulness about the Loire Canal scheme.

In addition to all these misfortunes, Balzac had to submit to the annoyance of several days' imprisonment in the Hotel des Haricots, for his refusal to serve in the Garde Nationale, a duty which was, he said, the nightmare of his life. The place of detention was not luxurious. There was no fire, and he was in the same hall for a time with a number of workmen, who made a terrible noise. Fortunately, he was soon moved to a private room, where he was warm and could work in peace. After this, in terrible pecuniary difficulties, and feeling acutely the loss of the woman who had been an angel to him in his former troubles, he left the Rue Cassini and fled from Paris, to avoid further detention by the civic authorities. He took refuge at Chaillot, and under the name of Madame Veuve Durand hid at No. 13, Rue des Batailles. Here he lodged for a time in a garret formerly occupied by Jules Sandeau, from the window of which there was a magnificent view of Paris, from the Ecole Militaire to the barrier of the Trone, and from the Pantheon to L'Etoile. From time to time Balzac would pause in his work to gaze on the ocean of houses below; but he never went out, for he was pursued by his creditors.

It is curiously characteristic of his love of luxury that, destitute as he was, he had no intention of occupying this modest garret for long, but that a drawing-room on the second floor, which would cost 700 francs, was already in preparation for his use. It was to No. 13, Rue des Batailles, that Emile de Girardin, who had just started *La Presse*, wrote asking him to contribute to its pages; and, in consequence, Balzac produced "La Vieille Fille," which began to appear on October 23rd, and shocked the subscribers very much. Here, too, at a most inopportune moment, Madame Hanska addressed to him a depressed and mournful letter, of which he complains bitterly. She was at this time extremely jealous of Madame Visconti, from whom she suspected that Madame de Mortsauf, in the "Lys dans la Vallee," had been drawn; and Balzac says he supposes that he must give up the Italian opera, the only pleasure he has, because a charming and graceful woman occupies the same box with him. In October he paid a sad little visit to La Boulonniere, which must have brought before him keenly the loss he had sustained; and after he spent a few days at Sache, where he was ill for a day or two as a result of mental worry and overwork.

Another blow was to fall on Balzac before the disastrous year 1836 came to a close. The "Lys dans la Vallee," on which Werdet had pinned all his hopes, had sold very badly, possibly owing to the hostility of the newspapers. As a climax to all Balzac's miseries, in October Werdet failed. This was doubly serious, as Balzac had signed several bills of exchange for his publisher, and was therefore liable for a sum of 13,000 francs. Werdet wrote a book abusing Balzac as the cause of his failure; and Balzac, on his side, was certainly unsympathetic about the misfortunes of a man whose interests, after all, were bound up with his own, and whom he politely called "childish, bird-witted, and obstinate as an ass." The truth seems to have been that, as Werdet aspired to be Balzac's sole publisher, he was obliged to buy up all the copies of Balzac's books which were already in the hands of publishers, and not having capital for this, he obtained money by credit and settled to pay by bills at long date. He also brought before the public a certain number of books by writers sympathetic to his client, and as these books were usually by young and unknown authors, their printing did not cover expenses. As a consequence of these imprudent ventures he was unable to meet his bills on maturity; and Balzac, being liable for some of them, was naturally furious, as *he* had to be in hiding from the creditors, while Werdet, as he remarked bitterly, was walking comfortably about Paris. Werdet was young and enthusiastic, and no doubt his imagination was fired by Balzac's picture of the glorious time in the future, when the great writer and his publisher should have both made their fortunes, and their carriages should pass each other in the Bois de Boulogne. There is no reason, however, to think that Balzac wilfully misrepresented matters, as Werdet insinuates. He was essentially good-hearted, as every one who knew him testifies; but his extraordinary optimism and power of self-deception, combined with the charm of his personality and the overmastering influence he exercised, made him a most dangerous man to be connected with in business; and Werdet, like many another, suffered from his alliance with the improvident man of genius.

Balzac also at this times suffered severely; but he had now completely recovered his energy. In his efforts to clear himself he worked thirty nights without going to bed, sending contributions to the *Chronique*, the *Presse*, the *Revue Musicale*, and the *Dictionnaire de la Conversation*, composing the "Perle Brisee," "La Vieille Fille," and "Le Secret des Ruggieri," besides finishing the last volumes of the "Etudes de Moeurs" and bringing out new editions of several of his books. As the result of his labours, he calculated, with his usual cheerfulness, that if he worked day and night for six months, and after that ten hours a day for two years, he would have paid off his debts and would have a little money in hand. In the end, he bound himself for fifteen years to an association formed by a speculator named Bohain: 50,000 francs being given him at once to pay off his most pressing debts, while, by the terms of the agreement, he provided a stipulated number of volumes every year, and was given 1,500 francs a month for the first year, 3,000 francs a month for the second year, 4,000 francs for the third, and so on. Besides this, he was to receive half the profits of each book after the publisher's expenses had been defrayed. As he was extremely pleased with this arrangement, which at any rate freed him from his immediate embarrassments, a faint ray of sunlight shone for him on the close of the sad year of 1836.

CHAPTER XI

1836 - 1840

It is curious to find that during the events recorded in the last chapter, when, to put the matter mildly, Balzac's spare time was limited, he yet managed to conduct a sentimental correspondence with "Louise," a lady he never met and whose name he did not know. Apparently, in the midst of his troubles, he was seized by an overmastering desire to pour out his feelings in writing to some kindred soul. Madame Hanska was far away, and could not answer promptly; besides, though passionately loved, she was not always sympathetic, the solid quality of her mind not responding readily to the quickness and delicacy of Balzac's emotions. Louise, to whom in 1844 he dedicated "Facino Cane," was close at hand; she was evidently mournful, sentimental, and admiring; she sent him flowers when he was in prison, and at another time a sepia drawing. Besides, her shadowy figure was decked for him with the fascination of the unknown, and there was excitement in the wonder whether the veil enveloping her would ever be lifted, and, like Madame Hanska, she would emerge a divinity of flesh and blood. However, in spite of Balzac's entreaties she refused to reveal her identity; and after about a year's correspondence, during which time Louise suffered from a great misfortune, the nature of which she kept secret, the letters between them ceased altogether.

Balzac had now left his garret, and was established in the drawing-room on the second floor of 13, Rue des Batailles, which is exactly described in "La Fille aux Yeux d'Or." The room was very luxurious, and the details had been thought out with much care.[*] One end of it had square corners, the other end was rounded, and the corners cut off to form the semicircle were connected by a narrow dark passage, and contained — one a camp bedstead, and the other a writing-table. A secret door led to this hiding-place, and here Balzac took refuge when pursued by emissaries from the Garde Nationale, creditors, or enraged editors. The scheme of colour in the room was white and flame-colour shading to the deepest pink, relieved by arabesques of black. A huge divan, fifty feet long and as broad as a mattress, ran round the horseshoe. This, like the rest of the furniture, was covered in white cashmere decked with flame-coloured and black bows, and the back of it was higher than the numerous cushions by which it was adorned. Above it the walls were hung with pink Indian muslin over red material, the flame-colour and black arabesques being repeated. The curtains were pink, the mantelpiece clock and candlesticks white marble and gold, the carpet and *portieres* of rich Oriental design, and the chandelier and candelabra to light the divan of silver gilt. About the room were elegant baskets containing white and red flowers, and in the place of honour on the table in the middle was M. de Hanski's magnificent gold and malachite inkstand. Balzac showed the glories of this splendid apartment with infantile pride and delight to visitors; and here, reckless of his pecuniary embarrassments, he gave a grand dinner to Theophile Gautier, the Marquis de Belloy, and Boulanger, and entertained them in the evening with good stories "a la Rabelais."

[*] See "Honore de Balzac" in "Portraits Contemporains," by Theophile Gautier.

About this time Balzac started the association he called the "Cheval Rouge," which was intended to be a mutual help society among a number of friends, who were to push and praise each other's compositions, and to rise as one man against any one who dared to attack a member of the alliance. The idea was a good one; but there was a comic side to it as conducted by Balzac, and the "Cheval Rouge," after five or six meetings, ceased to exist without having seriously justified its existence. Theophile Gautier, Jules Sandeau, and Leon Gozlan were among the members; and so dazzling were the pictures drawn by Balzac of the powers and scope of the society, that each one saw himself in imagination with a seat in the French Academy, and in succession peer of France, minister, and millionaire. It was sad that with these lofty aims the association should have been dissolved because most of its members were not able to pay their fifteen francs subscription. The first meeting was held at the Cheval Rouge, a very modest restaurant on the "Quai de l'Entrepot," from which the society took its name. The members were summoned by a card with a little red horse on it, and under this the words "Stable such a day, such a place." Everything was carried on with the greatest secrecy and mystery, and the arrangements, which were conducted by Balzac with much seriousness, afforded him intense pleasure. The "Cheval Rouge" might have been a dangerous political society from the precautions he took. In order to avoid suspicion one member was always to greet another member coldly in society; and Balzac would pretend to meet Gautier with much ceremony for the first time in a drawing-room, and then by delighted winks and grimaces would point out to him how well he was acting.

In March, 1837, Balzac paid a second visit to Italy; travelling through a part of Switzerland, stopping at Milan, Venice, Genoa, and Florence, and returning to Paris on May 3rd. His health was, he said, detestable at this time, and he required rest and change. He went alone, as Gautier, who had intended to be his companion, was kept in Paris by the necessity of writing criticisms on the pictures in the Salon. One object of Balzac's journey was to visit Florence to see Bartolini's bust of Madame Hanska, of which he evidently approved, as he asked M. de Hanski's permission to have a small copy made of it which he could always keep on his writing-table; but this was never sent to him. He was delighted with Venice, which he now saw for the first time; and in Florence was specially charmed with the pictures at the Pitti, though he found travelling by himself rather dull, and decided that his next journey should be undertaken at a time when Gautier could accompany him. At Genoa he met a wily merchant, to whom he unfortunately confided the last brilliant scheme for making his fortune which was floating through his active brain.

He had read in Tacitus that the Romans found silver in Sardinia; and it occurred to him, that, as the ancients were not learned in extracting metals, silver might still be found among the lead which was turned out of the mines as refuse. The Genoese merchant appeared much interested in Balzac's conversation, and remarked that, owing to the carelessness of the Sardinians, whole mountains of dross, containing lead, and most probably silver, were left in the vicinity of the mines. He was most obliging: he promised to send Balzac a specimen of the dross that it might be submitted to Parisian experts, and if the result were satisfactory, Balzac and he were to ask for a permit from the Government at Turin, and would work the mines together. When this had been arranged Balzac departed in high spirits, determined to keep his secret carefully, and feeling that at last he was on the high road to fortune. On the way back he was detained in quarantine for some time, and partly from economy, partly because he wanted to see Neufchatel, where he had first met Madame Hanska, he travelled back by Milan and the Splugen, and reached Paris in perfect health.

Here fresh misfortunes awaited him, as Werdet was bankrupt, and, as a consequence, his creditors pursued Balzac. Never in future would he be answerable or sign his name for any one, he cried in despair. He had forestalled the money allowed him by his treaty with Bohain, was working day and night, and in a few days would retire into an unknown garret, and live as he had done in the Rue Lesdiguieres. Nevertheless, in his anxiety to see Madame Hanska, he had begun to think out economical ways of getting to Ukraine. He was not very well at this time, and in August he went to Sache, to see whether his native air would revive him.

His next action would be astonishing to any one unacquainted with his extraordinary recklessness. In October 1837 he gave up the rooms at the

Rue Cassini, which he had kept during the time of his residence at Passy; and in order to escape what he termed "an atrocious law" on the subject of his abhorrence the Garde Nationale, he bought a piece of land in the Ville d'Avray, at Sevres, on which he began to build a house, planned by himself. This soon acquired celebrity as "Les Jardies," and gave much amusement to the Parisians, who were never tired of inventing stories about Balzac's villa. In March, 1838, before he settled in his new abode, he started on a journey to Sardinia to investigate matters himself about the mines. It was a year since the Genoese merchant had promised to send him a specimen of the dross, and as nothing had yet arrived, he was beginning to feel anxious.

The object of his journey was kept absolutely secret; owing to the dangers of the post even Madame Hanska being told only that "it is neither a marriage, nor anything adventurous, foolish, frivolous, or imprudent. It is a serious and scientific affair, about which it is impossible for me to tell you a word, because I am bound to the most absolute secrecy."[*] He had to borrow from his mother and from a cousin, and to pawn his jewellery to obtain money for his expedition. On the way he stayed with the Carrauds at Frapesle, where he was ill for a few days; and he went from there to pay his "comrade" George Sand a three days' visit at Nohant. He found her in man's attire, smoking a "houka," very sad, and working enormously; and he and she had long talks, lasting from five in the evening till five in the morning, and ranging over manners, morals, love affairs, and literature. She approved of "La Premiere Demoiselle," a play planned in February, 1837, which Madame Hanska had discouraged because she did not like the plot; and Balzac determined to work at it seriously now that "Cesar Birotteau" was finished. This brilliant picture of the Parisian *bourgeoisie* had been published in December, 1837, under the title of "Histoire de la Grandeur et de la decadence de Cesar Birotteau." Since then, Balzac had produced nothing new in book form, though he was writing "La Maison de Nucingen" for *La Presse*, and working at "Massimilla Doni," and at the second part of "Illusions Perdues." He was also preparing to bring out a "Balzac Illustre," which was to be a complete edition of his works with pictures; but of this only one volume, "La Peau de Chagrin," was ever published.

[*] "Lettres a l'Etrangere."

From Nohant he went to Marseilles, and from there he sent letters both to his mother and to Madame Carraud, written in a very different frame of mind from his usual one when he embarked on a scheme for making his fortune. "Now that I am almost at my destination, I begin to have a thousand doubts; anyhow, one cannot risk less to gain more. I do not fear the journey, but what a return if I fail!"[*]

He crossed from Marseilles to Ajaccio, and suffered much on the voyage, though he travelled on the mail steamer from Toulon, and spent a great deal of money by doing this. However, he was really trying to be economical, as on his way to Marseilles he had lived on ten sous' worth of milk a day, and when he reached there he put up at an hotel where his room cost fifteen sous and his dinner thirty.

The scenery of Corsica was, he said, magnificent; but he did not much appreciate Ajaccio, where he had to wait some time for a boat to take him to Sardinia, and said the civilisation was as primitive as that of Greenland. His only consolation about the delay was in the idea that he would have time to go on with "La Premiere Demoiselle," for which George Sand predicted a great success, while his sister told him it was superb. Therefore, as he had written the "Physiologie du Mariage" and "La Peau de Chagrin" against the advice of Madame de Berny, he determined to continue his play in spite of Madame Hanska's disapproval. His five days' journey to Sardinia was most uncomfortable, as he travelled in a rowing-boat belonging to French coral fishers. The food caught consisted of execrable soup, made from the fish caught by the fishermen during the voyage; and Balzac had to sleep on the bridge, where he was devoured by insects. To add to his misfortunes, the boat was kept for five days in quarantine in view of the port, and the inhabitants refused to give the occupants any food, or to allow them in a bad storm to attach their cables to the port-rings. This they managed at last to do, in spite of the objections of the governor, who, determined to assert his authority, decreed that the cable should be taken off as soon as the sea became calm: a regulation which, as Balzac said, was absurd, because either the people would by that time have caught the cholera, or they would not catch it at all.

When Balzac at last landed, he felt as though he were in Central Africa or Polynesia, as the inhabitants wore no clothes, and were bronzed like Ethiopians. He was much horrified at their misery and savage condition. Their dwellings he describes as dens without chimneys, and their food in many parts consisted of a horrible bread made of acorns ground, and mixed with clay.

No doubt he was not disposed to take a particularly favourable view of Sardinia, as it was to him the scene of a bitter disappointment. He had been right in his calculations about the value of the refuse from the mines: the dross contained 10 per cent of lead, and the lead 10 per cent of silver. But a Marseilles company as well as his Genoese friend had been beforehand with him, had obtained from the Government at Turin the right to work the mines, and were already in possession. Balzac's monetary sacrifices, and the hardships he had suffered on his journey, were in vain; he must return to sleepless nights of work, and must redouble his efforts in the endeavour to pay back the money he had borrowed for his expedition. He showed his usual pluck at this juncture; there were no complaints in his letters, and with singular forbearance he does not even abuse the faithless Genoese merchant. His expedition was useful to others, if not to himself; as he travelled on to Italy, and made a long stay at Milan in order to work for the interests of the Viscontis, whose property, without his efforts, would have been sequestrated owing to political complications. It is significant that Madame Hanska, who was always suspicious about Madame Visconti, was not informed of this reason for his long sojourn at Milan, which we hear of from a letter to his sister. Balzac was terribly low-spirited at this time; his whole life seemed to have been a failure, and he was approaching the age of forty, the date at which he had always determined to give up his aspirations, to fight no more, and to join the great company of the resigned. He was tired out, and very homesick. He admired the Cathedral, the churches, the pictures; but he was weary of Italy, and longed for France with its grey skies and cold winds. Behind this longing, and possibly the origin of it, was a passionate desire in his disappointment and disgust of life to be again near his "polar star."

It was a comfort when, the affairs of the Viscontis being at last satisfactorily arranged, he was able on June 6th to start on his journey back to France. He travelled by the Mont Cenis, and was nearly blinded by clouds of fine dust, so that he was unable to write for some days.

When he reached Paris he only remained for a short time in the Rue des Batailles, as in July, 1838, in defiance of his doctor's warnings about damp walls, he took up his residence at Les Jardies, having at the same time a *pied-a-terre* in Paris at the house of Buisson, his tailor, 108, Rue Richelieu. Les Jardies was a quaint abode. Built on a slippery hill, it overlooked the Ville d'Avray with smoky Paris below, and in the distance there was a view of the plain of Mont-rouge and the road to Orleans, which led also to Balzac's beloved Tours. The principal staircase was outside, because Balzac, in designing the house, found that a staircase seriously interfered with the symmetry of the rooms. Therefore he placed it in an inconspicuous position in a special construction at the back, and owing to the extremely steep slope the visitor entered by the top floor, and made his way down instead of up. There were three stories, the lowest containing the drawing-room and dining-room, the second a bedroom and dressing-room, and the third Balzac's study. All round the house, which was painted to represent bricks, was a verandah supported by black columns, and the cage in the rear which held the staircase was painted red. About sixty feet behind this curious habitation was the real living-place of Les Jardies, where Balzac kept his servants. Part of this he let at a later date to the Viscontis, and they had charge of his rich library, and of the beautiful furniture brought from the Rue des Batailles, which might, if kept by its owner, have been seized by his creditors.

The interior of this charming abode was intended to be adorned with the utmost magnificence, but it was never finished; there were no curtains, and no furniture to speak of. Years after, descriptions such as the following were still scrawled in charcoal on the bare stucco: "Here is a veneering of Parian marble"; "Here is a mantelpiece in cipolin marble"; "Here is a ceiling painted by Eugene Delacroix." Balzac laughed himself at these imaginary decorations, and was much delighted when Leon Gozlan wrote in large letters in his study, which was as bare as the other rooms, "Here is a priceless picture by Raphael." However, there was one thing at Les Jardies of which he was really proud; and that was his system of bell-ringing, which he considered a *chef-d'oeuvre*. Instead of having hanging wires with "big, stupid, indiscreet bells" at the end of them, *his* bells were hidden ingeniously in an angle of the wall; and his pride in this brilliant invention made him forget any possible deficiencies in the decorations and appointments of the mansion.

The great feature, however, at Les Jardies, and the torment, the delight, and the despair of Balzac's life, was the piece of land round the house where the garden ought to have been. He had beautiful plans about this when first he arrived at Les Jardies. The soil was then absolutely bare; but, as he remarked, it was possible to buy everything in Paris, and as money was, of course, no object with him, he intended in the autumn to have good-sized magnolias, limes, poplars, and willows transported there, and to make a little Eden of sweet scents, covered with plants and bushes. No doubt, in imagination he already saw his beautiful flowers, and wandered in this delightful and well-kept garden, which, as nothing with Balzac could possibly be ordinary, was to be "surprising." The reality, however, was sadly different from his expectations. In vain, by his orders asphalt paths were made in all directions, and landscape gardeners worked for months, trying with stones cunningly inserted to prop up the steep, slippery slope, and to form little terraces on which something might have a chance of growing. With the slightest shower, down tumbled these plateaus; and the work of building had to begin again. It was amusing, Leon Gozlan tells us, to see the amazement of the actor Frederick Lemaitre when he came to see Balzac; and found himself expected to walk up the side of a hill, with the ground at each step slipping under his feet. To support himself he stuck stones behind his heels, and Balzac meanwhile walked by his side with the calmness of a proprietor who is thoroughly used to the vagaries of his own territory, and scorns foreign assistance.

Occasionally, however, even Balzac came to the end of his equanimity. The wall, which separated his property from that of the neighbour below him, was a continual anxiety. In spite of all possible precautions it tumbled down constantly, and scattered stones and mortar over the ground on each side of it. After this had happened two or three times, and Balzac, while investigating the extent of the damage on one of these occasions, had fallen and injured his leg, so that he was in bed for forty days, a meeting of experts was held, and it was decided that the angle at which the wall had been built was not sufficiently acute. The error was rectified, and there were general rejoicings and congratulations; but the next day it rained, and in the evening news was brought to Balzac that the whole structure had toppled over, and was reposing in ruins in his neighbour's garden. This was serious, as the neighbour promptly sent in an enormous bill for damages done to his carrots and turnips; and it was probably on this occasion that Balzac wrote in March 1839 a despairing letter to Madame Carraud, containing the words: "To you, sister of my soul, I can confide my greatest secrets; I am now in the midst of terrible misery. All the walls of Les Jardies have fallen down through the fault of the builder, who did not make any foundations."[*] No builder, however, managed to effect the feat of making this unfortunate wall stand upright; and in the end, to allow it to come down in peace and comfort whenever it felt so disposed, Balzac bought the strip of his neighbour's land which bordered it, and after that, ceased to feel anguish at its vagaries.

[*] "Correspondance," vol. i. p. 453.

The wall was decidedly important, as Balzac's fortune was to be made by the contents of the garden at Les Jardies, and it would not have been satisfactory for strangers to be able to wander there at will. Balzac's new plan for becoming rich was to cover most of his territory with glass houses, and to plant 100,000 feet with pineapples. Owing to the warmth of the soil, he considered that these pineapples would not need much heat, and could be sold at five francs apiece, instead of the louis charged for them in Paris. They would therefore be quickly disposed of, and 500,000 francs would be made, which, deducting 100,000 francs for expenses, would mean a clear profit of 400,000 francs a year. "And this money will be made without a page of copy," said poor Balzac. He was, of course, absolutely confident about the success of this new undertaking, and Theophile Gautier, who tells the story,[*] says that a search was made for a shop in which to sell these pineapples of the future. This shop was to be painted black with lines of gold, and was to have on it in huge letters the announcement, "Ananas des

Jardies"; but Gautier managed to persuade Balzac in order to avoid useless expense, not to hire it till the next year, when the pineapples would have had time to grow. However, perhaps Balzac was discouraged by the sight of the snow falling silently on his slope, or possibly his desire to make a fabulous sum of money by a successful play had for a time blotted out all other ambitions; at any rate, we hear no more of the pineapples of Les Jardies.

[*] "Portraits Contemporains—Honore de Balzac," by Theophile Gautier.

Balzac's terribly embarrassed condition in 1837 caused him to return with new ardour to the idea which haunted him all his life, that of an immense theatrical success which should put an end for ever to his pecuniary embarrassments. References to projected plays, to the difficulty he found in writing them, and to his hope of finally freeing himself from debt by producing a masterpiece at the theatre, occur constantly in his letters. "Marie Touchet" and "Philippe le Reserve" —afterwards to become "Les Ressources de Quinola" —were the names of some of the plays he intended to write. In February, 1837, as we have already seen, he planned out "La Premiere Demoiselle," which he abandoned for the time, but which he worked at with much energy during his ill-fated expedition to Sardinia, and continued at Les Jardies during the summer and autumn of 1838. Before starting for Sardinia he wrote to Madame Carraud: "If I fail in what I undertake, I shall throw myself with all my might into writing for the theatre." He kept his word, and "La Premiere Demoiselle," a gloomy bourgeois tragedy, which soon received the name of "L'Ecole des Menages," was the result.

With the distrust in himself, which always in matters dramatic mingled with his optimistic self-confidence, Balzac determined to have a collaborator, and chose a young man named Lassailly, who was peculiarly unfitted for the difficult post. In doing this he only gave one instance out of many of the wide gulf which separated Balzac the writer, gifted with the psychological powers which almost amounted to second sight, and Balzac in ordinary life, many of whose misfortunes had their origin in an apparent want of knowledge of human nature, which caused him to make deplorable mistakes in choosing his associates.

The agreement between Balzac and his collaborator stipulated that the latter should be lodged and fed at the expense of Balzac, and should, on his side, be always at hand to help his partner with dramatic ideas. Balzac performed *his* part of the treaty nobly, and Lassailly remembered long afterwards the glories of the fare at Les Jardies; but his life became a burden to him from his incapacity to do what was expected of him, and he was nearly killed by Balzac's nocturnal habits. He was permitted to go to bed when he liked; but at two or three in the morning Balzac's peremptory bell would summon him to work, and he would rise, frightened and half stupefied with sleep, to find his employer waiting for him, stern and pale from his vigil. "For," Leon Gozlan says, "the Balzac fighting with the demon of his nightly work had nothing in common with the Balzac of the street and of the drawing-room."[*] He would be asked severely what help he could give, and, as a result of his terrified and drowsy stammerings would be sent to bed for another hour to see whether in that time inspiration would visit him. Six or eight times in the course of the night would this scene be repeated; and at last Lassailly, who was delicate, became seriously ill and had to leave Les Jardies, ever after looking back on the terrible Balzac and his appalling night-watches, as a nightmare to be recalled with a shudder.

[*] "Balzac en Pantoufles," by Leon Gozlan.

Balzac, deprived of Lassailly's valuable assistance, worked on alone; and at first everything seemed likely to go well with "L'Ecole des Menages."[*] The Renaissance, a new theatre which had opened on November 8th, 1838, with the first representation of Victor Hugo's "Ruy Blas," seemed willing to take Balzac's play to follow this; and M. Armand Pereme, a distinguished antiquary whom Balzac had met at Frapesle, was most active in conducting the negotiations. However, in the end the Renaissance refused the drama. Balzac was terribly dilatory, and irritated every one by not keeping his engagements, and he was also high-handed about the arrangements he considered necessary to the success of his tragedy. His unfortunate monetary embarrassments, too, made it necessary for him to ask for 16,000 francs before the play was written, a request which the Renaissance Theatre was rather slow in granting. However, the real reason for the rejection of the drama, which took place on February 26th, 1839—just at the time when Balzac was in despair because the wall at Les Jardies had fallen down— was want of money on the part of the managers of the theatre. The only thing that could save the Renaissance from ruin was a great success; and Alexandre Dumas, with whom the directors had formerly quarrelled, had now made peace with them, and had offered them "L'Alchimiste," which would be certain to attract large audiences. They accepted this in place of Balzac's play, and "L'Ecole des Menages," of which the only copy extant is in the possession of the Vicomte de Spoelberch de Lovenjoul, has never been acted.

[*] See "L'Ecole des Menages" in "Autour de Honore de Balzac," by the Vicomte de Spoelberch de Lovenjoul.

Balzac was in terrible trouble about the rejection of the drama from which he had hoped so much. He wrote to Madame Carraud[*] in March, 1839: "I have broken down like a foundered horse. I shall certainly require rest at Frapesle. The Renaissance had promised me 6,000 francs bounty to write a piece in five acts; Pereme was the agent, everything was arranged. As I wanted 6,000 francs at the end of February, I set to work. I spent sixteen nights and sixteen days at it, only sleeping three hours out of the twenty-four; I employed twenty workmen at the printer's office, and I managed to write, make and compose the five acts of 'L'Ecole des Menages' in time to read it on February 25th. The directors had no money, or perhaps Dumas, who had not acted fairly to them, and with whom they were angry, had returned to them; they would not hear my piece, and refused it. So here I am, worn out with work, sixteen days lost, 6,000 francs to pay, and nothing! This blow has crushed me, I have not yet recovered from it. My career at the theatre will have the same course as my literary career, my first work will be refused. A superhuman courage is necessary for these terrible hurricanes of misfortune."

[*] "Correspondance," vol. i. p. 454.

In the midst of his troubles, he thought with bitter regret of Madame de Berny, who would have understood everything, and have known how to help and console him. He was in a miserable state, was chased like a hare by creditors, and was on the point of lacking bread, candles, and paper. Then to add to his misery would come a sensible letter from the far-distant Madame Hanska, blaming his frivolity and levity; and, in his state of semi-starvation, poor Balzac would be almost driven frantic by words of reproach from his divinity.

A little earlier than this he had found time for an enormous amount of work which would seem completely out of his province, and had written letter after letter in the *Siecle,* and spent 10,000 francs, in defence of Peytel, a notary of Belley, who had been condemned to death on August 26th, 1839, for the murder of his wife and servant. Peytel appealed against his sentence, and Balzac, who had met him several times, espoused his cause with vehemence. There did not seem to be much satisfactory defence available for the prisoner, who admitted the fact that while driving in a carriage not far from Belley, he had shot both his wife and the coachman. Balzac, however, was urgent in upholding Peytel's contention that his crime had been homicide, not murder, and brought forward the plea of "no premeditation." His energetic efforts were of no avail: Peytel was executed at Bourg on November 28th, 1839, and Balzac, who had espoused his cause with quixotic enthusiasm, was genuinely sorry. He wrote to Madame Hanska in September: "I am extremely agitated by a horrible case, the case of Peytel. I have seen this poor fellow three times. He is condemned; I start in two hours for Bourg." On November 30th he continues: "You will perhaps have heard that after two months of unheard-of efforts to save him from his punishment Peytel went two days ago to the scaffold, like a Christian, said the priest; I say, like an innocent man."[*]

[*] "Lettres a l'Etrangere."

Another disappointment this year was the fact that Balzac considered it his duty, after presenting himself as candidate for the Academie and paying many of the prescribed visits, to retire in favour of Victor Hugo. As early as 1833 he had aspired to become some day "un des Quarante," and he then said half jokingly to his sister: "When I shall work at the dictionary of the Academy!"[*] He was never destined to receive the honour of admittance to this august body, though after his first attempt in 1839, when he himself withdrew, he again tried his fortune in 1843 and in 1849. His normal condition of monetary embarrassment was one reason for his failure, and no doubt some of the members of l'Academie Francaise disapproved of certain of his books, and perhaps did not admire his style. At any rate, as his enemy Saint-Beuve expressed it concisely: "M. de Balzac est trop gros pour nos fauteuils," and while men who are now absolutely unknown entered the sacred precincts without difficulty, the door remained permanently closed to the greatest novelist of the age.

[*] "Balzac, sa Vie et ses Oeuvres," par Mme. L. Surville (nee de Balzac).

CHAPTER XII

1840 - 1843

The sad fate of "L'Ecole des Menages" did not long discourage Balzac. At the beginning of 1840 he made an engagement to provide Harel, the speculative manager of the Theatre Porte-St-Martin, with a drama. The play was accepted before it was written; and in order to be near the theatre Balzac established himself in the fifth floor of the house of Buisson, his tailor, at the corner of the Rue Richelieu. His proceedings were, as usual, eccentric. One day Gautier, who tells the story, was summoned in a great hurry, and found his friend clad in his monk's habit, walking up and down his elegant attic, and shivering with impatience.

"'Here is Theo at last,' he cried, when he saw me. 'You idler! dawdle! sloth! gee up, do make haste! You ought to have been here an hour ago! To-morrow I am going to read to Harel a grand drama in five acts.'

"'And you want my advice,' I answered, settling myself comfortably in an armchair, ready to submit to a long reading.

"From my attitude Balzac guessed my thought, and said simply, 'The drama is not written.'

"'Good heavens!' said I: 'well, then you must put off the reading for six weeks.'

"'No, we must hurry on the drama to get the money. In a short time I have a large sum of money to pay.'

"'To-morrow is impossible; there is no time to copy it.'

"'This is the way I have arranged things. You will write one act, Ourliac another, Laurent-Jan the third, De Belloy the fourth, I the fifth, and I shall read it at twelve o'clock as arranged. One act of a drama is only four or five hundred lines; one can do five hundred lines of dialogue in a day and the night following.'

"'Relate the subject to me, explain the plot, sketch out the characters in a few words, and I will set to work,' I said, rather frightened.

"'Ah,' he cried, with superb impatience and magnificent disdain, 'if I have to relate the subject to you, we shall never have finished!'"[*]

[*] "Portraits Contemporains—Honore de Balzac," by Theophile Gautier.

After a great deal of trouble, Gautier managed to persuade Balzac to give him a slight idea of the plot, and began a scene, of which only a few words remain in the finished work. Of all Balzac's expected collaborators, Laurent-Jan, to whom "Vautrin" is dedicated, was the only person who worked seriously.

In two months and a half of rehearsals Balzac became almost unrecognisable from worry and overwork. His perplexities became public property, and people used to wait at the door of the theatre to see him rush out, dressed in a huge blue coat, a white waistcoat, brown trousers, and enormous shoes with the leather tongues outside, instead of inside, his trousers. Everything he wore was many sizes too big for him, and covered with mud from the Boulevards; and it was an amusement to the frivolous Parisians to see him stride along in these peculiar garments, his face bearing the impress of the trouble and overstrain he was enduring. He was at the mercy of every one. The manager hurried and harried him, because the only hope of saving the theatre from bankruptcy was the immediate production of a successful play. The actors, knowing the piece was not finished, each clamoured for a part to suit his or her peculiar idiosyncrasies, and Balzac was so overburdened, that occasionally in despair he was tempted to abandon his play altogether.

There was tremendous excitement in Paris about the approaching first representation of "Vautrin"; and foreign politics, banquets, and even the burning question of reform, paled in interest before the great event. All the seats were sold beforehand; and as there was a rush for the tickets, Balzac and Harel chose their audience, and thought that they had managed to secure one friendly to Balzac. Unfortunately, however, the seats were sold so early that many of them were parted with at a profit by the first buyers, and in the end a large proportion of the spectators were avowedly hostile to Balzac. March 14th, 1840, was the important date, and Balzac wrote to Madame Hanska: "I have gone through many miseries, and if I have a success they will be completely over. Imagine what my anxiety will be during the evening when 'Vautrin' is being acted. In five hours' time it will be decided whether I pay or do not pay my debts."[*]

[*] "Lettres a l'Etrangere."

He was very nervous beforehand, and told Leon Gozlan that he was afraid there would be a terrible disaster.

The plot of the play is extraordinary and impossible. Vautrin, the Napoleon among convicts, who appears in several of Balzac's novels, is the hero; he had declared war against society, and the scene of the drama, with Vautrin as the principal figure, passes in the aristocratic precincts of the Faubourg St. Germain. The theatre was crowded for the performance, and the first three acts, though received coldly, went off without interruption. At the fourth act, however, the storm burst, as Frederick Lemaitre, who evidently felt qualms about the success of his part, had determined to make it comic, and appeared in the strange costume of a Mexican general, with a hat trimmed with white feathers, surmounted by a bird of paradise. Worse still, when he took off this hat he showed a wig in the form of a pyramid, a coiffure which was the special prerogative of Louis Philippe! The play was doomed. The Duke of Orleans, who was in one of the boxes, left the theatre hurriedly; and it was difficult to finish the performance, so loud were the shouts, hisses, and even threats. The next day the following official announcement appeared in the *Moniteur*: "The Minister of the Interior has interdicted the appearance of the drama performed yesterday at the Theatre of the Porte St. Martin under the title of 'Vautrin.'" Balzac's hated foes, the journalists, of course rejoiced in his downfall, and accentuated the situation by declaring the piece to be not only disloyal, but revoltingly immoral. On the other hand, Victor Hugo, George Sand, and Mme. de Girardin, stood firmly by him, and Frederick Lemaitre, to whom Balzac evidently bore no malice for his large share in the disaster, was, he said, "sublime."

Leon Gozlan went to see Balzac the day after the performance, and found him outwardly calm, but his face was flushed, his hands burning, and his lips swollen, as though he had passed through a night of fever. He did not mention the scene of the night before, but talked eagerly of a plan to start a large dairy at Les Jardies, and to provide Paris and Versailles with rich milk. He had several other equally brilliant schemes on hand: he intended to grow vines, cultivate vegetables, sell manure; and by these varied means to assure himself of an income of eighteen thousand francs.

The Director of the Beaux-Arts was sent to offer Balzac money to make up for his loss; he says, however: "They came to offer me an indemnity, and began by proposing five thousand francs. I blushed to my hair, and answered that I did not accept charity, that I had put myself two hundred thousand francs in debt by writing twelve or fifteen masterpieces, which would count for something in the glory of France in the nineteenth century; that for three months I had done nothing but rehearse 'Vautrin,' and that during those three months I should otherwise have gained twenty-five thousand francs; that a pack of creditors were after me, but that from the moment that I could not satisfy all, it was quite indifferent to me whether I were tracked by fifty or by a hundred, as the amount of courage required for resistance was the same. The Director of the Beaux-Arts, Cave, went out, they tell me, full of esteem and admiration. 'This,' said he, 'is the first time that I have been refused.' 'So much the worse,' I answered."[*]

[*] "Lettres a l'Etrangere."

Balzac became very ill with fever and brain neuralgia the day after the performance of "Vautrin," and Madame Surville took him to her house and nursed him. When he left his bed it was, of course to find his affairs in a worse condition than ever, and he was, as he described himself, "a stag at bay." His friendship with Madame Visconti was a consolation to him in his troubles; he described her to Madame Hanska, who did not quite appreciate these raptures, as "one of the most amiable of women, of infinite and exquisite goodness. Of delicate, elegant beauty, she helps me to support life." Nevertheless, no friendships made up for the want of a wife, and home, the two things for which he yearned; and he writes sadly: "I have much need now of having my wounds tended and cured, and of being able to live without cares at Les Jardies, and to pass my days quietly between work and a wife. But it seems as if the story of every man will only be a novel to me."[*]

[*] "Lettres a l'Etrangere."

His despondency did not abate his powers of work, as from April to December he published "Z. Marcas," "Un Prince de la Boheme," and "Pierre Grassou"; while in 1841, among other masterpieces, appeared "La Fausse Maitresse," "Une Tenebreuse Affaire," "Un Menage de Garcon," "Ursule Mirouet," and "Les Memoires de deux Jeunes Mariees." He was almost at the end of his courage however, and talked seriously in the case of failure in his new enterprise—the *Revue Parisienne* —of going to Brazil on some mad errand which he would undertake because it *was* mad; and of either coming back rich or disappearing altogether.

A monthly magazine, of which one man was to be director, manager, editor, besides being sole contributor, was a heroic attempt at making a fortune; and this was what Balzac contemplated, and accomplished for a short time in the *Revue Parisienne*. His mode of working was not calculated to lessen the strain to which he subjected himself, as, never able to start anything till pressed for time, he left the work till near the end of the month, when the printers were clamouring for copy. Then there was no pause or slumber for him; his attention was concentrated on his varied and difficult subjects till the moment when he rushed with disordered garments to the printer's office. There, seated anywhere—on the corner of a table, at a compositor's frame, or before a foreman's bureau—he became completely absorbed in the colossal labour of reading and correcting his proofs. The first number of the *Revue Parisienne* appeared on July 25th, 1840; but it was only continued for three months, as Balzac decided that the task was too much for him. During its short life however, it furnished a magnificent and striking example of his extraordinary powers and mental attainments; as each of the numbers was the size of a small volume, and he provided novels, biography, philosophy, analysis, and criticism, and treated brilliantly each subject he attacked.

A question in which Balzac took the greatest interest was that of the rights of authors and publishers, under which Louis Philippe did not meet with much respect. Not only did the Belgians reproduce French works at a cheap rate by calmly dispensing with the duty of paying their authors; but publishers in the provinces often followed this pernicious practice, and it was difficult to prosecute them. A striking instance of this injustice was to be found in the case of "Paroles d'un Croyant," by M. de Lamennais, of which ten thousand pirated copies were sold in Toulouse, where only five hundred of the authorised edition had been sent by the publisher. No redress could be obtained because, though the fact was certain, legal proofs were apparently lacking; but in consequence of this glaring infraction of the rights of both author and publisher, on December 28th, 1838, Balzac became a member of the Societe des Gens-de-Lettres. This Society, which was insignificant when he first joined it, owed everything to his reputation, and to the energy with which he worked for its interests. On October 22, 1839, he spoke at Rouen in its behalf, in the first action brought by it against literacy piracy. Later in the same year he was elected President, and in May, 1840, he drew up the masterly "Code Litteraire de la Societe des Gens-de-Lettres"[*] to which reference has already been made. On September 5th, 1841, however, in consequence of a dispute concerning the drawing up by the Gens-de-Lettres of a manifesto to be presented to the deputies composing the Law Commission on Literary Property, Balzac withdrew from the Society. The ostensible reason for his resignation was, that at a committee meeting to discuss the Manifesto, doubts were thrown on his impartiality; but it seems probable from his letter[+] that some unwritten ground for complaint really caused his withdrawal. After Balzac's death, the Society des Gens-de-Lettres acknowledged with gratitude the debt owed him as one of the founders of the Society, and the help received from his intelligence and activity.

[*] This may be found in the Edition Definitive of Balzac's works, or in "Balzac Chez Lui," by Leon Gozlan.

[+] "Correspondance," vol. ii. p. 20.

In 1840, before he ceased to belong to the Societe des Gens-de-Lettres, he had left Les Jardies; and had hidden himself under the name of Madame de Brugnolle, his housekeeper, in a mysterious little house at No. 19, Rue Basse, Passy; to which no one was admitted without many precautions, even after he had given the password. Behind this was a tiny garden where Balzac would sit in fine weather, and talk over the fence to M. Grandmain, his landlord. In his new abode he established many of his treasures: his bust by David d'Angers, some of the beautiful furniture he was collecting in preparation for the home he longed for, and many of his pictures, those treasures by Giorgione, Greuze, and Palma, which were the delight of his heart. With great difficulty, by publishing books and articles in quick succession, he had prevented the sale of Les Jardies by his creditors. As he had no money to pay cab fares this entailed rushing from Passy to Paris on foot, often in pouring rain; with the result that he became seriously ill, and found it necessary to recruit in Touraine and Brittany.

On June 15th, 1841, a fictitious sale for 15,500 francs was made of Les Jardies, which had cost Balzac 100,000 francs; but he did not really part with the villa till later, when he had decided that it would not be suitable ultimately as a residence. To add to his troubles, he found it necessary to take his mother to live with him, an arrangement which gave rise to many little storms, and made writing a difficult matter. Madame Visconti's society gave him no consolation at this time,—he was disappointed in her; and decided that his abuse of Englishwomen in the "Lys dans la Vallee," was perfectly justified.

Fortunately, he was now feeling tolerably cheerful about money matters; as he had paid off the hundred thousand francs he owed from his treaty in 1836, and hoped in fifteen months to have made arrangements for discharging all his debts; while three publishers, Dubochet, Furme, and Hetzel & Paulin, had undertaken to publish a complete edition of his works with engravings. This was to be the first appearance of the long-dreamt-of "Comedie Humaine," the great work of Balzac's life.

However, for a time even this took secondary place, as on January 5th, 1842, a letter with a black seal arrived from Madame Hanska; and gave the important news of the death of M. de Hanski, which had taken place on November 10th, 1841. Balzac's letter in answer to this is pathetic to any one cognisant of his subsequent history. He begins with confidence:[*] "As to me, my dear adored one, although this event enables me to reach what I have desired so ardently for nearly ten years, I can, before you and God, say in justice, that I have never had anything in my heart but complete submission, and that in my most terrible moments I have not soiled my soul with evil wishes." Further on, he tells her that nothing in him is changed; and suddenly seized with a terrible doubt from the ambiguous tone of her letter, he cries, in allusion to a picture of Wierzchownia which always hung in his study: "Oh! I am perhaps very unjust, but this injustice comes from the passion of my heart. I should have liked two words for myself in your letter. I have hunted for them in vain—two words for the man who, since the landscape in which you live has been before his eyes, has never continued working for ten minutes without looking at it."

[*] "Lettres a l'Etrangere."

He longs to start at once to see her, but from the tone of her letter he gathers that he had better wait until she writes to him again, when he begs for the assurance that her existence will henceforward belong to him, and that no cloud will ever come between them. He is alarmed about her anxiety on the subject of her letters. They are quite safe, he says, kept in a box like the one in which she keeps his. "But why this uneasiness now? Why? This is what I ask myself in terrible anxiety!" He finishes with "Adieu, my dear and beautiful life whom I love so much, and to whom I can now say 'Sempre medesimo.'"

Madame Hanska, in reply to this letter, objected strongly to the breach of "les convenances" which would be committed if Balzac came to see her early in her widowhood; and it was not till July 17th, 1843, that he was at last permitted to meet her in St. Petersburg, and then he had not seen her since his visit to Vienna, eight years before.

However, he was now full of happy anticipations, and it was with the greatest enthusiasm that he looked forward to the appearance of "Les Ressources de Quinola," which had been accepted by the Odeon, and on which he founded the most extravagant hopes. The long night of trouble was nearly over, and a late happiness would dawn upon him, heralded by a brilliant success at the theatre, which would not only free him from debt, but would also enable him to offer riches to the woman he loved.

At the first hearing of this play in the green-room of the Odeon, the company had been rather disenchanted as we know, because, after reading four acts admirably, Balzac was forced to improvise the unwritten fifth, and this he did so badly that Madame Dorval, the principal actress, refused to act. However, on the same day Lireux, the director of the Odeon, came to the Restaurant Risbeck, where Balzac was dining with Leon Gozlan, and said that he would accept the play. Balzac at once insisted that for the first three representations he must have command of the whole of the theatre, but he promised that Lireux should share the receipts with him, and these he said would be enormous. He also stipulated that for his three special performances no journalists should be admitted, there being war to the knife between him and them. As the place of Balzac's abode was being kept strictly secret for fear of his creditors, the time of the rehearsal each day was to be communicated to him by a messenger from the theatre, who was told to walk in the Champs Elysees, towards the Arc de l'Etoile. At the twentieth tree on the left, past the Circle, he would find a man who would appear to be looking for a bird in the branches. The messenger was to say to him, "I have it," and the man would answer, "As you have it, what are you waiting for?" On receiving this reply the emissary from the Odeon would hand over the paper, and depart without looking behind him. The only comment that Lireux, who appears to have been a practical man, made on these curious arrangements was, that if the twentieth tree had been struck by lightning during the night, he supposed that the servant must stop at the twenty-first, and Balzac assented gravely to this proposition.

The great writer worked with his usual energy at the rehearsals, continually rewriting parts of the play, and besides this occupation spending hours in the theatre bureau, as he had determined to sell all the tickets himself. For the first night of "Les Ressources de Quinola" the audience was to be brilliantly representative of the aristocracy, beauty, and talent of France. The proscenium would, Balzac hoped, be occupied by ambassadors and ministers, the pit by the Chevaliers de St. Louis, and the orchestra stalls by peers; while deputies and state functionaries were to be placed in the second gallery, financiers in the third, and rich bourgeoisie in the fourth. Beautiful women were to be accommodated with particularly prominent places; the price of the seats was to be doubled or trebled; and to avoid the continual interruptions to which "Vautrin" was subjected, tickets were only to be sold to Balzac's assured friends. Therefore many persons who offered fabulous sums of money were refused admittance, and told that every seat was taken. By these means Balzac ultimately overreached himself, as people believed that all the seats were really sold, and that it was no use to apply for tickets. When, therefore, March 19th, 1842, the night of Balzac's anticipated triumph arrived, instead of a brilliant assemblage crowding the Odeon, it was three parts empty; and the small audience, who had paid enormously for their seats, and naturally expected a brilliant throng in the theatre, were in a critical and captious mood.

The scene of the play was laid in Spain in the time of Phillip II., and much of the dialogue was witty and spirited; but Balzac had mixed up serious situations and burlesque in a manner irritating to the audience, and there were many interruptions. Balzac was fortunately unaware of his want of success; he had completely disappeared, and it was not till half-past twelve, long after the finish of the performance, that he was discovered fast asleep at the back of a box. The fourth representation of "Les Ressources de Quinola" was specially tumultuous. Lireux, being now master of the theatre, invited all the journalistic world to be present, and they, furious at their exclusion during the first three nights, encouraged the general clamour. Some of the hooters were turned out, and the audience then amused themselves by ejaculating "Splendid!" "Admirable!" "Superb!" and "Sublime!" at every sentence, and by singing comic couplets, such as:

> C'est M. Balzac,
> Qu'a fait tout ce mic-mac!

During the intervals.

However, after two scenes had been entirely cut out, and several others suppressed, "Quinola" ran for nineteen nights. Many years afterwards, in 1863, it was acted at the Vaudeville, and was a great success. During his lifetime Balzac's plays received little applause —in fact, were generally greeted with obloquy; but when it was too late for praise or blame to matter, his apotheosis as a dramatist took place; and on this occasion his bust was brought to the stage, and crowned amid general enthusiasm.

The year 1842 is important in the annals of Balzac's life, as on April 23rd his novels were for the first time collected together to form the "Comedie Humaine," his great title to fame. The preface to this ranks among the celebrated prefaces of the world, and it was written at the suggestion of his friend Hetzel, who objected strongly to the prefaces signed Felix David, which had been placed in 1835 at the beginning of the "Etudes de Moeurs au XIXieme Siecle," and of the "Etudes Philosophiques." In an amusing letter Hetzel tells Balzac that a preface should be simple, natural, rather modest, and always good-humoured. "Sum up—sum up as modestly as possible. There is the true pride, when any one has done what you have. Relate what you want to say quite calmly. Imagine yourself old, disengaged from everything even from yourself. Speak like one of your own heroes, and you will make something useful, indispensable.

"Set to work, my fat father; allow a thin publisher to speak thus to Your Fatness. You know that it is with good intentions."[*]

[*] "Trois Lettres," in "Autour de Honore de Balzac," by the Vicomte de Spoelberch de Lovenjoul.

We may be grateful to Hetzel for this advice, which Balzac evidently followed; as the preface is written in a quiet and modest tone unusual with him, and he follows Hetzel's counsel, and gives a concise summary of his intention in writing the "Comedie Humaine."

He explains that he has attempted in his great work to classify man, as Buffon has classified animals, and to show that his varieties of character, like the differences of form in the lower creation, come from environment. The three great divisions of the Comedie Humaine are "Etudes de Moeurs," "Etudes Philosophiques," and "Etudes Analytiques"; and the "Etudes de

Moeurs" comprise many subdivisions, each of which, in Balzac's mind, is connected with some special period of life.

The "Scenes de la Vie Privee," of which the best-known novels are "Le Pere Goriot" (1834), "La Messe de l'Athee" (1836), "La Grenadiere" (1832), "Albert Savarus" (1842), "Etude de Femme" (1830), "Beatrix" (1838), and "Modeste Mignon" (1844), Balzac connects with childhood and youth. The "Scenes de la Vie de Province," to which belong among others "Eugenie Grandet" (1833), "Le Lys dans la Vallee" (1835), "L'Illustre Gaudissart" (1833), "Pierrette" (1839), and "Le Cure de Tours" (1832), typify a period of combat; while "Scenes de la Vie Parisienne," which contain "La Duchesse de Langeais" (1834), "Cesar Birotteau" (1837), "La Cousine Bette" (1846), "Le Cousin Pons" (1847), "Facino Cane" (1836), "La Maison de Nucingen" (1837), and several less-known novels, show the effect of Parisian life in forming or modifying character.

Next Balzac turns to more exceptional existences, those which guard the interests of others, and gives us "Scenes de la Vie Militaire," comprising "Une Passion dans la Desert" (1830), and "Les Chouans" (1827); and "Scenes de la Vie Politique," which contain "Un Episode sous la Terreur" (1831), "Une Tenebreuse Affaire" (1841), "Z. Marcas" (1840), and "L'Envers de l'Histoire Contemporaine" (1847). He finishes the "Etudes de Moeurs" with "Scenes de la Vie de Campagne," consisting of "Le Medecin de Campagne" (1832), "Le Cure de Village" (1837 to 1841), and "Les Paysans" (1844); and these are to be, Balzac says, "the evening of this long day. Here are my purest characters, my application of the principles of order, politics, morality."

There are no subdivisions to the "Etudes Philosophiques," among which we find "La Peau de Chagrin," written in 1830, and considered by Balzac a link between the "Etudes de Moeurs" and the "Etudes Philosophiques"; "Jesus-Christ en Flandre" (1831), "Massimilla Doni" (1839), "La Recherche de l'Absolu" (1834), "Louis Lambert" (1832), and "Seraphita" (1835). To the division entitled "Etudes Analytiques" belong only two books, "La Physiologie du Mariage" (1829), and "Petites Miseres de la Vie Conjugale" (1830 to 1845).

"The Comedie Humaine" was never finished, but, incomplete as it is, it remains a noble memorial of Balzac's genius, as well as an astonishing testimony of his extraordinary power of work. The last edition of it which was published in Balzac's lifetime appeared in 1846, and formed sixteen octavo volumes. It consists of eighty-eight novels and tales, and by far the greater number of these appeared in the first edition of 1842. A strong connection is kept up between the different stories by the fact that the same characters appear over and over again, and the reader finds himself in a world peopled by beings who, as in real life, at one time take the foremost place, and anon are relegated to a subordinate position; but who preserve their identity vividly throughout.

Balzac found it impossible to manage without a *pied-a-terre* in Paris, and for some reason he could no longer lodge with Bouisson, his tailor, so in 1842 he took a lodging in the same house with his sister, Madame Surville, at 28, Rue du Faubourg Poissonniere. Life was brightening for him; he was beginning by his strenuous efforts to diminish perceptibly his load of debt, and the star of hope shone brightly on his path.

After many doubts on the part of Madame Hanska, who was most particular in observing the proprieties, he was allowed in 1843 to meet her in St. Petersburg, and arrived on July 17th, after a rough passage from Dunkerque, during which his discomforts were nothing to him, so joyous was he at the thought of soon seeing his beloved one. Madame Hanska was established at the Hotel Koutaizoff, in the Rue Grande Millione, and Balzac took a lodging near, and thought St. Petersburg with its deserted streets a dreary place. All minor feelings were, however, merged in the happiness of being near Madame Hanska, of hearing her voice, and of giving expression to that passionate love which had possessed him for more than ten years. In his sight she was as young and beautiful as ever, and his fascinated eyes watched her with rapture, as she leant back thoughtfully in the little arm-chair in the blue drawing-room, her head resting against a cushion trimmed with black lace. He could recall every detail afterwards of that room, could count the points of the lace, and see the bronze ornaments filled with flowers, in which he used to catch his knees in his rapid pacings up and down; and his eyes would fill with tears, and the creations of his imagination fade and become unreal, beside the haunting pictures of his memory. He loved Madame Hanska with a love which had grown steadily since their first meeting, and which now was threatening to overmaster him, so that even work would become impossible. Nevertheless, though she was most charming and affectionate, and he stayed in St. Petersburg until September, nothing definite was settled.

Madame Hanska was a prudent person; her dearly-loved daughter Anna was growing up, and it was quite necessary to settle her in life before taking any decided step. Besides, though she hardly allowed this to herself, there is no doubt that she was rather alarmed at the prospect of becoming Madame Honore de Balzac. The marriage would be decidedly a *mesalliance* for a Rzewuska, and her family constantly and steadily exerted their influence to prevent her from wrecking her future. What, they asked her, would be her life with a husband as eccentric, extravagant, and impecunious, as they believed Balzac to be? They collected gossip about him in Paris, and told Madame Hanska endless stories, occasionally true, often false, and sometimes merely exaggerated, about his oddities, his love affairs, and his general unsuitability for alliance with an aristocratic family. It was no doubt pleasant to have a man of genius and of worldwide fame as a lover; but what would be her position if she took the fatal step, and bound herself to him for life? Madame Hanska listened and paused: she well understood her advantages as a great and moneyed lady; and she was under no illusions as to the harassed and chequered existence which she would lead with Balzac. She had often lent him money, his letters kept her well informed about the state of his affairs; and the idea of becoming wife to a man who was often forced to fly from his creditors, must have been extremely distasteful to a woman used to luxury and consideration. Maternal affection, love of her country, prudence, social and worldly considerations—besides the fear of the Czar's displeasure—were all inducements to delay; and even if she had felt towards Balzac the passionate love for the lack of which posterity has reproached her, it surely would have been the duty of an affectionate mother to think of her child's welfare before her own happiness. Later on, when Anna was married, and Balzac, broken in health and tortured by his longings, was kept a slave to Madame Hanska's caprices, the hard thing may be said of her, that she was in part the cause of the death of the man she pretended to love. In 1843, however, whatever motives incited her, her action in delaying matters appears under the circumstances to have been right; and Balzac seems to have felt that he had no just cause for complaint.

He wrote to Madame Hanska, at each of the stopping-places during his tiring overland journey back to France, and describes vividly the miserable, jolting journey through Livonia, where the carriage road was marked out by boughs thrown down in the midst of a sandy plain, and all around was depressing poverty and desolation. Berlin, peopled with Germans of "brutal heaviness," he detested, and he loathed the society dinner parties, with no conversation—nothing but tittle-tattle and Court gossip; and complained of the trains, which travelled he said no quicker than a French diligence. Nevertheless, in contrast to Russia, the great *voyant* was struck with the air of "liberte de moeurs" which prevailed throughout Germany. He liked Dresden, and enjoyed his visit to its picture gallery, where he especially admired a Madeleine and two Virgins by Correggio, as well as two by Raphael, one of them presumably the San Sisto Madonna. The gem of the whole collection, however, in his opinion, was Holbein's Madonna; and he longed to have Madame Hanska's hand in his while he gazed at it. As he was away from her, he was very restless, and soon tired of all he saw. He longed to be back in Paris, and to find distraction in his work. "Think of my trouble, my sadness, and my sorrow, and you will be full of pity and of indulgence for the poor exile,"[*] he writes.

[*] "Lettres a l'Etrangere."

CHAPTER XIII

1843 - 1846

On September 26th, 1843, during Balzac's absence in St. Petersburg, another play of which he was author was produced at the Gaite. It was called "Pamela Giraud," and the plot is contrived with an ability which proves Balzac's increased knowledge of the art of writing for the theatre. At the same time he has attempted no innovations, but he has kept to the beaten track; and the play is an old-fashioned melodrama with thrilling and heart-rending situations, and virtue triumphant at the end. Owing to Balzac's attack on journalism in the "Monographie de la Presse Parisienne," which had appeared in March, and finished with the words, "Si la presse n'existait pas, il faudrait ne pas l'inventer," the whole newspaper world was peculiarly hostile to him at this time, and his play received no mercy, and was a failure. Curiously enough, Balzac seemed rather pleased at this news, which reached him at Berlin, on his journey home to France. He had made use of the services of two practised writers for the theatre to fit his melodrama to the exigencies of the stage, and possibly this fact dulled his interest in it. At any rate he was strangely philosophical about its fate.

On November 28th, 1843, soon after his return to Paris, a vacancy was left in the Academy by the death of M. Vincent Campenon; and Charles Nodier and Victor Hugo proposed Balzac as a candidate for the empty seat. Balzac, however, soon withdrew, as he found that his impecunious condition would be a reason for his rejection, and he wrote promptly to Nodier and to M. de Pongerville, another member of the Academy, that if he could not enter L'Academie because of honourable poverty, he would never present himself at her doors when prosperity was his portion. In September, 1845, another vacancy occurred; but in spite of Madame de Girardin's entreaties that Balzac should again come forward as a candidate, he refused decidedly, and wrote to Madame Hanska that in doing this he knew himself to be consulting her wishes.

The year 1844 was not an unhappy one with Balzac, though his health was bad, and he speaks of terrible neuralgia; so that he wrote "Les Paysans" with his head in opium, as he had written "Cesar Birotteau" with his feet in mustard. Apparently Madame Hanska held out hopes that in 1845 his long probation might come to and end, as he writes: "Days of illness are days of pleasure to me, for when I do not work with absorption of all my moral and physical qualities, I never cease thinking of 1845. I arrange houses, I furnish them, I see myself there, and I am happy."[*] It was a joy to him to fulfil Madame Hanska's commissions, and thus to come in contact with people who had been at any time connected with her. Therefore, in spite of his busy life, he took much trouble over the arrangements for the entrance of Anna's former governess, Mlle Henriette Borel, into a religious house in Paris, and was present at her reception into the Couvent de la Visitation, Rue l'Enfer, in December, 1845. He was rather annoyed on this occasion, as he was working tremendously hard at the "Comedie Humaine," and at his "Petites Miseres de la Vie Conjugale," and the good nuns, who "thought the world turned only for themselves," told him that the ceremony would take place at one o'clock and would last an hour, whereas it was not over till four, and as he had to see Lirette afterwards, he could not get away till half-past five. However, he was consoled by the idea that he was representing his dear Countess and Anna, who were in Italy at the time, and he thought the service imposing and very dramatic. He was specially thrilled when the three new nuns threw themselves on the ground, were covered with a pall, while prayers for the dead were recited over them; and after this rose up crowned with white roses, as the brides of Christ. Lirette was radiant when she had taken the veil, and wished that every one would enter a religious house.

[*] "Correspondance," vol. ii. p. 102.

In July, 1844, Madame Hanska and her daughter made the acquaintance of the Comte Georges Mniszech, who appeared to be a very suitable _ parti_for Anna. Balzac naturally took a keen interest in all the prospective arrangements, and consulted anxiously with Madame Hanska about the young Comte's character, which must of course have proved perfect, before a treasure like the young Countess could be confided to his keeping. It is strikingly characteristic of Balzac's disinterestedness, that though he knew that the young Countess's marriage would remove the principal obstacle between him and Madame Hanska, he was most insistent in recommending caution till the young man had been for some time on probation. However, an engagement soon took place, and it seemed as though the great desire of Balzac's heart would in a short time be within his reach, and that happiness would shine upon him at last.

In 1844 he published among other books "Modeste Mignon," "Gaudissart II," a fragment of the first part of "L'Envers de L'Histoire Contemporaine," which he entitled "Madame de la Chanterie," the end of the first part of "Splendeurs et Miseres des Courtisanes," the third and last part of "Beatrix," and the first part of "Les Paysans." This began to appear in *La Presse* on December 3rd, and the disputes about its publication led to Balzac's final rupture with Emile de Girardin.

"Les Paysans" was never finished; but was intended to be the most considerable, as it is, even in its present fragmentary condition, one of the most remarkable of Balzac's novels. For eight years he had at intervals started on the composition of this vivid picture of the deep under-current of struggle which was going on between the peasant of France and the *bourgeoisie*; that deadly fight for the possession of the soil which resulted, as the great *voyant* plainly descried it must, in the Revolution of 1848, and the victory of the peasant. Balzac also intended to depict the demoralisation of the people by their abandonment of the Catholic religion; and the novel, in emulation of Victor Hugo and of Dumas, was to fill many volumes. The first version of it, entitled "Le Grand Proprietaire," was begun about 1835, and the Vicomte de Spoelberch de Lovenjoul in his interesting book entitled "La Genese d'un Roman de Balzac," gives the text of this, the MS. of which forms part of his collection. About the year 1836 or 1838, Balzac altered the title of his proposed novel to "Qui a Terre, a Guerre," and it was not till 1839 that he named the work "Les Paysans." In 1840 Balzac offered "Les Paysans," which he said was ready to appear in fifteen days, to M. Dujarier, the manager of *La Presse*, and received 1,650 francs in advance for the novel. However, in 1841 he substituted "Les Deux Freres," which was the first part of "La Rabouilleuse," for "Les Paysans," and offered the latter work as if finished to Le Messager and also to the publisher Locquin, under the title of "La Chaumiere et le Chateau."

In April, 1843, Balzac had paid back part of his debt to *La Presse* by publishing "Honorine" in its columns, but in September, 1844, he received 9,000 francs in advance for the still unwritten "Les Paysans." It was further arranged that when this debt had been worked out, he should be given sixty centimes a line for the remainder of the novel, and that *La Presse* should pay for composition and corrections. It will be noticed that Emile de Girardin, the autocratic chief of *La Presse*, had at last wearied of the bickering which had gone on between him and Balzac ever since their first relations of 1830, and in 1840 had handed over the task of dealing with the aggravating author to his subordinate Dujarier. The treaty concerning "Les Paysans" was therefore drawn up with Dujarier, and matters no doubt would have proceeded harmoniously, had not the latter been killed in a duel in March, 1845.

The first number of "Les Paysans" appeared on December 3rd, 1844, and then, owing to a most untoward concatenation of circumstances, there was a long pause in Balzac's contributions to *La Presse*. Madame Hanska had unfortunately decided for some time that she would in 1845 make one of those journeys which more than anything else threw Balzac and his affairs into inextricable confusion. Before M. de Hanski's death, however, Balzac was at any rate welcomed with effusion when, in his longing to see Madame Hanska, he left his affairs in Paris to take care of themselves. In those early days she was devotedly attached to him; besides, an adorer was a fashionable appendage for an elegant married woman, and the conquest of a distinguished man of letters like Balzac was something to be proud of. Now, however, there was no husband as a protector in the eyes of the world; and marriage, a marriage about which she felt many qualms, loomed large before her startled eyes. She had no intention of giving up the delightful luxury of Balzac's love; but might she not by judicious diplomacy, she sometimes asked herself, manage to enjoy this, without taking the last irrevocable step? Her position was not enviable, the state of feeling embodied in the words "she would and she wouldn't" always betokening in the subject a wearing variability of mind posture; but compared with the anguish of Balzac, whom she was slowly killing by her vacillations, her woes do not deserve much sympathy.

At St. Petersburg, possibly during one of their walks on the quay, or on a cozy evening when the samovar was brought up at nine o'clock, and placed on the white table with yellowish lines—she had promised Balzac that he might meet her next year at Dresden. However, when she arrived there, and found herself in a circle of her own relations, who according to Balzac poisoned her mind against him, she not only objected to his presence, but, in her sudden fear of gossip, she forbade him to write to her again during her stay at Dresden. She sent off another letter almost at once, contradicting her last command; but she would not make up her mind whether Balzac might come to her at Dresden, whether she would consent to meet him at Frankfort, or whether he should prepare a house for her and Anna in Paris. Balzac could settle to nothing. In order to work as he understood the word, it was necessary that he should exclude all outside disturbing influence, and hear only the voices of the world where Le Pere Goriot, old Grandet, La Cousine Bette, and their fellows, toiled, manoeuvred, and suffered. How could he do this, how could he even arrange his business affairs, when a letter might come by any post, telling him to start at once and meet his beloved one? Precious time was wasted, never to be recalled; and when Balzac, raging with impatience and irritation, dared very gently, and with words of affection, to express the feelings which devoured him, the divinity was offended, and he received a rebuke for his impatience and tone of authority.

In April, 1845, he writes: "Shall I manage to write two numbers of the 'Paysans' in twelve days? That is the problem, for I have not a single line written. Dresden and you, between you, turn my head; I do not know what will become of me. There is nothing more fatal than the state of indecision in which you have kept me for three months. If I had started on January 1st, and had returned on February 28th, I should have been more advanced in my work, and I should have had two good months, like the ones at St. Petersburg. Dear sovereign star, how do you expect me to conceive an idea or write a single phrase, with my heart and head agitated as they have been since last November? It has been enough to make a man mad! In vain I have stuffed myself with coffee: I have only succeeded in increasing the nervous trembling of my eyes, and I have written nothing; this is my situation to-day, April 10th; and I have *La Presse* behind me, sending to me every day, and the 'Paysans,' which is my first long work. I am between two despairs, that of not seeing you, of not having seen you, and the literary and financial trouble, the trouble of self-respect. Oh, Charles II. was quite right to say: 'But she?' in all the affairs submitted to him by his ministers.

"I can only write you this word, and it is full of sadness, for I must work and try to forget you for several days, to belong in the future more thoroughly and surely to you. It is noon; I start again at 'Les Paysans' for the tenth time, and all the muscles in my face work like those of an animal; Nature has had enough of work—she kicks over the traces. Ah! why have I debts? Why must I work whether I wish to or not? I am so unhappy, so tormented, so despondent, that I refuse to be hopeless; you must surely see that I am more than ever yours, and that I pass my life uselessly away from you, for the glory gained by inspired work is not worth a few hours passed with you! In the end I trust only in God and in you alone: in you who do not write me a word more for that; you who might at least console me with three letters a week, and who hardly write me two, and those so short!"[*]

[*] "Correspondance," vol. ii. p. 142.

However, on April 18th he received a letter from Madame Hanska containing the words, "I wish to see you," and rushed off at once to Dresden oblivious of everything but his one desire. *La Presse* apparently submitted to this interruption philosophically. Its readers had not found the opening of "Les Paysans" amusing, while *Le Moniteur de l'Armee* had strongly and rather absurdly objected to it, as likely to lower military prestige. *La Presse* had therefore decided in any case to put off the appearance of "Les Paysans" till February, and to begin the year 1845 with "La Reine Margot," by Alexandre Dumas.

Meanwhile Balzac was having a delightful time. Having joined Madame Hanska at Dresden, he travelled with her and the Comtesse Anna and Comte Georges Mniszech, who had lately become engaged, to Cannstadt, Carlsruhe, and Strasburg; and to his intense delight, in July, the Countess and her daughter came to him at Passy, and took up their abode in a little house near the Rue Basse, with a carefully chosen housemaid, cook, and man. The Czar had prohibited the journey to France, so they travelled incognito as Balzac's sister and niece, the Countess Anna taking the name of Eugenie, perhaps in remembrance of Balzac's heroine Eugenie Grandet. [*] In the morning they went by cab or on foot into Paris, and in the evening a carriage was at their disposal, and they visited the theatre and the opera. We can easily realise the excitement and joy Balzac felt in showing them all his treasures—the bust by David D'Angers, the precious Medici furniture of ebony encrusted with mother-of-pearl, the Cellini statuettes, and the pictures by Giorgione, Palma, Watteau, and Greuze.

[*] "La Genese d'un Roman de Balzac," by the Vicomte de Spoelberch de Lovenjoul.

July passed quickly in this mode of life, Balzac acting as cicerone to the two ladies, and their identity was fortunately not discovered. In August he conducted them as far as Brussels on their way back to Dresden, and together they visited Fontainebleau, Orleans, Bourges, his much-loved Tours, Blois, Rotterdam, La Hague, and Antwerp. At Brussels they were met by M. Georges Mniszech, who took charge of the two Countesses in Balzac's place. The latter felt obliged to write afterwards to the Count to apologise for his cold good-bye, and to explain that he had been forced to assume indifference, because he feared a complete breakdown unless he sternly repressed all appearance of feeling.

However, he was not away for long from Madame Hanska, as he spent from September 20th till October 4th with her at Baden-Baden, where she had been ordered for a course of the waters. The time there was the happiest in his life, as it seemed to him that he could now plainly see a picture of the future, which he prayed for and dreamed of in the midst of his crushing work.

On October 16th, 1845, he left Paris again, met Madame Hanska, her daughter, and prospective son-in-law at Chalons, and started with them on their Italian tour. It took a day to travel by boat from Chalons to Lyons, and another day to go by boat from Lyons to Avignon; but the time flew from Madame Hanska and Balzac, who were engrossed all the way in delightful talk. They arrived at Marseilles on October 29th, and stayed for two nights at the Hotel d'Orient, where Balzac's friend Mery had secured rooms for them.

They then went by sea to Naples, and there Balzac worked so hard at sight-seeing, saw so much, and talked so volubly, that he was quite exhausted. He remained a few days only at Naples, and had a very tiring journey back, as the sea was extremely rough; and when he reached Marseilles Mery insisted on taking him into society, so that he had no opportunity of resting even there. It was altogether a very expensive journey. He could not drink the water on board the boat coming home, and therefore was obliged to quench his thirst with champagne; and as the captain and the steward showed him extraordinary politeness, *they* had also to be given champagne, and invited to a lunch party at the Hotel d'Orient when the ship arrived at Marseilles. Balzac was evidently rather ashamed of this escapade, and begged Madame Hanska not to let Georges know anything of his extravagance, as he would be certain to make fun of it.

The bric-a-brac shops at Marseilles were another terrible cause of temptation, and one to which Balzac apparently succumbed without a struggle, consoling himself with the reflection that his purchases were "de vraies occasions a saisir."

When he arrived at Passy on November 17th, and retired to bed with an attack of fever as the result of all his fatigues, he might be expected to feel slightly depressed at the thought of the time he had wasted during the last few months, and of his small advance in the work of paying off his debts. As far as we can judge, however, these were not his reflections. He was dreaming of the past year, the happiest year of his life, because so much of it had been spent with Madame Hanska; and when his mind turned to more practical subjects, he thought of various projects for buying the house which was to be their future home, and of the way it should be decorated. His mind dwelt constantly on these preparations for his married life; and he continued to correspond with Mery, and to entrust him with delicate commissions which required much bargaining. At this Mery was not, according to his own account, very successful, as he remarks in an amusing letter to Balzac: "I call to witness all the marble false gods which decorate Lazardo's dark museum. I have neglected nothing to succeed with your message. I have paid indolent visits, I have taken the airs of a bored 'agathophile,' I have turned my back on the objects of your desire. All my efforts have been in vain. They obstinately continue to ask fabulous prices."[*]

[*] Letters from the collection of the Vicomte de Spoelberch de Lovenjoul, published in the *Revue Bleue* of December 5th, 1903.

In February, 1845,[*] Balzac had written cheerfully about the 30,000 francs for "Les Paysans" which he would obtain from the publisher, and the 10,000 from the journal; of the 15,000 francs which would come to him from "La Comedie Humaine," and the 30,000 from the sale of Les Jardies, besides 10,000 francs from his other works and 20,000 from the railway du Nord; and had calculated that his most pressing liabilities would soon be discharged. His figures and computations on the subject of money can never be relied on, and the railway du Nord was a most unfortunate speculation, and proved a constant drain on his resources. Nevertheless, there is no doubt that he was beginning to diminish perceptibly the burden of debt which pressed upon him, and that if Madame Hanska had not existed, and if on the other hand he had not himself embarked on some mad scheme or senseless piece of extravagance, he might in a few years have become a free man. These long months of expensive inaction rendered this happy solution to the troubles of his life impossible.

[*] "Correspondance," vol. ii. p. 123.

Meanwhile fresh misfortunes were gathering. On November 27th, 1845, Emile de Girardin, who since Dujarier's death had resumed business relations with Balzac, addressed to him a most discourteous letter. He apparently disbelieved in the terms of the agreement by which the great writer was to be paid sixty centimes a line for "Les Paysans," and demanded a certified copy of it;[*] and he also announced that for "Les Petites Miseres de la Vie Conjugale," which was about to appear in the *Revue*, he could not pay more than forty centimes, which was, he said, his maximum price to contributors. Later on, in March, 1846, Girardin despatched another message to complain of the delay in continuing "Les Paysans," and in this he remarked with bitter emphasis that as *La Presse* paid so highly for what was published in her pages, she had at least the right of objecting to being treated lightly. Balzac replied on March 16th, 1846, that *he* was the one who ought to bear malice, as Dujarier had upset his arrangements by interrupting the publication of "Les Paysans" to substitute "La Reine Margot," by Dumas, and that now his brain required rest, and that he was starting that very day for a month's holiday in Rome.

[*] "La Genese d'un Roman de Balzac," by the Vicomte de Spoelberch de Lovenjoul (from which the whole account of the dispute between Balzac and Emile de Girardin is taken).

If Balzac had remained in France it is doubtful whether he would have written much, as he had been in a miserably unsettled state all the winter of 1845 to 1846. His health was bad: he mentions continual colds and neuralgia, and on one occasion remarks that owing to complete exhaustion he has slept all through the day. Besides this, his suspense about Madame Hanska's ultimate decision made him absolutely wretched. He writes to her on December 17th, 1845: "Nothing amuses me, nothing distracts me, nothing animates me; it is the death of the soul, the death of the will, the weakening of the whole being; I feel that I can only take up my work again when I see my life determined, fixed, arranged."[*] Later on in the same letter he says: "I am crushed; I have waited too long, I have hoped too much; I have been too happy this year, and I do not want anything else. After so many years of misfortune and of work, to have been free as a bird, superhumanly happy, and to return to one's cell! . . . is it possible? . . . I dream: I dream by day and by night, and the thought of the heart driven back on itself prevents all action of the thought of the brain; it is terrible!"

[*] "Correspondance," vol. ii. p. 200.

On one occasion Madame Hanska wrote apparently reproaching him with talking indiscreetly about her; and without finishing the letter, the end of which was affectionate, and would have calmed his mind, he at once jumped out of the cab in which he was driving, and walked for hours about Paris. He was wearing thin shoes, and there were two inches of snow on the ground; but his agitation was so great at her unjust accusations, and his indignation so fierce at the wickedness of the people who had libelled him, that he hardly knew where he was going, and returned at last, still so excited by the anguish of his mind, that he was not conscious of bodily fatigue. Such crises, and the consequent exhaustion afterwards, were not conducive to work; particularly in a man whose heart was already affected, and who had overstrained his powers for years.

Possibly in the hope of obtaining distraction and relief from the anxious misery of thought, he went into society more than usual this year; and in spite the strained relations between him and Emile de Girardin, he often dined at the editor's house, and was on most friendly terms with Madame de Girardin. On January 1st, 1846, he wrote to Madame Hanska, "I dined, as I told you in my last letter, with Nestor Roqueplan, the director of the Theatre des Varietes, the last Wednesday of December, and the last day of the month with the illustrious Delphine. We laughed as much as I can laugh without you, and far from you. Delphine is really the queen of conversation; that evening she was especially sublime, brilliant, charming. Gautier was there as well; I left after having a long talk with him. He said that there was no hurry for 'Richard, Coeur d'Eponge'; the theatre is well provided at present. Perhaps Gautier and I will write the piece together later on."[*]

[*] "Correspondance," vol. ii. p. 212.

Balzac's mind was still running on the theatre. Owing to failing health and to his unfortunate love affair, he now found it more difficult to concentrate his mind than formerly, and the incessant work of earlier years was no longer possible; so that the easy road to fortune offered by a successful play became doubly attractive. "Richard Coeur d'Eponge," however, never appeared; and except several fragments, which are in the hands of the Vicomte de Spoelberch de Lovenjoul, it is doubtful whether it was written, though Balzac often discussed the plot with Gautier.

What, after all, were novels, essays, or plays, of what interest were scenes, plots, or characters, what was fame, what was art itself, compared with Madame Hanska? How was it possible for a man to work, with the gloriously disquieting prospect before him that in so many months, weeks, days, he should meet his divinity? The phantoms of his imagination faded to insignificance, and then to utter nullity, beside the woman of flesh and blood, the one real object in a world of shadows. On March 17th, 1846, he started on his journey to Rome, and everything became a blank, except the intoxicating thought that each hour diminished the distance between him and the woman he loved. She evidently received him with enthusiasm, and showed so much affection, that though nothing definite was settled, he felt that her ultimate decision to marry him was certain; and was only deferred to a more convenient season, when her daughter Anna should have become La Comtesse Mniszech. Therefore the whole world brightened for him, and he became again full of life and vigour. He stayed for a month in the Eternal City, was presented to the Pope, admired St. Peter's extremely, and said that his time there would for ever remain one of the greatest and most beautiful recollections of his life. As the route by sea was crowded by travellers who had spent Holy Week in Rome, and all wanted to return at the same time, he travelled back by Switzerland; and explored fresh country and hunted for curiosities on the way. Several pictures were to follow him from Italy: a Sebastian del Piombo, a Bronzino, and a Mirevelt, which he describes as of extreme beauty; and with his usual happy faith in his own good luck, he hoped to pick up some other bargains such as "Hobbemas and Holbeins for a few crowns," in the towns through which he would pass on his journey. A definite engagement did not take place till some months later; but some tacit understanding must now have been allowed by Madame Hanska, as there began to appear from this time in Balzac's letters exact descriptions of the Sevres china, the inlaid furniture, and the bric-a-brac, which he was buying evidently with her money as well as his own, to adorn their future home together. As usual, on his return he found his affairs in utter confusion, was pursued by creditors, and was absolutely without money. As a last misfortune, his housekeeper, Madame de Brugnolle, in whose name the habitation at Passy had been rented, and who generally managed his business affairs, was busy preparing for her approaching marriage, and had naturally no time to spare for her supposed lodger's difficulties. Altogether Balzac felt that the world was a harassing place.

However, his health was admirable, "et le talent! . . . oh! je l'ai retrouve dans sa fleur!"[*] He was full of hope and confidence; and although the shares of the railway du Nord continued to fall in value, he considered that with steady work at his novels, and with the help of a successful comedy, he would soon have paid off his debts, and would have a little house of his own, with room for his beautiful things; which, owing to want of space, and also to fear of his creditors, were never unpacked. It was necessary to prove that he was as young, as fresh, and as fertile as ever, and with this object in view, in June, 1846, he began the two books which were to form the series entitled "L'Histoire des Parents Pauvres." The first, "La Cousine Bette," appeared in the *Constitutionnel* from October to December, 1846, and is intended to represent "a poor relation oppressed by humiliations and injuries, living in the midst of three or four families of her relations, and meditating vengeance for the bruising of her amour-propre, and for her wounded vanity!"[*] The second received several names in turn. It was first called "Le Vieux Musicien," next "Le Bonhomme Pons," and then "Le Parasite," a title on which Balzac said he had decided definitely. However, Madame Hanska objected, as she declared that "Le Parasite" was only suitable for an eighteenth-century comedy, and the book appeared in April, 1847, as "Le Cousin Pons." Though intensely tragic, it is not as horrible or revolting as its pendant, the gloomy "Cousine Bette"; and Balzac has portrayed admirably the simple old man with his fondness for good dinners; "the poor relation oppressed by humiliations and injuries, pardoning all, and only revenging himself by doing kindnesses." Side by side with him is the touching figure of his faithful friend Schmucke, the childlike German musician, who dies of grief at the death of Pons. In writing these two remarkable books, his last important works, Balzac proved conclusively that his hand had not lost its cunning, and that the slow rate of literary production during the last few years of his life was caused by his unhappy circumstances, and not by any failure in his genius.

[*] "Correspondance," vol. ii. p. 243.

After all, the year 1846 ended for him with agitation which increased his heart disease. His beloved trio, whom he had christened the "troupe Bilboquet," after the vaudeville "Les Saltimbanques," had now moved to Wiesbaden; and thither their faithful "Bilboquet," the "vetturino per amore," as Madame de Girardin laughingly called him, rushed to meet them. He found "notre grande et chere Atala" rather crippled with rheumatism, and not able to take the exercise which was necessary for her, but in his eyes as beautiful as ever. The "gentille Zephirine," otherwise the Countess Anna, was gay, charming, and beautifully dressed; and "Gringalet," the Count, was completely occupied—when not making love—with his collection of insects, on which he spent large sums. About this collection Balzac made many rather heavy jokes, calling the Count a "Gringalet sphynx-lepidoptere-coleoptere-ante-diluvien,"[*] but in an anxious desire to ingratiate himself with Madame Hanska's family, he often despatched magnificent specimens of the insect species from Paris to add to it.

[*] "Correspondance," vol. ii. p. 287.

Balzac travelled about a little with the Hanski family, and remained with them till September 15th, when he was obliged to go back to Paris. Either at this time, or when he returned for the wedding of the Comtesse Anna and the Comte Georges Mniszech, which took place at Wiesbaden on October 13th, 1846, a secret engagement was contracted between him and Madame Hanska.

He was now terribly anxious that there should be no further delay about his marriage, and on his way back from Germany on one of these two occasions, he applied to M. Germeau, then prefect of Metz,[*] who had been at school with him at Vendome, to know whether the necessary formalities could be abridged, so that the wedding might take place at once. This was impossible; and though the great obstacle to their union was now removed, Madame Hanska refused to be parted from her beloved daughter, and insisted on accompanying the newly married couple on their honeymoon. Her determination caused Balzac terrible agony of mind, as she was unwell, and was suffering a great deal at the time, and he therefore wished her to remain quietly somewhere in France; moreover, despair seized him at her hesitation to become his wife, when the course at last seemed clear. His trouble at this time appears to have had a serious effect on his health, and some words spoken half in malice, half in warning by Madame de Girardin, must have sounded like a knell in his ears. He tells them apparently in jest to Madame Hanska to give her an example of the nonsense people talk in Paris. In his accuracy of repetition, however, we can trace a passionately anxious desire to force Madame Hanska herself to deny the charges brought against her; and perhaps lurking behind this, a wish unacknowledged even to himself, to shame her if—even after all that had passed—she were really not in earnest.

[*] See "Une Page Perdue de Honore de Balzac," p. 276, by the Vicomte de Spoelberch de Lovenjoul.

He says: "Madame de Girardin told me that she heard from a person who knew you intimately, that you were extremely flattered by my homage; that from vanity and pride you made me come wherever you went; that you were very happy to have a man of genius as courier, but that your social position was too high to allow me to aspire to anything else. And then she began to laugh with an ironical laugh, and told me that I was wasting my time running after great ladies, only to fail with them. Hein! Isn't that like Paris!"[*]

[*] "Correspondance," vol. ii. p. 295.

The reader of Balzac's life is forced to the sad conclusion that Parisian gossip had on this occasion sketched the situation tolerably correctly; though the truth of the picture was no doubt denied with much indignation by Madame Hanska.

CHAPTER XIV

1846 - 1848

Much of Balzac's time, whenever he was in Paris in 1845 and 1846, was taken up with house-hunting; and some of his still unpublished letters to Madame Hanska contain long accounts of the advantages of the different abodes he had visited. He was now most anxious to be permanently settled, as there was no room for his art treasures in the Rue Basse; but as Madame Hanska's tastes had to be consulted as well as his own, it was necessary to be very careful in his choice. However, in October, 1846, he at last found something which he thought would be suitable. This was the villa which had formerly belonged to the financier Beaujon, in the Rue Fortunee, now the Rue Balzac. The house was not large, it was what might now be described as a "bijou residence," but though out of repair, it had been decorated with the utmost magnificence by Beaujon, and Balzac's discriminating eye quickly discerned its aesthetic possibilities.

In front of the house was a long narrow courtyard, the pavement of which was interrupted here and there by flower-beds. This courtyard was bordered by a wall, and above the wall nothing could be seen from the road but a cupola, which formed the domed ceiling of the financier's boudoir. Some of the inside adornments possessed a delightful fitness for the uses to which they were destined. For instance, what could have been a more graceful compliment to the Mniszechs than to lodge them during their visits to Paris, which would of course be frequent, in a set of rooms painted with brilliant exotic butterflies, poised lightly on lovely flowers? Apparently foreseeing, as Balzac remarks, that a "Lepidopterian Georges" would at some time inhabit the mansion, Beaujon had actually provided a beautiful bedroom and a little drawing-room decorated in this way.[*] It seemed quite providential!

[*] "Correspondance," vol. ii. p. 289.

Balzac was very happy superintending the building operations, deciding exactly where his different treasures would look best in his new abode, and hunting for fresh acquisitions to make every detail perfect. Later on, his letters from Russia to his mother when she was taking charge of the house — then furnished and decorated — show how dearly he loved all his household goods, and how well he was acquainted with their peculiarities; how he realised the danger, unless it were held by the lower part,[*] of moving the greenish-grey china vase with cracked glaze, which was to stand on one of the consoles in black wood and Buhl marqueterie; and how he thought anxiously about the candle ornaments of gilt crystal, which were only to be arranged *after* the candelabra had been put up in the white drawing-room. In 1846 and 1847, his letters are instinct with the passion of the confirmed collector, who has no thought beyond his bric-a-brac. His excitement is intense because Madame Hanska has discovered that a tea service in his possession is real Watteau, and because he has had the "incredible good fortune" to find a milk jug and a sugar basin to match it exactly. When we remember that the man who thus expresses his delight was in the act of writing "Les Parents Pauvres," and of evoking scenes of touching pathos and gloomy horror, we are once more amazed at the extraordinary versatility of Balzac's mind and genius.

[*] "Correspondance," vol. ii. p. 337.

The deep thinker, the pessimistic believer in the omnipotence of vice and in the helpless suffering of virtue, who drags to light what is horrible from among the dregs of the people, seems to have nothing in common with the charming, playful figure of "le vieux Bilboquet," who gave Madame Hanska's daughter and her son-in-law a big place in his heart, and was never jealous when, avowedly for their sakes, his wishes, feelings, and health were unconsidered; whose servants, hard-worked though they were, adored him; and who never forgot his friends, or failed to help them when adversity fell upon them.

At the beginning of 1847, peace for a time visited Balzac's restless spirit. In February he went to Germany to fetch Madame Hanska, and leaving the Mniszechs to go back alone to Wierzchownia, she travelled with him to Paris, and remained there till April. It is significant, as the Vicomte de Spoelberch de Lovenjoul remarks,[*] that during the time of her stay in Paris, when Balzac's mind was no longer disturbed by his constant longing to see her, he accomplished the last serious bout of work in his life, beginning the "Depute D'Arcis" in *L'Union*, "La Cousine Bette" in the *Constitutionnel*, and "La Derniere Incarnation de Vautrin" in *La Presse*.

[*] "La Genese d'un Roman de Balzac," p. 194

He had other duties at the same time, being occupied with what *he* calls the most beautiful work of his life, that of preventing "a mother separated from so adorable a child as her Grace the Countess Georges, from dying of grief." He writes to the Mniszechs on February 27th, 1847[*]: "Our dear adored Atala is in a charming and magnificent apartment (and not too dear). She has a garden; she goes a great deal to the convent" (to see Mlle. Henriette Borel). "I try to distract her and to be as much as possible Anna to her; but the name of her dear daughter is so daily and continually on her lips, that the day before yesterday, when she was enjoying herself immensely at the Varietes—in fits of laughter at the 'Filleul de Tout le Monde,' acted by Bouffe and Hyacinthe—in the midst of her gaiety, she asked herself in a heartbroken voice, which brought tears to my eyes, how she could laugh and amuse herself like this, without her 'dear little one.' I allow, dear Zephirine, that I took the liberty of telling her, that you were amusing yourself enormously without her, with your lord and master, His Majesty the King of the Coleoptera; that I was sure that you were at this time one of the happiest women in the world; and I hope that Gringalet, on whom I drew this bill of exchange, will not contradict me. I have four tolerably strong attractions to bring forward against the thought of you: 1st, the Conservatoire; 2nd, the Opera; 3rd, the Italian Opera; 4th, the Exhibition."

[*] "Correspondance," vol. ii. p. 312.

Balzac's hands were certainly pleasantly full at this time. His power of writing, which had temporarily deserted him, seemed now to have returned in full vigour; and he had made forty or fifty thousand francs in three months, so was hopeful of paying off his debts, a point on which Madame Hanska wisely laid much stress. She still refused to decide anything definitely about the date of their marriage; but the house was to a great extent her property, and at this time she identified herself completely with Balzac in all the arrangements to do with it. Though he kept on his rooms in the Rue Basse and left his effects there, he moved in April 1847 to the Rue Fortunee, that he might be better able to superintend the building and decorating, and might himself keep watch over his treasures, which must gradually be unpacked and bestowed to the best advantage. About the middle of April he conducted Madame Hanska to Forbach on her way back to Wierzchownia, and himself returned to Paris to finish the house, put his affairs in order, and then follow her to Wierzchownia. There he hoped the wedding would quickly take place, and that Monsieur and Madame Honore de Balzac would return to Paris, and would live to a ripe old age in married happiness; he writing many masterpieces, she helping with advice, and forming a salon where her social position, cleverness, and charm would surround her with the highest in the land. The prospect was intoxicating; surely no one was ever so near the attainment of his most radiant visions!

On Balzac's return to Paris, however, he was confronted by realities of the most terrible nature.

When he arrived at the Rue Basse, he found to his horror that the lock of his precious casket had been forced, and some of Madame Hanska's letters had been abstracted. It was a case of blackmail, as the thief demanded 30,000 francs, in default of which the letters would at once be handed over to the Czar. If this were to happen, Balzac's hopes of happiness were annihilated, and the consequences to Madame Hanska would be even more serious. Unless approached with the utmost caution, the Czar would certainly refuse his consent to the marriage of a Russian subject with a foreigner, and would be furious if he were to discover a secret love affair between the French novelist and one of his most important subjects. Yet how could Balzac find 30,000 francs?

Already in the grip of heart disease the agony he endured at this time took him one stage further down the valley of death. In the end he managed by frightening the thief, to effect the return of the letters without any immediate payment; but the anguish he had passed through, and the thought of the terrible consequences only just evaded, decided him to burn all the letters he had received from Madame Hanska. It was a terrible sacrifice. He describes in an unpublished letter to her his feelings, as he sat by the fire, and watched each letter curl up, blacken, and finally disappear. He had read and re-read them till they had nearly dropped to pieces, had been cheered and comforted by the sight of them when the world had gone badly, and had owned them so long that they seemed part of himself. There was the first of all, the herald of joy, the opening of a new life; and almost as precious at this moment seemed the one which discovered to him the identity of his correspondent, and held out hopes of a speedy meeting. One after another he took them out of the box which had held some of them for many years, and each seemed equally difficult to part with. However, as he wrote to Madame Hanska, he knew that he was doing right in destroying them, and that the painful sacrifice was absolutely necessary.

Meanwhile, Emile de Girardin was naturally becoming impatient about the continuation of "Les Paysans," which he had never received.[*] He wrote to Balzac at the end of April, 1847, that the printer had been ready for the finish of the book since the November before, and that unless Balzac could produce it in June, the idea of its appearance in *La Presse* must be given up altogether; and in this case he must ask the author to settle with M. Rouy about the advances of money already made to him. He further remarked with scathing though excusable distrust in Balzac's fulfilment of his business engagements, that he refused to continue to bring out the work at all, unless he were absolutely certain that it was completely written and that no further interruption would ensue. Friendly social relations still subsisted, however, between Balzac and the Girardins, as, about the same time that Emile penned this uncompromising epistle, the following note reached Balzac,[+] the last he ever received from the peace-making Madame de Girardin:

"It is the evening of my last Wednesday. Come, cruel one. Mrs. Norton will be here. Do you not wish me to have the glory of having presented you to this English 'Corinne'? Emile tells me that 'La Derniere Incarnation de Vautrin' is admirable. The compositors declare that it is your *chef-d'oeuvre*.

"Only till this evening, I implore you.

"DELPHINE GAY DE GIRARDIN"

[*] "La Genese d'un Roman de Balzac," by the Vicomte de Spoelberch de Lovenjoul, from which the whole account of Balzac's rupture with Girardin is taken.

[+] "La Genese d'un Roman de Balzac," by the Vicomte de Spoelberch de Lovenjoul, p. 262

Balzac on his side, was now most anxious to finish "Les Paysans," especially as his penniless state at this time would render it most difficult for him to pay back the money advanced to him by *La Presse*. He was in special difficulties, as he had lately borrowed ten or fifteen thousand francs from the impecunious Viscontis, giving them as guarantee some shares in the unfortunate Chemin de Fer du Nord, and as the railway was a failure, and these shares were a burden instead of a benefit, Balzac was bound in honour to relieve his friends of their troublesome possession, and to pay back what he owed them. This necessity was an additional incentive to action, and Balzac's letters to Madame Hanska about this time, contain several indications of his anxiety about "Les Paysans." On June 9th he speaks of his desire to bring it to a close; and on the 15th he writes that he must certainly finish it at once, to avoid the lawsuit with which he has been for so long threatened by *La Presse*. However, he seems to have experienced an unconquerable difficulty in its composition, as in that of "Seraphita," the other book about which he had cherished a peculiarly lofty ideal. Therefore in July the termination of "Les Paysans" had not yet reached the office of *La Presse*, and on the 13th of the month Balzac received the following letter:[*]

"PARIS, July 13th, 1847

"'Le Piccinino' will be finished this week. Only seven numbers of 'Les Paysans' are completed in advance. We are therefore at the mercy of an indisposition, of any chance incident, things of which it is necessary for me to see the possibility, and to which I must not expose myself.

"Really you high dignitaries of the periodical are insupportable, and you will manage so cleverly that the periodical will some day fail you completely.

"For my part, my resolution on this matter is taken, and firmly taken, and if I had not a remainder of the account to work out, I would certainly not publish 'Les Paysans,' as I have not received the last line.

"EMILE DE GIRARDIN"

[*] "La Genese d'un Roman de Balzac," by the Vicomte de Spoelberch de Lovenjoul, p. 268.

Balzac's answer to this missive is lost. It must have been despatched at once, and was evidently not conciliatory, as it was answered on the same day in the following terms:

"PARIS, July 13th, 1847.

"I only publish 'Les Paysans' because we have an account to settle. Otherwise I certainly should not publish it, and the success of 'La Derniere Incarnation de Vautrin' would certainly not impel me to do it.

"Therefore if you are able without inconvenience to pay back to the *Presse* what it advanced to you, I will willingly give up 'Les Paysans.' Otherwise I will publish 'Les Paysans,' and will begin on Monday next, the 19th. But I insist that there shall be no interruption. I count on this.

"EMILE DE GIRARDIN"

Girardin's bitter resentment is excusable, when we remember that it was in September, 1844, nearly three years before, that Balzac had received 9,000 francs in advance for "Les Paysans." Since then only one number of the promised work had been produced, and the great writer's only explanation for his long delay in finishing the book was the inadequate one, that Dujarier had interrupted "Les Paysans" after the first chapters had been published, to be able to begin Alexandre Dumas' novel "La Reine Margot," before the end of 1844.

In Balzac's reply, written next day, he definitely withdrew "Les Paysans" from publication, and said that he would pay what he owed *La Presse* within the space of twenty days, and would not charge for what had not yet been printed; though it had been written and composed specially for *La Presse*, and at the request of the *Presse*. As to Emile de Girardin's insinuations about the failure of "La Derniere Incarnation de Vautrin," Balzac remarked that this had been written for *L'Epoque*, not for *La Presse*, and that it had not been necessary for Girardin to purchase it from the moribund journal, unless he had approved of it. Girardin had hurt him on his tenderest point when he branded his works as failures. With pride and bitterness in his heart he went through the accounts with Mr. Rouy, and found that out of the 9,000 francs received from *La Presse*, he still owed 5,221 francs 85 centimes. How he raised the money it is impossible to guess, but on August 5th he paid 2,500 francs, and on September 1st 2,000 more, so that only 721 francs 85 centimes remained of his debt, and he made his preparations to start for Wierzchownia with his mind at rest.

He heard from Emile de Girardin again, as we shall see later on, but he had seen Madame de Girardin for the last time. She did not forget him, however, and the news of his death was so terrible a shock that she fainted away. She died in 1855, and was deeply mourned by her friends. Theophile Gautier, in his admiring account of her, says that for some years before her death, she became a prey to depression and discouragement at the conditions surrounding her. It may have been that her brilliant, exciting life led naturally to a partly physical reaction, and that she became too tired by the emotions she had gone through, to adapt herself with buoyancy to the ever variable conditions of existence. At all events she is a refreshing figure in the midst of much that is unsatisfactory—a woman witty, highly gifted, a queen of society, who was yet kindly, generous, and absolutely free from literary jealousy.

Before the middle of September when Balzac left for Wierzchownia, we hear once of him again. He was still dreaming of the theatre as a means of relief from all his embarrassments,[*] and on a hot day in August, 1847, he went to Bougival, to pay a visit to M. Hostein, the director of the Theatre Historique, a new theatre which had not yet been opened six months. There, sitting in the shade on the towing path by the river, he unfolded to the manager his design of writing a grand historical drama on Peter I. and Catherine of Russia, to be entitled "Pierre et Catherine." Nothing was written, it was all still in his head; but he at once sketched the first scene to the manager, and talked with enthusiasm of the enormous success which would be caused by the novelty of introducing the Russian peasant on the stage. The play could be written very quickly; and M. Hostein,[+] carried away by Balzac's extraordinarily persuasive eloquence, already began to reflect about suitable scenery, dresses, and decorations, for the framing of his masterpiece. However, to his disappointment Balzac returned in a few days, to announce that there would be some delay in the production of his play, as he wished to study local colouring on the spot, and was on the point of starting for Russia. He said that when he returned to Paris in the spring, he would bring M. Hostein a completed play, and with this promise the manager was obliged to be satisfied.

[*] "Honore de Balzac," by Edmond Bire.

[+] "Historiettes et Souvenirs d'un Homme de Theatre," by M. Hostein.

Balzac was in an enormous hurry to reach Wierzchownia, and set himself with much energy to the task of finishing the house in the Rue Fortunee. His efforts in this direction were doubtless the reason that the writing of "Pierre et Catherine" was postponed till the *moujik* could be studied in his native land. At last, however, the work of decoration was complete, and his mother left in charge, with minute directions about the care of his treasures. He had toiled with breathless haste, and managed after all to start earlier than he had expected. Once on the journey his northern magnet drew him with ever-increasing strength, and regardless of fatigue, he travelled for eight days in succession without stoppage or rest, and arrived ten days before his letter announcing his departure from Paris. The inhabitants of the chateau were naturally much surprised at his sudden appearance, and Balzac considers that they were touched, or rather—though he does not say this—that *She* was touched by his *empressement*.

He was much delighted with his surroundings. Wierzchownia was a palace, and he was interested and amused with the novelty of all he saw. He writes: "We have no idea at home of an existence like this. At Wierzchownia it is necessary to have all the industries in the house: there is a confectioner, a tailor, and a shoemaker."[*] He was established in a delicious suite of rooms, consisting of a drawing-room, a study, and a bedroom. The study was in pink stucco, with a fireplace in which straw was apparently burnt, magnificent hangings, large windows, and convenient furniture. In this Louvre of a Wierzchownia there were, as Balzac remarks with pleasure, five or six similar suites for guests. Everything was patriarchal. Nobody was bored in this wonderful new life. It was fairy-like, the fulfilment of Balzac's dreams of splendour, an approach of reality to the grandiose blurred visions of his hours of creation. He who rejoiced in what was huge, delighted in the fact that the Count Georges Mniszech had gone to inspect an estate as big as the department of Seine-et-Marne, with the object of dismissing a prevaricating bailiff. It gave him intense satisfaction to record the wonders of this strange new life: to tell those at home of the biting cold, which rendered his pelisse of Siberian fox of no more protection than a sheet of blotting-paper; or to mention casually that all the letters were carried by a Cossack across sixty "verstes" of steppes.

[*] "Correspondance," vol. ii. p. 324.

The Russians were eager to show their admiration of the celebrated French novelist, and Balzac experienced the truth of the adage, that a prophet is not without honour save in his own country. On the journey out the officials were charmingly polite to him, and when he went to Kiev to pay his respects to the Governor-General, and to obtain permission for a lengthy sojourn in Russia, he was overwhelmed with attentions. A rich moujik had read all his books, burnt a candle for him every week to St. Nicholas, and had promised a sum of money to the servants of Madame Hanska's sister, if they could manage that he might see the great man. This atmosphere of adoration was very pleasant to one whose reward in France for the production of masterpieces, seemed sometimes to consist solely in condemnation and obloquy. Balzac enjoyed himself for the time, and rested from his literary labours, except for working at the second part of "L'Envers de l'Histoire Contemporaine," which is called "L'Initie," and writing the play which he had promised Hostein as a substitute for "Pierre et Catherine."

His ever-active brain had now evolved a plan for transporting sixty thousand oaks to France, from a territory on the Russian frontier belonging to Count Georges Mniszech and his father. He was anxious that M. Surville should undertake the matter, as, after abstruse and careful calculations— which have the puzzling veneer of practicality always observable in Balzac's mad schemes—he considered that 1,200,000 francs might be made out of the affair, and that of course the engineer who arranged the transport would reap some of the benefit. The blocks of wood would be fifteen inches in diameter at the base, and ten at the top. They would first be conveyed to Brody, from there by high road to Cracow, and thence they would travel to France by the railway, which would be finished in a few days. Unfortunately, there were no bridges at Cologne over the Rhine, or at Magdeburg over the Elbe; but Balzac was not discouraged by the question of the transshipment of sixty thousand oaks, any more than in his old days in the Rue Lesdiguieres, he had been deterred from the idea of having a piano, by the attic being too small for it. M. Surville was to answer categorically, giving a detailed schedule of the costs of carriage and of duty from Cracow to France; and to this, Balzac would add the price of transport from Brody to Cracow. He discounted any natural astonishment his correspondent would feel, at the neglect hitherto of this certain plan for making a fortune, by remarking that the proprietors were Creoles, who worked their settlements by means of moujiks, so that the spirit of enterprise was entirely absent.[*] M. Surville, however, received this brilliant proposition without enthusiasm, and did not even trouble to write himself about the matter, but sent back an answer by his wife, that the price of transporting the freight from one railway to another at Breslau, Berlin, Magdeburg, and Cologne, would render the scheme impossible. Balzac showed unusual docility at this juncture; he was evidently already half-hearted about the enterprise, and remarked that since his first letter he had himself thought of the objections pointed out by M. Surville, and had remembered hearing that a forest purchased in Auvergne, had ruined the buyer, owing to the difficulty of transport.

[*] "Correspondance," vol. ii. p. 321.

Balzac was very happy at Wierzchownia, though the fulfilment of the great desire of his life seemed still distant. Madame Hanska's hesitation continued: she considered herself indispensable to her children; besides, owing to the unfortunate state of the Chemin de Fer du Nord, Balzac's pecuniary affairs would certainly be in an embarrassed condition for the next two years. Living in the same house with her, seeing her every day, and feeling sure of her affection, and of a certain happy consummation to his long probation, would not after all have been very painful, except for one great drawback, which increased continually as time went on; and that was the terrible effect of the inclement climate on Balzac's health. He had suffered from heart disease for some years, and in a letter to his sister, he traces its origin to the cruelty of the lady about whom she knows — possibly Madame de Castries. His abuse of coffee, however, and the unnatural life which he had led with the object of straining the tension of every power to its uttermost, and thus of forcing the greatest possible quantity and quality of literary work out of himself, had done much to ruin his robust constitution. Nevertheless, if he had been able to take up his abode with his wife in the Rue Fortunee, and to enjoy the freedom from anxiety which her fortune would have assured to him; if he had been happy with her, and surrounded by his beautiful things, had at last lived the life for which he had so long yearned, it seems as though several years at least might have remained to him. The enormous labours of his earlier years would indeed have been impossible,[*] but "Les Parents Pauvres" had shown that his intellect was now at its best, and material for many masterpieces was still to be found in that capacious brain and fertile imagination. However, the rigours of the Russian climate, aided no doubt by the privations and anxieties Balzac suffered in Paris after the Revolution of 1848, and by the barbarous treatment which he underwent at the hands of the doctor at Wierzchownia, rendered his case hopeless; and at this time only one more stone was destined to be laid on the unfinished edifice of the "Comedie Humaine."

[*] "Balzac, sa Vie, son Oeuvre," by Julien Lemer.

In February, 1848, it was absolutely necessary that Balzac should go to Paris, as money must at once be found, to meet the calls which the ill-fated Chemin de Fer du Nord was making on its shareholders. Balzac suffered terribly from cold on the journey, and arrived at the Rue Fortunee at a most unfortunate time, just before the Revolution of February, 1848.

In consequence of the disturbed state of the political atmosphere, the outlook for literature was tragic; and Balzac, who was in immediate want of money, found himself in terrible straits. Living with two servants in his luxurious little house, surrounded by works of art which had cost thousands of francs, he was almost dying of hunger. His food consisted of boiled beef, which was cooked and eaten hot once a week, and the remaining six days he subsisted on the cold remains. It seemed impossible to raise money for his present pressing necessities. He managed to sell "L'Initie,"[*] at a ridiculously small price, to an ephemeral journal called *Le Spectateur Republicain*, but only received in return bills at a long date, and it was doubtful whether he was ever paid the money due to him.

[*] "La Genese d'un Roman de Balzac," by the Vicomte de Spoelberch de Lovenjoul.

Nevertheless, whatever effects his privations may have had on his health, they did not subdue his spirits, as both Lemer and Champfleury,[*] who each spent several hours with him in the Rue Fortunee, talk of his undiminished vivacity, his hearty fits of laughter, and his confident plans for the future. Lemer, who had known him before, does indeed remark that he seemed much aged; but Champfleury, who saw him for the first time, is only struck with his strength, animal spirits, and keen intelligence. In the midst of the despondent unhealthy tendencies of the literary talent of his day, he was still, with his *joie de vivre*, a man apart. *Naif*, full of a charming pride, he loved literature "as the Arab loves the wild horse he has found a difficulty in subduing." Nevertheless, material prosperity, as ever, occupied an important place in the foreground of his scheme of life, and his mind was still running on the theatre, as the great means of gaining money. He warned Champfleury not to follow his example, which led after the production of many books to an existence of deplorable poverty, but to write only three novels a year, so that ten months annually should be left for making a fortune by working for the theatre, "car il faut que l'artiste mene une vie splendide."[+]

[*] "Balzac, sa Vie, son Oeuvre," by Julien Lemer.

[+] "Grandes Figures d'Hier et d'Aujourd'hui," by Champfleury.

Schemes still coursed each other through his quick-moving brain. He wished to create an association of all the great dramatists of the day, who should enrich the French stage with plays composed in common. He was rather despondent about this, however, as he said that most writers were cowardly and idle, and he as afraid they would therefore refuse to join his society. Scribe was the only one who would work; "Mais quelle litterature que 'Les Memoires d'un Colonel de Hussards!'" he exclaimed in horror.[*]

Another plan for becoming colossally rich of which he talked seriously, was to gain a monopoly of all the arts, and to act as auctioneer to Europe: to buy the Apollo Belvedere, for instance, let all the nations compete for it against each other, and then to sell to the highest bidder.

[*] "Notes Historiques sur M. de Balzac," by Champfleury.

He took a gloomy view of the political situation, because, though he had a great admiration for Lamartine, he feared that the poet would not have sufficient strength of mind, to take advantage of the great majority he would doubtless have in the next Assemblee Constituante, and to make himself the chief of a strong government, when he might justify his magnificent *role*, by presiding at the accomplishment of the great social and administrative reforms, demanded by justice, and material, moral, and intellectual progress. In one of his remarks was a touch of sadness. He told Lemer that, at the present crisis, all authors should sacrifice their writing for a time, and throw themselves with energy into politics. "Et pour cela il faut etre jeune," he added with a sigh; "et moi, je suis vieux!"

However, on March 18th, 1848, a letter written by him appeared in the *Constitutionnel*, in which he stated that he would stand as deputy if requested to do so.[*] In consequence, the "Club de la Fraternite Universelle" wrote to inform him that his name had been put on the list of candidates for election, and invited him to explain his political views at a meeting of the Club. In the *Constitutionnel* of April 19th Balzac answered this request by refusing to go to the meeting, and at the same time announced that he had no intention of canvassing, and wished to owe his election solely to votes not asked for, but given voluntarily. He further commented on the fact that from 1789 to 1848 France had changed its constitution every fifteen years, and asked if it were not time, "for the honour of our country, to find, to found, a form, an empire, a durable government; so that our prosperity, our commerce, our arts, which are the life of our commerce, the credit, the glory, in short, all the fortune of France, shall not be periodically jeopardised?"

[*] "Honore de Balzac," by Edmond Bire.

Naturally, these uncompromising views did not meet with favour from the "citoyens membres du Club de la Fraternite Universelle," and Balzac was not elected a member of the Assemblee Nationale.

CHAPTER XV

1848 - 1849

During his stay in Paris, which lasted from February till the end of September, Balzac was careful not to admit any strangers to the mysterious little house in the Rue Fortunee. Even his trusted friends were only shown the magnificence of his residence with strict injunctions about secrecy, so afraid was he that the news of his supposed riches should reach the ears of his creditors. He was only the humble custodian, he said, of all these treasures. Nothing belonged to him; he was poorer than ever, and was only taking charge of the house for a friend. This was difficult to believe, and his acquaintances, who had always been sceptical about his debts, laughed, and said to his delight, yet annoyance, that he was in reality a millionaire, and that he kept his fortune in old stockings.

Theophile Gautier, after remarking how difficult it was to gain an entrance to this carefully-guarded abode, describes it thus: "He received us, however, one day, and we were able to see a dining-room panelled in old oak, with a table, mantelpiece, buffets, sideboards, and chairs in carved wood, which would have made a Berruguete, a Cornejo Duque, or a Verbruggen envious; a drawing-room hung with gold-coloured damask, with doors, cornices, plinths, and embrasures of ebony; a library ranged in cupboards inlaid with tortoiseshell and copper in the style of Buhl; a bathroom in yellow breccia, with bas-reliefs in stucco; a domed boudoir, the ancient paintings of which had been restored by Edmond Hedouin; and a gallery lighted from the top, which we recognised later in the collection of 'Cousin Pons.' On the shelves were all sorts of curiosities — Saxony and Sevres porcelain, sea-green horns with cracked glazing; and on the staircase which was covered with carpet, were great china vases, and a magnificent lantern suspended by a cable of red silk."[*]

[*] "Portraits Contemporains: Honore de Balzac," by Theophile Gautier.

The gallery, the holy of holies of this temple of Art, where the treasures laboriously collected and long concealed, were at last assembled, is described exactly in "Le Cousin Pons." It was a large oblong room, lighted from the top, the walls painted in white and gold, but "the white yellowed, the gold reddened by time, gave harmonious tones which did not spoil the effect of the canvases."[*]

[*] "Le Cousin Pons," by Honore de Balzac.

There were fourteen statues in this gallery mounted on Buhl pedestals, and all round the walls were richly decorated ebony buffets containing *objets d'art*, while in the centre stood carved wooden cases, which showed to great advantage some of the greatest rarities in human work —costly jewellery, and curiosities in ivory, bronze, wood, and enamel. Sixty-seven pictures adorned the walls of this magnificent apartment, among them the four masterpieces, the loss of which is the most tragic incident in the melancholy story of poor old Pons. There were a "Chevalier de Malte en Priere," by Sebastian del Piombo; a "Holy Family," by Fra Bartolommeo; a "Landscape," by Hobbema; and a "Portrait of a Woman," by Albert Durer. Apparently they were in reality mediocre as works of art, but they were a source of the utmost pride and delight to their owner, who said enthusiastically of one of them—the Sebastian del Piombo—that "human art can go no further." When we know that in the novel Balzac is speaking of his own cherished possessions, we think of his own words, "Ideas project themselves with the same force by which they are conceived,"[*] and can understand the reason of the positive pain we feel, when the poor old Cousin Pons is bereft of his treasures. The great *voyant* was transported by his powerful imagination into the personality of the old musician, and the heartrending situation he had evoked must have been torture to him; though with the courage and conscientiousness of the true artist he did not hesitate in the task he had set himself, but ever darkened and deepened the shadows of his tragedy towards the close.

[*] "Le Pere Goriot," by Honore de Balzac.

It is not surprising to hear that this sumptuous house cost 400,000 francs, but it is astonishing, and it gives the inhabitant of steady-going England an idea of the inconvenience of revolutions, that its owner and occupant should in 1848 have been starving in the midst of magnificence, and that it should have been impossible for him to find a purchaser for some small curiosity, if he had wished to sell it to buy bread. Part of the cost of the house had been defrayed by Madame Hanska, but Balzac had evidently overstepped her limits, and had involved himself seriously in debt. One of the alleged reasons given by the lady for the further deferment of her promise to become Madame Honore de Balzac, was the state of embarrassment to which Balzac had reduced himself by his expenditure in decoration; and, in his despair and disgust, the home he had been so happily proud of, and which seemed destined never to be occupied, soon became to him "that rascally plum box."

At this time, however, he was still tasting the joys of ownership, and was, as usual, hopeful about the future. His dreams of theatrical success seemed at last destined to come true.[*] Hostein, who had rushed to the Rue Fortunee as soon as he heard of the arrival of the great man, to ask for the play promised him in place of "Pierre et Catherine," found Balzac as usual at his desk, and was presented with a copy-book on which was written in large characters, "Gertrude, tragedie bourgeoise." The play was read next day in Balzac's drawing-room to Hostein, Madame Dorval, and Melingue; and Hostein accepted it under the name of "La Maratre," Madame Dorval expressing much objection to its first title. Eventually, to Madame Dorval's and Balzac's disappointment, Madame Lacressoniere, who had much influence with Hostein, was entrusted with the heroine's part; and the tragedy was produced at the Theatre-Historique on May 25th, 1848. In spite of the disturbed state of the political atmosphere, which was ruinous to the theatres, the play met with considerable success; and the critics began to realise that when once Balzac had mastered the *metier* of the theatre, he might become a great dramatist. About this time, Cogniard, the director of the Porte-Saint-Martin, received a letter with fifty signatures, asking for a second performance of "Vautrin." He communicated this request to Balzac, who stipulated that if "Vautrin" were again put on the stage, all caricature of Louis Philippe should be avoided by the actor who played the principal part. He added that when he wrote the play he had never intended any political allusion. However, "Vautrin" was not acted till April, 1850, when, without Balzac's knowledge, it was produced at the Gaite. Balzac, who heard of this at Dresden, on his journey to Paris from Russia, wrote to complain of the violation of his dramatic rights, and in consequence the play was withdrawn from the boards of the Gaite.

[*] "Honore de Balzac," by Edmond Bire.

During his stay in Paris in 1848, Balzac sketched out the plots of many dramas. The director of the Odeon, in despair at the emptiness of his theatre after the political crisis of June, offered Victor Hugo, Dumas, and Balzac[*] a premium of 6,000 francs, and a royalty on all receipts exceeding 4,000 francs, if they would produce a play for his theatre; and in response to this offer Balzac promised "Richard Sauvage," which he never wrote. The manager of the Theatre Francais, M. Lockroy, also made overtures to the hitherto despised dramatist; and Balzac thought of providing him with a comedy entitled "Les Petits Bourgeois," but abandoned the idea. "Is it," he wrote to Hippolyte Rolle, "the day after a battle when the *bourgeoisie* have so generously shed their blood for menaced civilisation; is it at the time when they are in mourning, that they should be represented on the stage?"[+]

[*] "Honore de Balzac," by Edmond Bire.

[+] "Correspondance," vol. ii. p. 332.

At this time, however, Balzac had in his portfolio a play quite ready to be acted—one which had several times changed its title, being called by its author successively "Mercadet," "Le Speculateur," and "Le Faiseur." It was read and accepted by the Comedie Francaise on August 17th, 1848, under the name of "Le Faiseur"; and when Balzac returned to Russia at the end of September, he asked his friend Laurent-Jan to take charge of the comedy during his absence. Evidently he heard that matters were not going very smoothly, as in December he wrote to Laurent-Jan from Wierzchownia to say that if the Comedie Francaise refused "Mercadet"—which had been "recue a l'unanimite" on August 17th—it might be offered to Frederick Lemaitre; and a few days later, hearing that the piece was "recue seulement a corrections," by the Comedie Francaise, he withdrew it altogether. "Le Faiseur" or "Mercadet" was then offered to the Theatre Historique, and Balzac already saw in imagination his sister and his two nieces attending the first night's performance, decked out in their most elegant toilettes. As he was in Russia, and his mother did not go to the theatre, they would be the sole representatives of the family; and Hostein must therefore provide them with one of the best boxes in the theatre. If there were hissings and murmurings, as Balzac expected from past experiences, his younger niece Valentine would be indignant; but Sophie would still preserve her dignity, "and you, my dear sister. . . . But what can a box do against a theatre?"

Nevertheless, though Hostein accepted "Le Faiseur," he announced that his clients preferred melodrama to comedy, and that, in order to fit it for his "theatre de boulevard," the play would require modifications which would completely change its character. Balzac naturally objected to these proposed alterations, as they sounded infinitely more sweeping than the "corrections" of the Comedie Francaise, and the play was never acted during his life. On August 23rd, 1851, however, as we have already seen, "Mercadet le Faiseur," with certain modifications made by M. Dennery, and also with omissions —for the play as Balzac originally wrote it was too long for the theatre—was received with tremendous acclamations at the Gymnase; and on October 22nd, 1868, it was acted at the Comedie Francaise, and again in 1879 and in 1890.

Mercadet, first played by Geoffroy, who conceived Balzac's creation admirably, and at the Comedie Francaise less successfully by Got, is a second Figaro, with a strong likeness to Balzac himself. He is continually on the stage, and keeps the audience uninterruptedly amused by his wit, good-humour, hearty bursts of laughter, and ceaseless expedients for baffling his creditors. The action of the play is simple and natural, and the dialogue scintillates with *bon mots*, gaiety, and amusing sallies. The play had been conceived and even written in 1839 or 1840, and never did Balzac's imperishable youth shine out more brilliantly than in its execution. It is curious to notice that his innate sense of power as a dramatist, which never deserted him, even when he seemed to have found his line in quite a different direction, was in the end amply justified.

His vivacity and hopefulness never forsook him for long. Even in his terrible state of health in 1849, and in spite of his disappointment at the non-appearance of "Le Faiseur," he was in buoyant spirits, and informed his sister in one of his letters, that he was sending a comedy, "Le Roi des Mendiants," to Laurent-Jan, as soon as he could manage to transport it to St. Petersburg. There, the French Ambassador would be entrusted with the charge of despatching it to Paris, as manuscripts were not allowed to travel by post.[*] About three weeks later,[+] he wrote to ask his mother to tell Madame Dorval that he was preparing another play, with a great *role* in it designed specially for her. However, owing to Balzac's failing health the drama never took form, and Madame Dorval died on April 20th, 1849, about three weeks after his letter was despatched.

[*] "Correspondance," vol. ii. p. 393.

[+] "Correspondance," vol. ii, p. 397.

At the time of his stay in the Rue Fortunee in 1848, he was, however, satisfied about "Mercadet," which had, as we have seen, been accepted by the Comedie Francaise; and the production of which would help, he doubtless hoped, to relieve him from his monetary difficulties. Ready money was an ever-pressing necessity. Emile de Girardin, in his political activity during the Revolution of 1848, had not forgotten his personal resentments, and soon after Balzac's arrival in Paris he requested him to pay at once the 721 francs 85 centimes which he still owed *La Presse*.[*] This Balzac could not possibly do, and most probably he forgot all about the matter. Not so his antagonist, who on October 7th, 1848, after Balzac had returned to Russia, demanded immediate payment; and four days afterwards applied to the Tribunal of the Seine for an order that the debt should be paid from the future receipts of "Le Faiseur," which was at that time in rehearsal at the Theatre Francais. This demand was granted, but as after all the play was withdrawn, Emile de Girardin did not receive his money. However, he was paid in the end, as he wrote Balzac a receipt dated December 30th, 1848, for 757 francs 75 centimes, a sum which included legal expenses as well as the original debt.

[*] "La Genese d'un Roman de Balzac," by the Vicomte de Spoelberch de Lovenjoul.

There were to be two elections to the Academie Francaise in January, 1849, as M. Chateaubriand's and M. Vatout's armchairs were both vacant; and Balzac determined again to try his fortune. He wrote the required letter before his departure to Russia, and this was read at a meeting of the illustrious Forty on October 5th, 1848.[*] Apparently, Balzac's absence from France, which prevented him from paying the prescribed visits, militated against his chances of success, as his ardent supporter, M. Vacquerie, wrote in *L'Evenement* of January 9th, 1849: "Balzac is now in Russia. How can he be expected to pay visits? He will not become a member of the Academie because he has not been in Paris? And when posterity says, 'He wrote "Splendeurs et Miseres des Courtisanes," "Le Pere Goriot," "Les Parents Pauvres," and "Les Treize,"' the Academie will answer: 'Yes, but he went on a journey.'"

[*] "Honore de Balzac," by Edmond Bire.

At the first election, which took place on January 11, 1849, the Duc de Noailles was at the head of the list, with twenty-five papers in his favour, and Balzac received two; at the second, on January 18th, when M. de Saint-Priest was the successful candidate, two members of the Academy again voted for Balzac at the first round of the ballot, but at the third and deciding round his name was not included at all. Balzac wrote to Laurent-Jan to ask for the names of his supporters, as he wished to thank them; and about the same time, in a letter to his brother-in-law, M. Surville, he let it be understood that he would never again present himself as a candidate for admission to the Academie Francaise, as he intended to put that body in the wrong.

This is anticipation; we must return to the end of September, 1848, when Balzac, after having arranged the necessary business matters, hurried back to Madame Hanska. For the better guardianship of his treasures, he left his mother with two servants installed in the Rue Fortunee, and he expected to return to Paris by the beginning of 1849. His family did not hear from him for more than a month after his arrival, when his mother received a letter full, as usual, of directions and commissions, but giving no news of his own doings. He was evidently ill at the time he wrote, and a few days afterwards was seized with acute bronchitis, and was obliged to put off his projected return to Paris.

Balzac's health all through the winter was deplorable, and under the direction of the doctor at Wierzchownia, he went through a course of treatment for his heart and lungs. This doctor was a pupil of the famous Franck, the original of Benassis in the "Medecin de Campagne," and Balzac appears to have had complete faith in him, and to have been much impressed by his dictum, that French physicians, though the first in the world for diagnosis, were quite ignorant of curative methods. Balzac's passion at this time for everything Russian, must have been peculiarly trying to his family. It surely seemed to them madness that he should separatè himself from his country, should gradually see less and less of his friends, and should show an inclination to be ashamed of his relations, for the sake of a woman crippled with rheumatism, and no longer young, who, however passionately she may have loved him in the past, seemed now to have grown tired of him. Sophie and Valentine Surville were no doubt delighted to receive magnificent silk wraps from their uncle, trimmed with Russian fur; but the letter accompanying the gift must, we think, have rather spoiled their pleasure, or at any rate was likely to have hurt their mother's feelings. It was surely hardly necessary to inform "ma pauvre Sophie" that it was in vain for her to compete with the Countess Georges in proficiency on the piano, as the latter had "the genius of music, as of love"; and a long string of that wonderful young lady's perfections must have been rather wearying to those who had not the felicity of being acquainted with her. Apparently the young Countess possessed deep knowledge without pedantry, and was of delicious naivete, laughing like a little child; though this did not prevent her from showing religious enthusiasm about beautiful things. Further, she was of angelic goodness, intensely observant, yet extremely discreet, most respectful to her adored mother, very industrious, and she lived only for duty. "All these advantages are set off by a proud air, full of good breeding, an air of ease and grandeur which is not possessed by every queen, and which is quite lost in France, where every one wishes to be equal. This outward distinction, this look of being a great lady, is one of the most precious gifts which God, the God of women, can bestow on them."[*] To paint her character aright, Balzac says, it would be necessary to blend in one word virtues which a moralist would consider it impossible to find united in a single human being; and her "sublime education" was a crown to the whole edifice of her perfections.

[*] "Correspondance," vol. ii. p. 345.

The only consolation which an impartial though possibly unprincipled observer, might have offered at this point to the unfortunate Sophie and Valentine, would be the fact that the young Countess was evidently extremely plain, as even Balzac's partiality only allows him to say: "Physically she possesses grace, which is more beautiful even than beauty, and this triumphs over a complexion which is still brown (she is hardly sixteen years old), and over a nose which, though well cut, is only charming in the profile."

Let us hope, however, that our pity is after all wasted on the nieces, and that in their joy at the idea of receiving handsome presents, they either skipped the unwelcome portions of their distinguished uncle's letter, or that, knowing the cause of his raptures, if they *did* read, they laughed and understood.

His Polar Star is seldom mentioned by name in Balzac's letters; she is generally "the person with whom I am staying," and he says little about her, except that she is very much distressed at the amount of his debts, and that the great happiness of his life is constantly deferred. Two fires had taken place on the estate, and the Countess was in addition burdened with three lawsuits: one about some property which should have come to her from an uncle, and about which it would be necessary for her to go to St. Petersburg. Balzac's letters as usual abound in allusions to his monetary difficulties, while the Survilles had been almost ruined by the Revolution of 1848, so that the outlook for the family was black on all sides.

All this time Balzac's relations were becoming more and more discontented with his doings, as well as with the general aspect of his affairs. Honore was evidently pursuing a chimera, and because of his illusions, many burdens were imposed on them. Madame de Balzac the principal sufferer, was tired of acting as custodian at the Rue Fortunee, where she was expected to teach Francois how to clean the lamps, and received careful instructions about wrapping the gilt bronzes in cotton rags. It seemed as though her son were permanently swallowed up by that terrible Russia, about which, as he remarked impatiently, she would never understand anything; and she longed to retire to her little lodgings at Suresnes, and to do as she pleased. Laure, too, had her grievances, though possibly she kept them to herself and strove to act as peacemaker. She and her family were in terrible monetary straits, and the sight of the costly house, which seemed destined never to be occupied, must have been slightly exasperating. She was quite willing to be useful to Honore, and did not mind when troublesome commissions were entrusted to her; but it was no doubt galling to notice that—though her daughters were expected to write continually, and were supposed to be amply rewarded for their labours, by hearing of the delight with which the young Countess listened to their letters—a strong motive lurking behind Balzac's anxiety to hear often from his family, was the desire to impress Madame Hanska favourably with the idea of their affection for himself, and their unity. At the same time, a sad presentiment warned her, that if ever her brother were married to this great lady, his family and friends would see little more of him. The prospect cannot have been very cheerful to poor Laure, as either Honore would return to France brokenhearted and overwhelmed with debt, or he would gain his heart's desire, and would be lost to his family.

The tone of Balzac's letters to his relations at this time has been adversely criticised, and it is true that the reader is sometimes irritated by the frequency of his requests for service from them, and his continual insistence on the wonderful perfections of the Hanski family, and their grandeur and importance. Occasionally, too, his letters show an irritability which is a new feature in his character. We must remember, however, in judging Balzac, that he was nearly driven wild by the position in which he found himself. It was necessary that he should always be bright, good-natured, and agreeable to the party at Wierzchownia, and his letters to his family were therefore the only safety-valve for the impatience and despair, which, though he never utters a word of reproach against Madame Hanska, must sometimes have taken possession of him.

His was a terrible dilemma. Ill and suffering, so that he was not able to work to diminish his load of debt, desperately in love with a cold-hearted woman, who used these debts as a lever for postponing what on her side was certainly an undesirable marriage; and enormously proud, so that failure in his hopes would mean to him not only a broken heart, but also almost unbearable mortification; Balzac, crippled and handicapped, with his teeth set hard, his powers concentrated on one point, that of winning Madame Hanska, was at times hardly master of himself. There was indeed some excuse for his irritation, when his family wrote something tactless, or involved themselves in fresh misfortunes, just as matters perhaps seemed progressing a little less unfavourably than usual. Their letters were always read aloud at the lunch table at Wierzchownia, and often, alas! their perusal served to prove anew to Madame Hanska, the mistake she had made in contemplating an alliance with a member of a family so peculiarly unlucky and undesirable.

At last the smouldering indignation between Balzac and his relations burst into a flame. The immediate cause of ignition was a letter from Madame de Balzac, complaining that Honore had not written sufficiently often to her; and further, that he did not answer his nieces' epistles. These reproaches were received with much indignation, as Balzac remarked in his answer, which was dated February, 1849, that he had written seven times to his mother since his return to Wierzchownia in September, and that he did not like to send letters continually, because they were franked by his hosts. He goes on to say rather sadly, that it will not do for him to trespass on the hospitality offered him, because, though he has been royally and magnificently received, he has still no rights but those of a guest. On the subject of his neglect to write to his nieces, he is very angry, and cries in an outburst of irritability: "It seems strange to you that I do not write to my nieces. It is you, their grandmother, who have such ideas on family etiquette! You consider that your son, fifty years old, is obliged to write to his nieces! My nieces ought to feel very much honoured and very happy when I address a few words to them; certainly their letters are nice, and always give me pleasure."[*] A postscript to the letter contains the words: "Leave the house in the Rue Fortunee as little as possible, I beg you, because, though Francois is good and faithful, he is not very clever, and may easily do stupid things."

[*] "Correspondance," vol. ii. p. 373.

Balzac followed this with another letter, which apparently impressed on his mother that to please the Wierzchownia family she must behave very well to him; and this communication naturally annoyed Madame de Balzac even more than the preceding one.

In reply, she wrote a severe reprimand to her son, in which she addressed him as "vous," and remarked that her affection in future would depend on his conduct. In fact, as Balzac wrote hotly to Laure, it was the letter of a mother scolding a small boy, and he was fifty years old! Unfortunately, too, it arrived during the *dejeuner*, and Balzac cried impulsively, "My mother is angry with me!" and then was forced to read the letter to the party assembled. It made a very bad impression, as it showed that either he was a bad son, or his mother an extremely difficult person to get on with. Fate had chosen an unfavourable moment for the arrival of this missive, which, later on, when her wrath had abated, Madame de Balzac announced that she had written partly in jest. Balzac had at last been allowed to write to St. Petersburg, to beg the Czar's permission for his marriage with Madame Hanska, and this had been very decidedly refused. Madame Hanska was not at this time prepared to hand over her capital to her daughter, and thus to take the only step, which would have induced her Sovereign to authorise her to leave his dominions. She therefore talked of breaking off the engagement, and of sending Balzac to Paris, to sell everything in the Rue Fortunee. She was tired of struggling; and in Russia she was rich, honoured, and comfortable, whereas she trembled to think of the troublous life which awaited her as Madame Honore de Balzac. Madame de Balzac's letter further strengthened her resolve. Apparently, in addition to evidence about family dissensions, it contained disquieting revelations about the discreditable Henri, and the necessity for supporting the Montzaigle grandchildren; and the veil with which Balzac had striven to soften the aspect of the family skeletons was violently withdrawn. He was in despair. At this juncture his mother's communication was fatal! She had done irreparable mischief!

The long letter he wrote to Madame Surville,[*] imploring her to act as peacemaker, and insisting on the benefits which his marriage would bring to the whole family, would be comical were it not for the writer's real trouble and anxiety; and the reader's knowledge that, underlying the common-sense worldly arguments—which were brought forward in the hope of inducing his family to help him by all the means in their power—was real romantic love for the woman who had now been his ideal for sixteen years.

[*] "Correspondance," vol. ii. p. 378.

He put the case to Madame Surville as if it were her own, and asked what her course would be if she were rich, and Sophie an heiress with many suitors. Sophie, according to her uncle's hypothesis, was in love with a young sculptor; and her parents had permitted an engagement between the two. The sculptor, however, came to live in the same house with his *fiancee*, and his family wrote him letters which he showed to Madame Surville, containing damaging revelations about family matters. As a culminating indiscretion, his mother wrote to this sculptor, "who is David, or Pradier, or Ingres," a letter in which she treated him like a street boy. What would Laure do in these circumstances? Balzac asks. Would she not in disgust dismiss the sculptor, and choose a more eligible *parti* for Sophie? "Unsatisfactory marriages," he remarks sagely, "are easily made; but satisfactory ones require infinite precautions and scrupulous attention, or one does not get married; and I am at present most likely to remain a bachelor."[*]

[*] "Correspondance," vol. ii. p. 328.

He appeals to Madame Surville's self-interest. "Reflect on the fact, my dear Laure, that not one of us can be said to have arrived at our goal, and that if, instead of being obliged to work in order to live, I were to become the husband of a most intellectual, well born and highly connected woman, with a solid though small fortune—in spite of this woman's desire to remain in her own country and to make no new relations, even family ones—I should be in a much more favourable position to be useful to you all. I know that Madame Hanska would show kindness to and feel keen interest in your dear little ones."

Surely, he says, it will be an advantage to the whole family, when he has a *salon* presided over by a beautiful, clever woman, imposing as a queen, where he can assemble the *elite* of Parisian society. He does not wish to be tyrannical or overbearing with his family, but he informs them that it will be of no use to place themselves in opposition to such a woman. He warns them that she and her children will *never forgive* those who blame him to them. Further on in his lengthy epistle, he gives instructions in deportment, and tells his relations that in their intercourse with Madame Hanska they must not show servility, haughtiness, sensitiveness, or obsequiousness; but must be natural, simple, and affectionate. It was no wonder that the Balzac family disliked Madame Hanska! And the poor woman cannot be considered responsible for the feeling evoked!

Towards the end of his letter, however, the reader forgives Balzac, and realises that the cry of a desperate man, ill and suffering, yet still clinging with determined strength to the hope which means everything to him, must not be criticised minutely. "Once everything is lost, I shall live no longer; I shall content myself with a garret like that of the Rue Lesdiguieres, and shall only spend a hundred francs a month. My heart, soul, and ambition will be satisfied with nothing but the object I have pursued for sixteen years: if this immense happiness escapes me, I shall no longer want anything, and shall refuse everything!"

CHAPTER XVI

1849 - 1850

The quarrel between Balzac and his family was quickly made up, and it was settled that his mother should—if she wished to do so—return at once to Suresnes; and come up every day to the Rue Fortunee, taking carriages for this purpose at Balzac's expense. However, having made a small commotion, and asserted her dignity by the announcement that she felt perfectly free to leave the Rue Fortunee whenever she chose to do so, Madame de Balzac's resentment was satisfied; and she remained there till a month before Balzac's return in May, 1850, when illness necessitated her removal to her daughter's house.[*] The nieces, of whom Balzac was really extremely fond, "sulked" no longer, but wrote letters which their uncle praised highly, and which he answered gaily and amusingly. The shadowy cloud, too, which had prevented the brother and sister from seeing each other clearly, dispersed for ever; and one of Honore's letters to Laure about this time contains the loving words, "As far as you are concerned, every day is your festival in my heart, companion of my childhood, and of my bright as well as of my gloomy days."[+]

[*] "Une Page perdue de Honore de Balzac," by the Vicomte de Spoelberch de Lovenjoul.

[+] "Correspondance," vol. ii. p. 420.

It is curious to notice that Balzac's thoughts now turned to those faithful friends of his youth, who had in late years passed rather into the background of his life. He wrote a long letter to Madame Delannoy, who had been a mother to him in the struggling days of his half-starved youth. He had paid off the debt he owed her, but he said he would never be able to thank her adequately for her tenderness and goodness to him. He thought also of Dablin, his early benefactor; and he remembered the old days at Frapesle, and wrote Madame Carraud a most affectionate letter, sending messages of remembrance to Borget and to the Commandant Carraud, and inquiring about his old acquaintance Periollas. The Carrauds, like others in those revolutionary days, had lost money; and Balzac explained that though owing to his illness he had been forbidden to write, he felt obliged to disobey his doctor's commands, that Madame Carraud should not believe that true friends can ever fail each other in trouble. He says: "I have never ceased thinking about you, loving you, talking of you, even here, where they have known Borget since 1833. . . . How different life is from the height of fifty years, and how far we are often from our hopes! . . . How many objects, how many illusions have been thrown overboard! and except for the affection which continues to grow, I have advanced in nothing!"[*]

[*] "Correspondance," vol. ii. p. 422.

The annals of this last year of Balzac's life, are a record of constantly disappointed hope and of physical suffering. One after another he was forced to give up his many plans, and to remain in suffering inaction. He had intended to go to Kiev to present himself to the Governor-General, but this expedition was put off from month to month owing to his ill health. A visit to Moscow on his way back to Paris, was another project which had to be abandoned, as he was never well enough to make his proposed visit to France till he took his last painful and difficult journey in April, 1850, and sight-seeing was then impossible. His hopefulness, however, never left him, and his projected enterprises, whether they took the shape of writings or of travels, were in his eyes only deferred, never definitely relinquished. The wearing uncertainty about Madame Hanska's intentions was the one condition of his life which continued always, if continuance can be considered applicable to anything so variable as that lady's moods. In April, 1849, Balzac wrote to his sister: "No one knows what the year 1847, and February, 1848, and above all the doubt as to what my fate will be, have cost me!"[*]

[*] "Correspondance," vol. ii. p. 392.

Sometimes, Madame Hanska, cruelly regardless of the agony she caused the sick man by her heedless words, would threaten to break off the engagement altogether. On other occasions, Balzac would write to his family to say that, for reasons which he was unable to give in his letters, the question of the marriage was *postponed indefinitely*; and once he made the resolution that he would not leave Wierzchownia till the affair was settled in one way or another. In a crisis of his terrible malady he wrote: "Whatever happens, I shall come back in August. One must die at one's post. . . . How can I offer a life as broken as mine! I must make my situation clear to the incomparable friend who for sixteen years has shone on my life like a beneficent star."[*]

[*] "Correspondance," vol. ii. p. 401.

The relations between Balzac and Madame Hanska at this time are mysterious. He shows his usual caution in his letters to his family, and the reader is conscious that much was passing at Wierzchownia, on which

Balzac is absolutely silent, and that many events that he *does* record are carefully arranged with the intention of conveying certain impressions to his hearers. One of his motives is clear. He was nervously afraid that gossip about his secret engagement, and possibly approaching marriage, should be spread abroad prematurely; and that the report might either frighten Madame Hanska into dismissing him altogether, or might reach the ears of her relations, and cause them to remonstrate with her anew on the folly of her proceedings.

Other discrepancies are puzzling. All through 1849 Balzac, as we have seen, was very ill. He was suffering from aneurism of the heart, a complaint which the two doctors Knothe told him they could cure. With perfect faith in their powers, Balzac wrote to his sister expressing regret that, owing to the ignorance of the French doctors Soulie had been allowed to die of this malady, when he might have been saved if Dr. Knothe's treatment had been followed. The younger doctor, however, soon gave up Balzac's case as hopeless; but the father, who was very intimate with the Wierzchownia family, always expressed himself confidently about his patient's ultimate recovery; and Balzac wrote: "What gratitude I owe to this doctor! He loves violins: when once I am at Paris I must find a Stradivarius to present to him."[*]

[*] "Correspondance," vol. ii. p. 404.

Dr. Knothe's principal prescription was pure lemon juice. This was to be taken twice a day, to purify and quicken the circulation of the blood in the veins, and to re-establish the equilibrium between it and the arterial blood. Either as a consequence of this treatment, or in the natural course of the illness, a terrible crisis took place in June, 1849, during which Balzac's sufferings were intense; and for twenty-five hours the doctor never left him. After this he was better for a time, and though his eyesight had become so weak that he was unable to read at night, he could walk, go upstairs, and lie flat in bed. In October he was seized with what he called Moldavian fever, a disease which came, he said, from the swamps of the Danube, and ravaged the Odessa district and the steppes; and again he became dangerously ill. In January, 1850, the fever was followed by a terrible cold in his lungs, and he was obliged to remain for ten days in bed. However, he was cheered by the society of Madame Hanska and Madame Georges Mniszech, who showed "adorable goodness" in keeping him company during his imprisonment.

After hearing all this, it is startling to read in a letter from Madame Honore de Balzac to her daughter written from Frankfort on May 16th, 1850,[*] that it is awkward that she should know nothing of the regimen to which Balzac has been subjected by Dr. Knothe; because when they arrive in Paris, his own doctor is certain to ask for particulars! The most indifferent hostess could not fail, one would think, to interest herself sufficiently about the welfare of the solitary and expatriated guest under her roof, to consult with the doctor about him when he was dangerously ill. More especially would she feel responsibility, when it was owing to her own action that the patient was cut off from all other advice, except that of a medical man who was her peculiar *protege*. He would thus be completely in her charge; and she would naturally be nervously anxious, for her own comfort and satisfaction, to acquaint herself with the course of the malady, and with the treatment used to subdue it. If we add to these considerations the fact that the sufferer was not a mere acquaintance, was not even only a great friend; but was the man who loved her, the man whose wife she had promised to become, Madame Hanska's ignorance appears totally inexplicable.

[*] Unpublished letter in the possession of the Vicomte de Spoelberch de Lovenjoul.

We must remember, however, that we only have *Balzac's* account of his illness, and of his interviews with the doctor; and that the malady being heart disease, it is possible that Dr. Knothe considered it his duty to deceive his patient—possible therefore that Madame Hanska knew before her marriage that Balzac was a dying man, and that the doctor's prescriptions were useless.

Owing to the burning of her letters, we have only Balzac's enthusiastic and lover-like descriptions to guide our idea of Madame Hanska; and she remains to some extent a shadowy figure, difficult to realise. Several characteristics, however, stand out clearly: among them her power of hiding her thoughts and feelings from those to whom she was most deeply attached; also an occasional self-control, which seems strangely at variance with her naturally passionate and uncontrolled nature. She was extremely proud; and the wish, while pleasing herself, to do nothing which would lower her in the eyes of the world, exercised a powerful influence over her actions. Intellectually brilliant, a clever woman of business, and mentally active; she was yet on some occasions curiously inert, and carried the state of mind embodied in the words "live and let live," to dangerous lengths. She must have possessed great determination, as even Balzac's adoration, and his undoubted powers of fascination, could not move her from the vacillations which, designedly or no, kept *him* enchained at her feet while *she* remained free.

Among much however, in her character that we cannot admire, she possessed one virtue in perfection—that of maternal love. The bond of affection between the mother and her daughter Anna was strong and enduring, and Madame Hanska would willingly have sacrificed everything for her beloved child's happiness. This was the true, engrossing love of her life; her affection for Balzac not having remained in its first freshness, as his love for her had done. On the contrary, it was at this time slightly withered, and had been partially stifled by prudential considerations, so that it was difficult to discover among the varied and tangled growths which surrounded it.

It is an interesting problem whether Balzac, in spite of his brave words, realised that Madame Hanska no longer cared for him. When he wrote that he was sure that none of these deferments proceeded from want of love, did he pen these words with a wistful attempt to prove to himself that the fact was as he stated? After eighteen months in the same house with Madame Hanska, could he *really* believe that only material difficulties kept her apart from him? Or did he at last understand: and though stricken to death, cling still, for the sake of his pride and his lost illusions, to what had been for so long his one object in life? We do not know.

The only thing of which we are certain is, that if the fact of Madame Hanska's indifference *had* slowly and painfully dawned upon Balzac, he would never have told, and would have used words to hide his knowledge.

On the other hand, there is sometimes a ring of truth about his words, which seem to prove that he had not yet tasted the full bitterness of the tragedy of his life. On November 29th, 1849, he wrote to Madame Surville[*]: "It is the recompense of your life to possess two such children; you must not be unjust to fate; you ought to be willing to accept many misfortunes. The case is the same with me and Madame Hanska. The gift of her affection accounts to me for all my troubles, my worries, and my terrible labours. I have been paying in advance for the price of this treasure: as Napoleon says, everything is paid for here, nothing is stolen. I seem, indeed, to have paid very little. Twenty-five years of work and struggle are nothing compared to a love so splendid, so radiant, so complete. I have been fourteen months in a desert, for it *is* a desert; and it seems to me that they have passed like a dream, without an hour's weariness, without a single dispute; and that after five years to travel together, and sixteen years of intimate acquaintance, our only troubles have been caused by the state of our health and by business matters."

[*] "Correspondance," vol. ii. p. 426.

When he wrote these words, Balzac must have at last felt tolerably confident about a happy solution to his troubles. However, in a later letter to his mother, he says that the Wierzchownia party are going to Kiev for the great Fair, that he will avail himself of this occasion for the renewal of his passport, and that he will not know till he arrives there, whether the great event will at last take place. In any case, he will start for France directly after the party return to Wierzchownia in the beginning of February; and as caution is still highly important, his mother must judge from his directions about the Rue Fortunee, whether he is coming back alone, or is bringing his bride with him. She is, in any case, not to be sparing about fires in the library and the picture gallery; and can write to him at Berlin, and at Frankfort, on his way home.

The great Fair at Kiev, which was called the "Foire des Contrats," was a notable occasion for gaiety; and extensive preparations were made beforehand for the enjoyment of a thoroughly festive time. A house was hired by Madame Hanska and the Mniszechs, and furniture, carriages, and servants, were despatched in advance. The weather, however, was an important consideration; and on this occasion, owing to the inclemency of the season, the roads were unfortunately impassable, so that the pleasure trip had to be deferred from the middle till the end of February. This was no doubt a sad disappointment to the Countess Anna, who thereby missed much enjoyment, and the delay must have caused intense irritation to the impatient Balzac, but Madame Hanska's feelings on the subject remain, as usual, enigmatical.

When the Wierzchownia party at last arrived at Kiev, Madame Georges Mniszech found plenty of gaiety awaiting her, and enjoyed herself immensely, going out to balls in costumes of regal magnificence. Her partners were often very rough, and on one occasion Balzac relates that a handkerchief belonging to the young Countess, which had cost more than 500 francs, was torn to pieces in a figure of the mazurka, in which men contend for the dancer's handkerchief. However, "La mere adorable" at once repaired the deficiency in her daughter's trousseau by presenting her with one of the best of her own, "twice as nice, with only linen enough to blow one's nose on, all the rest being English point lace."

Balzac was unable to be present at any of these festivities, as the journey to Kiev had caused him acute suffering; and two days after his arrival, while he was paying his State visits to the authorities,[*] he caught the most violent cold he had ever had, and spent the time of his stay at Kiev in his bedroom, where his only pleasure was to see the Countess Anna before she started for her parties, and to admire her beautiful clothes. He ascribes his malady to "a terrible and deleterious blast of wind called the 'chasse-neige,' which travels by the course of the Dnieper, and perhaps comes from the shores of the Black Sea," and which managed to penetrate to him, though he was wrapped up with furs so that no spot seemed left for the outside air to reach. He was now very ill, and the slightest agitation, even a sentence spoken rather loudly in his presence, would bring on a terrible fit of suffocation. He still hoped to return to Paris before long, and clung to the idea that his wife would accompany him; but he said it would be impossible to travel without a servant, as he was unable to carry a parcel or to move quickly. As he remarks, "Tout cela n'est pas gai!"

[*] "Correspondance," vol. ii. p. 436.

However, his expedition and its attendant suffering were not useless,[*] as the "four or five successive illnesses and the sufferings from the climate, which I have laughed at for her sake, have touched that noble soul; so that she is, as a sensible woman, more influenced by them, than afraid of the few little debts which remain to be paid, and I see that everything will go well." On March 11th, 1850, he writes from Berditchef that "everything is now arranged for the affair his mother knows of," but that the greatest discretion is still necessary. Madame de Balzac is given minute directions about the flowers which are to decorate the house in the Rue Fortunee, as a surprise to Madame Honore; and as we read, we can imagine Balzac's pride and delight when he wrote the name. His ailments and sufferings are forgotten, and the letter sounds as though written by an enthusiastic boy. He will send from Frankfort to let Madame de Balzac know the exact day that he and his bride will reach Paris; and in order that the mystery may be preserved, will merely say, "Do not forget on such a day to have the garden arranged,"[+] and his mother will understand what he means. The whole house is evidently photographed in his mind like the houses in his novels. He knows the exact position of each vase: of the big jardiniere in the first room, the one in the Japanese drawing-room, the two in the domed boudoir, and the two tiny ones in the grey apartment. They are all to be filled with flowers; but the marquetry jardiniere in the green drawing-room, evidently the future Madame Honore's special abode, is to be filled with "belles, belles fleurs!"

[*] "Correspondance," vol. ii. p. 438.

[+] "Correspondance," vol. ii. p. 444.

The wedding took place at seven o'clock on the morning of March 14th, 1850, at the church of Saint Barbe at Berditchef. In the unavoidable absence of the Bishop of Jitomir, the ceremony was performed by the Abbe Comte Czarouski, whom Balzac calls a holy and virtuous priest, and likens to Abbe Hinaux, the Duchesse d'Angouleme's confessor.

The Countess Anna accompanied her mother, and was in the highest spirits; and the witnesses were the Comte Georges Mniszech, the Comte Gustave Olizar brother-in-law to the Abbe Comte Czarouski, and the cure of the parish of Berditchef. Madame Honore de Balzac had given her capital to her children, but received in exchange a large income, a fact which she wisely concealed because of Balzac's creditors; and Balzac speaks with admiration of her noble generosity and disinterestedness, in this denuding herself of her fortune.

The newly-married couple travelled back to Wierzchownia, arriving, quite tired out, at half-past ten at night; and the next morning, as soon as he woke, Balzac wrote to inform his mother of the great event. He explained, with a well-adjusted prevision of future discord, if the elder Madame de Balzac's dignity were not sufficiently considered, that his wife had intended writing herself to offer her respects, but that her hands were so swollen with rheumatic gout that she could not hold a pen. He further informed his family, who had hitherto been kept in ignorance of the fact, that from the same cause she was often unable to walk. However, this did not depress him, as he remarked with his usual cheerfulness, that she would certainly be cured in Paris, where she would be able to take exercise and would follow a prescribed treatment. On the same day he penned a delighted letter to his sister, containing the exultant words: "For twenty-four hours, therefore, there has now existed a Madame Eve de Balzac, *nee* Rzewuska, *or* a Madame Honore de Balzac, *or* a Madame de Balzac the younger." He could hardly believe in his own good fortune, and the joyful letter finishes with the words, "Ton frere Honore, au comble du bonheur!"

Two days later, Balzac wrote to Madame Carraud a letter in which he said: "Three days ago I married the only woman I have ever loved, whom I love more than ever, and whom I shall love till death. This union is, I think, the recompense which God has had in reserve for me after so much adversity, so many years of work, so much gone through and overcome. I did not have a happy youth or happy springtide; I shall have the most brilliant of summers and the sweetest of autumns." In his newly-found happiness he did not forget that his old friend was now in straitened circumstances, but begged her from himself and Madame Honore to consider their house as her own: "Therefore, whenever you wish to come to Paris you will come to us, without even giving us notice. You will come to us in the Rue Fortunee as if to your own home, just as I used to go to Frapesle. This is my right. I must remind you of what you said to me one day at Angouleme, when, having broken down after writing 'Louis Lambert,' I was afraid of madness, and talked of the way in which people afflicted in this manner were neglected. On that occasion you said, 'If you were to become mad I should take care of you!' I have never forgotten those words, or your look and expression. I am just the same now as I was in July, 1832. It is because of those words that I claim you to-day, for I am nearly mad with happiness."[*]

[*] "Correspondance," vol. ii. p. 448.

In another part of the letter he tells her: "Ah! I never forget your maternal love, your divine sympathy with suffering. Therefore, thinking of all you are worth, and of the way in which you are struggling with trouble, I, who have so often waged war with that rough adversary, tell you that, knowing your unhappiness, I am ashamed of *my* happiness; but we are both too great for these littlenesses. We can say to each other that happiness and unhappiness are only conditions in which great hearts live intensely, that as much strength of mind is required in one position as in the other, and that misfortune with true friends is perhaps more endurable than happiness surrounded by envy."

Balzac was not, after all, destined to start on his journey homeward as quickly as he had intended. His health was terribly bad, his eyes had become so weak that he could neither read nor write, and the chronic heart and lung malady was gaining ground so rapidly, that his breathing was affected if he made the slightest movement. It was absolutely necessary that he should rest for a time at Wierzchownia before attempting any further exertion. Another delay was caused by the young Countess being attacked by measles. Her devoted mother, who in her crippled state could not attempt any active nursing, sat by her daughter's bedside all day, and refused to leave Wierzchownia till her anxiety about her darling's health should be over.

It was, therefore, not till the end of April that M. and Madame Honore de Balzac started for what proved to be a terrible journey. They did not arrive in Dresden till about May 10th, having taken three weeks to go to a distance which ought naturally to have been accomplished in five or six days. The roads were in a fearful condition, and their lives were in danger not once, but a hundred times a day. Sometimes fifteen or sixteen men were required to hoist the carriage out of the mud-holes into which it had fallen. It is a wonder that Balzac survived the torture of the journey, and it must have been very trying to the rheumatic Madame Honore. When at last they arrived at Dresden they were both utterly exhausted, while Balzac was extremely ill, and felt ten years older than when he started. His sight was so bad that he could not see the letters that he was tracing on the paper, and was obliged to apologise to his correspondents for his extraordinary hieroglyphics, while he told Madame Surville that the swollen condition of his wife's hands still rendered it impossible for her to write.

However, Madame Honore was well enough to amuse herself by visits to the jewellers' shops, where she bought a magnificent pearl necklace, a purchase of which Balzac evidently approved, as he remarked that it was so beautiful that it would make a saint mad! On his part, he was greeted on his arrival by a new vexation; as letters from Paris told him of "Vautrin" being put on the stage without his permission, and, as we have seen, he wrote with much indignation, to put a stop to this infringement of his rights.

An interesting letter already referred to, which is now in the possession of the Vicomte de Spoelberch de Lovenjoul, is dated from Frankfort, the travellers' next stopping-place. It is written to the Countess Anna, and was begun by Balzac, and finished by his wife. About Balzac's part of the letter there is not much to remark, except that he was evidently very fond of his step-daughter, that he told her how ill he was, and that the handwriting is the scrawl of a man who could not see. His high spirits indeed have disappeared, but this change of tone is easily accounted for by the state of his health. It is Madame Honore's part of the letter which strikes the reader as curiously inadequate. It is dated May 16th, only five days after Balzac's letter from Dresden informing his family of his wife's inability to hold a pen, and is perfectly written; so that her rheumatic gout must have abated suddenly. She begins her letter by commenting placidly on the sadness of seeing the sufferings of our "poor dear friend," says she tries in vain to cheer him, and contrasts regretfully the difference between her feelings during this journey, and her happiness when she last visited the same places, with her darling child at her side. The principal subject in her present rather wearying life, is the wonderful pearl necklace, which she takes out of its case conscientiously every day, that the air may preserve the whiteness of the pearls. She states, indeed, that she does not care much about it, and has only bought it to please her husband; but it seems to have pressed the unfortunate husband rather into the background, and to have become the chief centre of its owner's thoughts and solicitude.

The chilling unsatisfactory impression the letter leaves on the reader, however, is not conveyed so much by what is said by Balzac's newly-married wife, as by what she leaves unsaid. It must be remembered that the Countess Eve possessed the power of expressing herself with the utmost warmth, and with even exaggerated emphasis, when she saw fit occasion for the display of feeling. We must also keep the fact in mind, that in writing to the daughter who was her intimate friend, she would naturally give some indications of her real self; and though it might be impossible for one of her curiously secretive temperament to lift the veil altogether, and to open her heart without reserve, she would be likely in some way to enable the reader to realise her mental attitude. Therefore it is disconcerting and disquieting to discover that the one noticeable characteristic of the letter, is utter want of feeling. No anxiety is expressed about the growing illness of the sick man, not a word tells of fears so terrible that she hardly dares breathe them, about the ultimate result of his malady; on the contrary, everything is taken as a matter of course, and as though the writer had expected it beforehand.

There is not even a recognition of Balzac as her husband; he is merely "our poor dear friend," a person for whom she feels vague pity, and in whom Anna's degree of interest is likely to be the same as her own.

Balzac was only married for about five months, and very little is known of his life during that time. It is certain, however, that his marriage did not bring him the happiness which he had expected, and Madame Hanska's letter from Frankfort helps to explain the reason of the tragedy. Perhaps he had raised his hopes too high for fulfilment to be a possibility in this world of compromise, and very likely his sufferings had made him irritable and exacting. Nevertheless, so quick a wearing out of the faithful and passionate love which had lasted for sixteen years, and so sudden a killing of the joy which had permeated the man's whole being when he had at last attained his goal, seems a hard task for a woman to accomplish; and can only be explained by her employment of the formless yet resistless force of pure indifference.

Balzac's awakening, the knowledge that the absolute perfection he had dreamed of was only an ideal created by his own fancy, must have been inexpressibly bitter. Utter moral collapse and vertigo were his portion, and chaos thundered in his ears, during his sudden descent from the heights clothed with brilliant sunshine, to the puzzling depths, where he groped in darkness and sought in vain for firm footing. "Our poor dear friend" seems, for the moment, to have merited even more sympathy than the measure accorded to him by his wife, in her intervals of leisure after caring for her pearl necklace.

Balzac's mother had, as we have already seen, taken up her abode with Madame Surville, long before the often-deferred appearance in Paris of her son and daughter-in-law; but Honore had given directions, that at any rate she was to leave the Rue Fortunee before he and his bride arrived. It would, he said, compromise her dignity to help with the unpacking, and Madame Honore should visit her mother-in-law next day to pay her respects. Balzac was anxious that the first meeting should take place at Laure's house rather than at Madame de Balzac's lodging at Suresnes, as it was now impossible for him to mount any steps, and there were fewer stairs at No. 47, Rue des Martyrs than at his mother's abode.[*] His health, he wrote, was so deplorable that he would not remain for long in Paris, but would go with his wife to Biarritz to take the waters.

[*] "Correspondance," vol. ii. p. 456.

The travellers did not after all arrive in Paris till near the end of May. This is proved by a letter from Madame de Balzac[*] to a friend, written on the 20th of that month, in which she says that they are now expected every day, but that their progress is a slow one, owing to her son's illness and the heavy condition of the roads. She adds that she has now been in bed for three months, so Laure must evidently have acted as her deputy, in the task of superintending Francois' preparations in the Rue Fortunee. No doubt Francois worked strenuously, as he, like all Balzac's servants, was devoted to his master, though on this occasion he unwittingly provided him with a ghastly home-coming.

[*] "Une Page perdue de Honore de Balzac," by the Vicomte de Spoelberch de Lovenjoul.

The travellers did not arrive at the Rue Fortunee till late at night.[*] The house was brilliantly lit, and through the windows they could see the flowers with which the rooms were decorated; but in vain they rang at the courtyard gate—no one appeared to let them in. It was a miserable arrival, and utterly inexplicable, as Balzac had planned the arrangements most carefully beforehand, going minutely into commissariat details, that his bride might find everything absolutely comfortable on her arrival in her new home. It was impossible to force an entrance, so M. and Madame Honore de Balzac, utterly worn out by the fatigues of the journey, and longing for rest, were obliged to sit in the carriage and spend the time in agitation and vain conjecture, while a messenger was despatched for a locksmith. When the door was at last opened, a terrible solution to the problem presented itself. The excitement and strain of the preparations, and of the hourly expectation of the travellers, had completely upset the mental balance of the unfortunate Francois, and he had gone suddenly mad! It was a sinister omen, a wretched commencement to Balzac's home life; and he, always superstitious, was no doubt doubly so in his invalided and suffering condition. Francois Munch was sent to a lunatic asylum, where he was cared for at his master's expense.

[*] "Un Roman d'Amour," by the Vicomte de Spoelberch de Lovenjoul.

CHAPTER XVII

1850 AND AFTER

When Balzac's friends came to visit him in the Rue Fortunee, they were much shocked by the change in his appearance. His breathing was short, his speech jerky, and his sight so bad that he was unable to distinguish objects clearly. Nevertheless, as Gautier says,[*] every one felt such intense confidence in his wonderful constitution that it seemed impossible to think of a probably fatal result to his malady. Balzac himself, optimistic as ever, clung persistently to his hope of speedy recovery. His fame was now at its zenith, the series entitled "Les Parents Pauvres" had awakened the utmost enthusiasm; and the *elite* of the Parisian world were eager to flock to the Rue Fortunee to stare at the curiosities collected there, and to make the acquaintance of Balzac's rich and distinguished Russian wife.

[*] "Portraits Contemporains: Honore de Balzac," by Theophile Gautier.

However, in his native country, Balzac was destined never to receive a full guerdon of adulation and admiration; for though he was visited by a few friends, the doctors insisted on keeping him otherwise in the strictest retirement.

Theophile Gautier relates that he went to the Rue Fortunee to say good-bye to his friend before starting for Italy, and, though disappointed not to see him, was relieved about his health when told that he was out driving. However, a little later, a letter was brought to Gautier which had been dictated by Balzac to his wife, in which he explained that he had only gone to the Customhouse to get out some luggage, and had done this against the express orders of his doctors. However, he spoke cheerfully of his health, saying that he was feeling better, and that the next day the doctors intended to attack the chronic malady from which he was suffering. For two months at least he expected to be kept like a mummy, and not to be allowed to speak or to move; but there were great hopes of his ultimate recovery. If Gautier came again, he hoped for a letter beforehand naming the day and hour, that he might certainly be at home; as in the solitude to which he was doomed by the doctors, his friend's affection seemed to him more precious than ever. All this was written in Madame de Balzac's handwriting, and under it Balzac had scrawled: "I can neither read nor write!"[*] Gautier left for Italy soon after this, and he never saw his friend again. He read the news of Balzac's death in a newspaper when he was at Venice, taking an ice at the Cafe Florian, in the Piazza of St. Mark; and so terrible was the shock, that he nearly fell from his seat. He tells us that he felt for the moment unchristian indignation and revolt, when he thought of the octogenarian idiots he had seen that morning at the asylum on the island of San Servolo, and then of Balzac cut off in his prime; but he checked himself, for he remembered that all souls are equal in the sight of God.

[*] "Portraits Contemporains: Honore de Balzac," by Theophile Gautier.

Victor Hugo also visited the invalid, and says that even a month before his death he was perfectly confident about his recovery, and was gay and full of laughter, discussing politics, stating his own legitimist views with decision, and accusing his visitor of being a demagogue. He said: "I have M. de Beaujon's house without the garden, but I am owner of the gallery leading to the little church at the corner of the street. A door on my staircase leads into the church. One turn of the key, and I am at Mass. I care more for the gallery than for the garden."[*]

[*] "Choses Vues," by Victor Hugo.

When Victor Hugo got up to go, Balzac accompanied him with difficulty to this staircase, to point out the precious door; and called to his wife, "Mind you show Hugo all my pictures." Though Balzac does not appear to have been very intimate with the great romantic poet in former years, he seems to have found special pleasure in his society at this time. Hugo was at the seaside when Balzac next sent for him. He hurried back,[*] however, at the urgent summons, and found the dying man stretched on a sofa covered with red and gold brocade. Balzac tried to rise, but could not; his face was purple, and his eyes alone had life in them. Now that happiness in his married life had failed him, his mind had reverted to the yet unfinished "Comedie Humaine"; and he talked long and sadly of projected herculean labours, and of the fate of his still unpublished works. "Although my wife has more brains than I, who will support her in her solitude, she whom I have accustomed to so much love?" "Certainly," Victor Hugo remarks drily, "she was crying a great deal."

[*] See letter written by Madame Hamelin to the Countess Kisselef quoted in "Histoire des Oeuvres de Balzac," by the Vicomte de Spoelberch de Lovenjoul, p. 406.

Nevertheless, though Balzac did at last realise his dangerous state, he had no idea that his end was approaching so near, and he still hoped to be able to add a few more stones to the edifice of the "Comedie Humaine," that great work, which was now again the principal object of his life, the one bright vision in a world of disappointment. In August, however, an agonising suspicion began for the first time to visit him momentarily, a terrible fear to assail him. What if there were not time after all? What if the creations which floated through his mind while he lay suffering and helpless, were never destined to be put into shape? What if his opportunity for work on earth were really over? It was a horrible idea; a fancy, he told himself, born only of weakness. Destiny *must* intend him to finish his appointed task. Robbed of everything else he had longed for, that one consolation surely remained. He would ask the doctor, would be content with no vague and soothing generalities, but would insist on knowing the exact truth. It could not—ah, it could not be as black as the nightmares of his imagination!

He approached the subject cautiously on the doctor's next visit.[*] Perhaps, he said, he had after all never realised sufficiently the acuteness of his malady. He certainly felt terribly ill, and knew that he was losing ground; while, in spite of all his efforts, he was unable to eat anything. His duty required that he should bequeath a certain legacy to the public, and he had calculated carefully, and had discovered that he would be able in six months to accomplish his task. Could the doctor promise him that length of time? There was no answer to this searching question, but a shake of the head from the pitying doctor. "Ah," cried Balzac sorrowfully, "I see quite well that you will not allow me six months. . . . Well, at any rate, you will at least give me six weeks? . . . Six weeks with fever is an eternity. Hours are like days . . . and then the nights are not lost." Again the doctor shook his head, and Balzac once more lowered his claims for a vestige of life. "I have courage to submit," he said proudly; "but six days . . . you will certainly give me that? I shall then be able to write down hasty plans that my friends may be able to finish, shall tear up bad pages and improve good ones, and shall glance rapidly through the fifty volumes I have already written. Human will can do miracles." Balzac pleaded pathetically, almost as though he thought his interlocutor could grant the boon of longer life if he willed to do so. He had aged ten years since the beginning of the interview, and he had now no voice left to speak, and the doctor hardly any voice for answering. The latter managed, however, to tell his patient that everything must be done to-day, because in all probability to-morrow would not exist for him; and Balzac cried with horror, "I have then only six hours!" fell back on his pillows, and spoke no more.

[*] The following account of Balzac's interview with his doctor is taken from an article written by Arsene Houssaye in the *Figaro* of August 20th, 1883. It is right to add that the Vicomte de Spoelberch de Lovenjoul, the great authority on Balzac, throws grave doubts on the accuracy of the story.

He died the next day, and Victor Hugo gives us one more glimpse of him.[*] The poet was told by his wife, who had visited Madame de Balzac during the day, that Balzac's last hour had come; and directly after dinner he took a cab and drove rapidly to the Rue Fortunee. "I rang. It was moonlight, occasionally veiled by clouds. The street was deserted. No one came. I rang a second time. The door was opened. A servant appeared with a candle. 'What does Monsieur want?' she said. She was crying.

[*] "Choses Vues, 1850: Mort de Balzac," by Victor Hugo.

"I gave my name. I was shown into the room on the ground floor. On a pedestal opposite the fireplace was the colossal bust of Balzac by David. In the middle of the salon, on a handsome oval table, which had for legs six gilded statuettes of great beauty, a wax candle was burning. Another woman came in crying, and said: 'He is dying. Madame has gone to her own rooms. The doctors gave him up yesterday.' After going into medical details, the woman continued: 'The night was bad. This morning at nine o'clock Monsieur spoke no more. Madame sent for a priest. The priest came, and administered extreme unction. Monsieur made a sign to show that he understood. An hour afterwards he pressed the hand of his sister, Madame Surville. Since eleven o'clock the death rattle has been in his throat, and he can see nothing. He will not last out the night. If you wish it, Monsieur, I will call M. Surville, who has not yet gone to bed.'

"The woman left me. I waited several minutes. The candle hardly lighted up the splendid furniture of the salon, and the magnificent paintings by Porbus and Holbein which were hanging on the walls. The marble bust showed faintly in the obscurity, like the spectre of a dying man. A corpse-like odour filled the house.

"M. Surville came in, and confirmed all that the servant had told me. I asked to see M. de Balzac.

"We crossed a corridor, went up a staircase covered with a red carpet and crowded with artistic objects—vases, statues, pictures, and stands with enamels on them. Then we came to another passage, and I saw an open door. I heard the sound of difficult, rattling breathing. I entered Balzac's room.

"The bedstead was in the centre of the room. It was of mahogany, and across the foot and at the head were beams provided with straps for moving the sick man. M. de Balzac was in this bed, his head resting on a heap of pillows, to which the red damask sofa cushions had been added. His face was purple, almost black, and was inclined to the right. He was unshaved, his grey hair was cut short, and his eyes open and fixed. I saw his profile, and it was like that of the Emperor Napoleon.

"An old woman, the nurse, and a servant, stood beside the bed. A candle was burning on a table behind the head of the bed, another on a chest of drawers near the door. A silver vase was on the stand near the bed. The women and man were silent with a kind of terror, as they listened to the rattling breathing of the dying man.

"The candle at the head of the bed lit up brilliantly the portrait of a young man, fresh-coloured and smiling, which was hanging near the fireplace. . . .

"I lifted the coverlet and took Balzac's hand. It was covered with perspiration. I pressed it. He did not respond to the pressure. . . .

"I went downstairs again, carrying in my mind the memory of that livid face, and, crossing the drawing-room, I looked again at the bust — immovable, impassive, proud, and smiling faintly, and I compared death with immortality."

Balzac died that night, Sunday, August 17th, 1850, at half-past eleven, at the age of fifty-one.

The dying man's almost complete isolation is strange, and the servant's news that M. Surville had not *yet* gone to bed has a callous ring about it. Perhaps, however, the doctors had told Madame de Balzac and Madame Surville that Balzac was unconscious, and they had therefore withdrawn, utterly exhausted by the fatigues of the night before. In any case, it seems sad, though possibly of no moment to the dying man, that several of his nearest relations should have deserted him before the breath had left his body. Our respect for the elder Madame de Balzac is decidedly raised, because, though there had occasionally been disagreements between her and her son, the true mother feeling asserted itself at the last, and she alone watched with the paid attendants till the end came.

However, some one was busy about the arrangements, as Balzac's portrait was taken by Giraud directly after his death, and a cast was made of his beautifully-shaped hand. His body was taken into the Beaujon Chapel before burial, so that he passed for the last time, as Victor Hugo remarks, through that door, the key of which was more precious to him than all the beautiful gardens which had belonged to the old Farmer-General.

The funeral service was held on Wednesday, August 20th, at the Church of Sainte Philippe du Roule. The rain was descending in torrents, but the procession, followed by a large crowd, walked the whole way across Paris to the Cemetery of Pere-la-Chaise, where the interment took place. The pall-bearers were Victor Hugo, Alexandre Dumas, Monsieur Baroche, and Sainte-Beuve. At the grave Victor Hugo spoke, finishing with the words: "No, it is not the Unknown to him. I have said this before, and I shall never tire of repeating it: it is not darkness to him, it is Light! It is not the end, but the beginning; not nothingness, but eternity! Is not this the truth, I ask you who listen to me? Such coffins proclaim immortality. In the presence of certain illustrious dead, we understand the divine destiny of that intellect which has traversed earth to suffer and to be purified. Do we not say to ourselves here, to-day, that it is impossible for a great genius in this life to be other than a great spirit after death?"[*]

[*] "Funerailles de Balzac," in "Actes et Paroles," by Victor Hugo.

The Cemetery of Pere-la-Chaise had been one of Balzac's favourite haunts in the old half-starved days of the Rue Lesdiguieres. "Here I am back from Pere-la-Chaise," he wrote to his sister in 1820,[*] "and I have brought with me some good big inspiring reflections. Decidedly, the only fine epitaphs are these: La Fontaine, Messena, Moliere, a single name, which tells all and makes one dream." Probably Madame Surville remembered these words and repeated them to Madame Honore de Balzac, for the monument erected to Balzac is a broken column with his name inscribed on it.

[*] "Correspondance," vol. i. p. 24.

The fortunes of the inhabitants of the Rue Fortunee were not happy after Balzac's death. Madame Honore de Balzac's contemporaries considered that she as not really as overwhelmed with sorrow at her husband's death as she appeared to be, and that when she wrote heartbroken letters, she slightly exaggerated the real state of her feelings; but she assumed gallantly the burdens laid upon her by the state of pecuniary embarrassment in which her husband died. If Balzac had lived longer and had been able to work steadily, there is little doubt that he would in a few years have become a free man, as the Vicomte de Spoelberch de Lovenjoul tells us[*] that in the years between 1841 and 1847, after which date his productions became very rare, he had enormously diminished the sum he owed.

[*] "La Genese d'un Roman de Balzac," by the Vicomte de Spoelberch de Lovenjoul.

Under Balzac's will his widow might have refused to acknowledge any liability for his debts, but she set to work bravely, with the aid of MM. Dutacq and Fessart, to make as much money as she could out of Balzac's published works, and to bring before the public those that were still unpublished. In this way, "Mercadet le Faiseur" was acted a year after Balzac's death, and "Les Petits Bourgeois" and "Le Depute d'Arcis" were published, the latter being finished, according to Balzac's wish, by Charles Rabou. "Les Paysans," which was to have filled eight volumes, and of which, as we have already seen, only a few chapters were written, presented great difficulty; but at last Madame de Balzac, aided by Champfleury and by Charles Rabou, managed to give some consistency to the fragment, and it appeared in the *Revue de Paris* in April, May and June, 1855. Unfortunately, however, no information was given as to the unfinished state in which it had been left by Balzac, and therefore no explanation was offered of the insufficiency of the *denouement*, and the inadequacy of the last chapters. Madame de Balzac worked hard, and long before her death in April, 1882, the whole of Balzac's debts were paid off.

This was most creditable to her; but side by side with her admirable conduct in this respect, she seems to have either actively abetted, or at any rate acquiesced in mad extravagance on the part of Madame Georges Mniszech, who with her husband, had come to live in the Rue Fortunee after Balzac's death. Perhaps Madame de Balzac was too busy with her literary and business arrangements, to pay attention to what was happening, or possibly maternal devotion prevented her from denying her beloved daughter anything she craved for. At all events the results of her supineness were lamentable, especially as M. Georges Mniszech was not capable of exercising any restraint on his wife; he being for some years before his death in 1881, in the most delicate state of health, both mental and physical.

Madame Georges Mniszech—after years of the wild Russian steppes, suddenly plunged into the fascinations of shopping in Paris, and left to her own devices—seems to have shown senseless folly in her expenditure. Additions were made to the house in the Rue Fortunee, though Balzac's rooms were left untouched; and the Chateau de Beauregard, at Villeneuve-Saint-Georges, was bought as a country residence. Madame de Balzac and her daughter were, however, rich, and could quite afford to live comfortably, and even luxuriously. Their ruin seems to have been brought about by reckless expenditure on things which were of absolutely no use, and were only bought for the amusement of buying. Several sales of pictures took place, and on February 9th, 1882,[*] the Chateau de Beauregard and its contents were sold by order of the President of the Civil Tribunal of Corbeil.

[*] "Life of Balzac," by Frederick Wedmore.

Madame de Balzac died in April of the same year; and the very day of her funeral, Madame Georges Mniszech's creditors pushed her and her maid into the street, and rifled the house in the Rue Fortunee. The booty was transported to the auction-room known as l'Hotel Drouot, and there a sale was held by order of justice of Balzac's library, his Buhl cabinets, and some of his MSS., including that of "Eugenie Grandet," which had been given to Madame Hanska on December 24th, 1833. During the shameless pillage of the house, the vultures who ransacked it found evidence of the most reckless, the most imbecile extravagance, proof positive that the wisdom, prudence, even the principles of poor Balzac's paragon the Countess Anna, had been routed by the glitter and glamour of the holiday city. One room was filled with boxes containing hats, and in another, piles of costly silks were heaped, untouched since their arrival from the fashionable haberdasher or silk mercer.[*] Balzac's treasures, the curiosities he had amassed with so much trouble, the pictures of which he had been so proud, were ruthlessly seized; while precious manuscripts and letters, which would perhaps have brought in a hundred thousand francs if they had been put up for sale, were thrown out of the window by the exasperated throng.

[*] "Journal des Goncourts," vol. viii. P. 48.

The Vicomte de Spoelberch de Lovenjoul rescued a page of the first of Balzac's letters to Madame Hanska which has been found up to this time, from a cobbler whose stall was opposite the house. The cobbler, when once started on the quest by the Vicomte, discovered many other letters, sketches, and unfinished novels, which had been picked up by the neighbouring shopkeepers, and were only saved in the nick of time from being used to wrap up pounds of butter, or to make bags for other household commodities. It was an exciting chase, requiring patience and ingenuity; and Balzac's former cook held out for years, before she would consent to sell a packet of letters which the Vicomte coveted specially. Sometimes incidentally there were delightful surprises, and occasionally real joys; as on the occasion when the searcher found at a distant grocer's shop, the middle of the letter, of which the first page had been saved from destruction at the hands of the cobbler.

The bitter dislike Balzac had evoked in the literary world, and his occasional obscurity and clumsy style, have militated very strongly against his popularity in his native land, where perfection in the manipulation of words is of supreme importance in a writer. While in France, however, Balzac's undoubted faults have partially blinded his countrymen to his consummate merits as a writer, and they have been strangely slow in acknowledging the debt of gratitude they owe to him, the rest or the world has already begun to realise his power of creating type, his wonderful imagination, his versatility, and his extraordinary impartiality; and to accord him his rightful place among the Immortals. Nevertheless we are still too near to him, to be able to focus him clearly, and to estimate aright his peculiar place in literature, or the full scope of his genius.

Some very great authorities claim him as a member of the Romantic School; while, on the other hand, he is often looked on—apparently with more reason—as the first of the Realists. His object in writing was, he tells us, to represent mankind as he saw it, to be the historian of the nineteenth century, and to classify human beings as Buffon had classified animals. No doubt this scheme was very imperfectly carried out: certainly the powerful mind of Balzac with its wealth of imagination, often projected itself into his puppets, so that many of his characters are not the ordinary men and women he wished to portray, but are inspired by the fire of genius. This fact does not, however, alter the aim of their creator. He intended to be merely a chronicler, a scientific observer of things around him; and though his works are tinged to a large extent with the Romanticism of the powerful school in vogue in his day, this object marks him plainly as the forerunner of the Realists, the founder of a totally new conception of the scope and range of the novel.

Theophile Gautier's words should prove to the modern reader, the debt of gratitude he owes to the inaugurator of a completely original system of fiction. Speaking of Balzac's impecunious and ambitious heroes, Gautier cries:[*] "O Corinne, who on the Cape of Messina allowest thy snowy arm to hang over the ivory lyre, while the son of Albion, clothed in a superb new cloak, and with elegant boots perfectly polished, gazes at thee, and listens in an elegant pose: Corinne, what wouldst thou have said to such heroes? They have nevertheless one little quality which Oswald lacked—they live, and with so strong a life that we have met them a thousand times." Balzac's own words, speaking of his play "La Maratre,"[+] might also serve for a motto for his novels: "I dream of a drawing-room comedy, where everything is calm, quiet, and amiable. The men play whist placidly by the light of candles with little green shades. The women talk and laugh while they work at their embroidery. They all take tea together. To sum up, everything announces good order and harmony. Well, underneath are agitating passions; the drama stirs, it prepares itself secretly, till it blazes forth like the flame of a conflagration."

[*] "Portraits Contemporains: Honore de Balzac," by Theophile Gautier.

[+] "Historiettes et Souvenirs d'un Homme de Theatre," by H. Hostein.

Balzac is essentially a Realist, in his use of the novel as a vehicle for the description of real struggling life; with money and position, the principal desiderata of modern civilisation, powerful as determining factors in the moulding of men's actions. Life, as portrayed in the old-fashioned novel, where the hero and heroine and their love affairs were the sole focus of attraction, and the other characters were grouped round in subordinate positions, while every one declined in interest as he advanced in years, was not life as Balzac saw it; and he pictures his hero's agony at not having a penny with which to pay his cab fare, with as much graphic intensity, as he tells of the same young gentleman's despair when his inamorata is indifferent to him.

Nevertheless, if we compare Balzac with the depressing writers of the so-called Realist School, we shall find that his conception of life differed greatly from theirs. In Flaubert's melancholy books, even perfection of style and painstaking truth of detail do not dissipate the deadly dulness of an unreal world, where no one rises above the low level of self-gratification; while Zola considers man so completely in his physical aspect, that he ends by degrading him below the animal world. Balzac, on the other hand, believed in purity, in devotion, and unselfishness; though he did not think that these qualities are triumphant on earth. In his pessimistic view of life, virtue generally suffered, and had no power against vice; but he knew that it existed, and he believed in a future where wrongs would be righted.

He is a poet and idealist, and thus akin to the Romanticists—though he lacks their perfection of diction—in his feeling for the beauty of atmospheric effects, and also in his enthusiasm for music, which he loved passionately. The description of Montriveau's emotions when the cloistered Duchesse de Langeais plays in the church of Spain—and Balzac tells us that the sound of the organ bears the mind through a thousand scenes of life to the infinite which parts earth from heaven, and that through its tones the luminous attributes of God Himself pierce and radiate—is totally unrealistic both in moral tone, and in its accentuation of the power of the higher emotions. His intense admiration for Sir Walter Scott—an admiration which he expresses time after time in his letters—is a further proof of his sympathy for the school of thought, which glorified the picturesque Middle Ages above every other period of history.

Whichever school, however, may claim Balzac, it is an undisputed fact that he possessed in a high degree that greatest of all attributes —the power of creation of type. Le Pere Goriot, Balthazar Claes, Old Grandet, La Cousine Bette, Le Cousin Pons, and many other people in Balzac's pages, are creations; they live and are immortal. He has endowed them with more splendid and superabundant vitality than is accorded to ordinary humanity.

To do this, something is required beyond keenness of vision. The gift of seeing vividly—as under a dazzling light—to the very kernel of the object stripped of supernumerary circumstance, is indeed necessary for the portrayal of character; but although Dickens, as well as Balzac, possessed this faculty to a high degree, his people are often qualities personified, or impossible monsters. For the successful creation of type, that power in which Balzac is akin to Shakespeare, it is necessary that a coherent whole shall be formed, and that the full scope of a character shall be realised, with its infinite possibilities on its own plane, and its impotence to move a hairsbreadth on to another. The mysterious law which governs the conduct of life must be fathomed; so that, though there may be unexpected and surprising developments, the artistic sense and intuition which we possess shall not be outraged, and we shall still recognise the abiding personality under everything. Balzac excels in this; and because of this power, and also because—at a time when Byronic literature was in the ascendant, and it was the fashion to think that the quintessence of beauty could be found by diving into the depths of one's own being—he came forward without pose or self-consciousness, as a simple observer of the human race, the world will never cease to owe him a debt of gratitude, and to rank him among her greatest novelists.